The Ghosts of Truk Lagoon

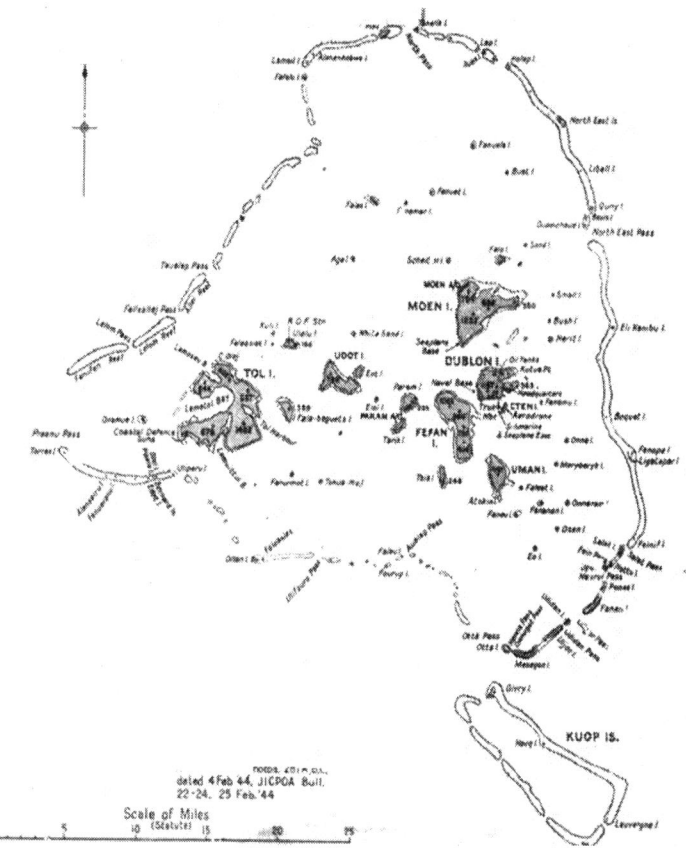

Dedication

This book is dedicated to the brave men and women, both American and Japanese, who fought and perished in the waters of Truk Lagoon during Operation Hailstone. Their courage, sacrifice, and resilience in the face of unimaginable hardship serve as a profound reminder of the human cost of war. It is also dedicated to the divers and researchers who continue to explore the submerged remnants of this pivotal battle, preserving its memory and ensuring that the stories of those lost are not forgotten. Their work contributes to a deeper understanding of a critical turning point in the Pacific Theater, allowing us to learn from the past and honor the fallen. This book is a testament to their dedication and their tireless efforts in preserving the rich history of Truk Lagoon, transforming a haunting underwater graveyard into a poignant tribute to the enduring spirit of those who served. May their discoveries continue to illuminate the complexities and consequences of this defining moment in World War II naval history, ensuring a lasting tribute to the bravery, sacrifice, and resilience of all those involved.

Preface

Operation Hailstone, the February 1944 assault on Truk Lagoon, stands as a pivotal moment in the Pacific Theater of World War II.

This meticulously researched account aims to provide a comprehensive and nuanced understanding of the battle, moving beyond simple narratives of victory and defeat. Through extensive archival research, including primary source materials such as operational orders, intelligence reports, and personal accounts (where available), this book delves into the strategic considerations that led to the operation, the technological advantages that contributed to the American success, and the human cost borne by both sides. The narrative explores the surprising lack of significant Japanese resistance, analyzing the factors that contributed to their weakened state and the effectiveness (or lack thereof) of their defensive strategies. Furthermore, the book moves beyond the immediate aftermath of the battle to examine its lasting legacy, highlighting its contribution to the Allied advance across the Pacific and its transformation of Truk Lagoon into an underwater graveyard – a haunting, yet compelling, testament to the destructive power of war and the enduring human spirit. Ultimately, this is more than a military history; it is a story of courage, sacrifice, and the profound impact of a single battle on the course of a global conflict.

Introduction

Truk Lagoon, a seemingly idyllic atoll in the heart of Micronesia, served as a crucial Japanese naval base during World War II. Its strategic location, sheltered by a complex network of islands and reefs, made it a formidable stronghold. However, this seemingly impenetrable fortress was dealt a devastating blow in February 1944 during Operation Hailstone, a massive American air and sea assault that crippled Japan's Pacific operations. This book examines the meticulously planned and executed operation that effectively neutralized the lagoon as a major Japanese base, irrevocably shifting the balance of power in the Pacific. We will explore the strategic importance of Truk Lagoon, examining its role as a vital hub for Japanese naval and air forces. The narrative details the extensive intelligence gathering efforts by the US Navy, highlighting the critical decision-making processes that culminated in Operation Hailstone. Beyond the strategic planning, we delve into the tactical execution of the operation, analyzing the impressive power of American carrier-based aviation and the devastating impact of the airstrikes. We will explore the surprisingly light Japanese resistance, examining the factors that contributed to their weakened state, including prior losses, logistical challenges, and intelligence failures. This book also examines the significant human cost of the battle, exploring the losses suffered by both the American and Japanese forces. It offers a glimpse into the experiences of the sailors and airmen involved, bringing to life the courage, fear, and sacrifice of those who fought in this pivotal conflict. Finally, the book will explore the present-day state of Truk Lagoon, a haunting underwater graveyard and a popular destination for shipwreck divers, serving as a somber yet compelling reminder of the consequences of war and the enduring legacy of Operation Hailstone.

Truks Geographic Location and Defenses

Truk Lagoon, situated in the heart of the Caroline Islands in Micronesia, possessed a geographic location of immense strategic value during World War II. Its sheltered waters, formed by a vast ring of coral reefs and islets, created a natural harbor of unparalleled size and security. This atoll, approximately 40 miles in diameter, encompassed a lagoon of approximately 500 square miles, providing ample space for a sizable fleet. The numerous islands, varying in size from small coral outcroppings to larger, more substantial landmasses, offered multiple anchorages, defensive positions, and sites for the development of airfields and support facilities. This intricate network of waterways and islands provided natural camouflage and protection from aerial reconnaissance and attack, at least initially. The lagoon's entrance channels, although navigable, were relatively narrow and easily defensible, further enhancing its inherent security.

The Japanese recognized Truk's strategic potential early in the war. Its central location in the Pacific allowed for efficient deployment of forces to various operational theaters. From Truk, Japanese naval units could readily operate across a vast swathe of the Pacific, projecting power towards the Gilbert and Marshall Islands, the Solomons, and even reaching further into the vast expanse of the Pacific Ocean. This central position made it a vital hub for supply and logistical support, allowing for the efficient movement of personnel, materials, and equipment to other Japanese-held territories in the region. Its strategic importance was matched only by its natural defensive capabilities, a combination that proved irresistibly attractive to the Japanese Navy's strategic planners.

The development of Truk as a major Japanese naval base was a gradual yet impressive undertaking, accelerating significantly as the war progressed. Beginning as a smaller, more modestly equipped base, Truk grew rapidly into a vast, fortified stronghold. Japanese engineers and construction crews worked tirelessly to transform the atoll into a comprehensive operational center. Extensive dockyards and repair facilities were constructed, enabling the maintenance and repair of ships, submarines, and aircraft. The islands were fortified with artillery batteries, anti-aircraft guns, and other defensive installations, creating a layered defense system intended to deter any potential enemy attack. This intricate system of fortifications was complemented by the creation of numerous airfields, providing bases for a substantial number of fighter planes, bombers, and reconnaissance aircraft.

The infrastructure supporting Truk's operational capabilities was equally impressive. Massive fuel storage depots, ammunition dumps, and supply warehouses were built to sustain the large number of warships, submarines, and aircraft stationed there. The lagoon's waters teemed with support craft – patrol boats, minesweepers, and transports – all vital to the base's functionality. The logistical complexities of supplying this far-flung bastion were substantial, requiring extensive maritime transport networks and sophisticated supply chains, demonstrating the Japanese commitment to Truk's strategic role. The sheer size and complexity of the base reflected Japan's unwavering belief in its strategic importance and its role as a cornerstone of their Pacific defense strategy. The sheer scale of the operation is underscored by contemporary accounts and photographs from the period, revealing the extensive infrastructure and the bustling activity that characterized the base at its zenith.

Evidence from captured Japanese documents and postwar interviews with surviving personnel shed light on the daily life and operational routines at Truk. The base represented a self-contained world, with its own administrative structure, support personnel, and even civilian population. The atmosphere was one of cautious vigilance, reflecting the constant threat of Allied attack. While the daily routines involved maintaining the fleet, conducting training exercises, and preparing for potential combat operations, the psychological toll of living under the ever-present threat of air raids is palpable in many of the accounts. The base's strategic importance was often emphasized in morale-building efforts by the command, underscoring its crucial role in the overall Japanese war effort.

However, despite the careful precautions and defensive measures undertaken by the Japanese, the sheer scale and complexity of the base made it potentially vulnerable to a concentrated attack.

American intelligence-gathering efforts played a crucial role in the planning and execution of Operation Hailstone. Intelligence agencies meticulously pieced together information about Truk's strength, infrastructure, and defenses. Naval reconnaissance missions, code-breaking activities, and aerial photography played a key part in building a comprehensive picture of the Japanese base.

Reports from captured Japanese personnel and intercepted communications proved invaluable in understanding the operational routines, organizational structure, and defensive capabilities of the Truk garrison. The resulting intelligence assessments provided the US Navy with crucial insight into the base's defenses, alerting them to the potential challenges of an attack while also highlighting potential vulnerabilities. The analysis was painstaking and thorough, using a multi-faceted approach combining aerial observation, electronic interception, and human intelligence.

The compilation of this intelligence was not without its challenges.

The lagoon's natural defenses hampered visual reconnaissance, whilst the Japanese demonstrated their own adeptness at deception, camouflaging installations and dispersing aircraft to mislead any aerial surveillance. The intricate network of islands and waterways provided effective cover for Japanese naval assets, masking their actual numbers and positions from even the most meticulous aerial scrutiny. However, advanced code-breaking techniques and the deployment of long-range reconnaissance planes began to unravel the complexities of Truk's defenses. The intelligence community developed a remarkably precise understanding of the base's layout, the types and numbers of ships and aircraft present, and even details about the locations of fuel and ammunition depots. This intricate and comprehensive intelligence gathering process played a critical role in the US Navy's successful execution of Operation Hailstone, demonstrating the importance of intelligence in the context of a major naval operation. The meticulous work of intelligence analysts paved the way for a well-planned and highly successful attack.

The strategic decision to launch a pre-emptive strike against Truk Lagoon, codenamed Operation Hailstone, was a pivotal moment in the Pacific War. The operation represented a significant commitment of American naval resources and reflected the growing confidence of the US Navy in their ability to project power across the vast expanse of the Pacific. The decision was based on a careful assessment of the risks and rewards, considering the strategic implications of neutralizing such a vital Japanese base. This decision-making process involved weighing the potential benefits against the cost of committing substantial resources. It was a calculated gamble with high stakes, one that involved considerable debate and discussion within the highest echelons of the US Navy. Ultimately, the strategic calculus favored the risk, as the potential rewards of crippling a major Japanese base outweighed the inherent dangers of the operation. The decision ultimately demonstrated the growing strategic confidence of the US Navy command in their capabilities.

The Growth of Truk as a Japanese Naval Base

The transformation of Truk Lagoon from a relatively minor Japanese outpost to a formidable naval bastion was a testament to Japanese engineering prowess and strategic vision. The initial Japanese presence in Truk was modest, consisting primarily of a small naval detachment and rudimentary facilities. However, as the war in the Pacific intensified, the strategic importance of Truk became increasingly apparent. Its central location, sheltered lagoon, and readily defensible approaches made it an ideal location for a major naval base, capable of supporting operations throughout the vast expanse of the Pacific Ocean. The expansion began with the construction of substantial docking facilities capable of accommodating a wide range of vessels, from destroyers and cruisers to submarines and support ships. These facilities were not merely basic piers; they were sophisticated dockyards equipped with repair shops, machine shops, and dry docks, capable of performing major repairs and maintenance on even the largest warships. The construction of these facilities involved significant logistical challenges, as materials had to be transported across thousands of miles of ocean.

The Japanese commitment to Truk's development extended beyond the dockyards. Massive fuel storage depots were constructed to ensure a continuous supply of fuel for the large fleet based there.

These fuel reserves were crucial for the operation of warships, submarines, and aircraft, and their presence underlined the importance of Truk as a forward operating base. Likewise, substantial ammunition dumps and supply warehouses were established, ensuring that the base was adequately stocked with the necessary munitions and supplies to support its considerable garrison. These storage facilities were strategically dispersed across several islands within the lagoon, reducing the risk of a single catastrophic event wiping out the entire supply chain. The sheer scale of these logistical endeavors is remarkable, showcasing the meticulous planning and the considerable resources committed to transforming Truk into a powerful naval fortress. The construction of extensive networks of roads and railways facilitated the internal movement of personnel, equipment, and supplies across the various islands of the lagoon.

Concurrently with the development of the logistical infrastructure, the Japanese military invested heavily in the fortification of the lagoon's defenses. Artillery batteries were strategically positioned on the islands surrounding the lagoon, providing a formidable ring of fire designed to repel any naval attack. These batteries were complemented by a comprehensive network of anti-aircraft guns, positioned to defend against air raids, a constant threat as the war progressed. The islands themselves were fortified with trenches, bunkers, and other defensive installations, creating a layered defense system designed to withstand prolonged sieges. The sheer number of defensive emplacements at Truk is staggering, reflecting the Japanese commitment to establishing an impregnable stronghold. The construction of these fortifications involved immense effort, and records show the deployment of significant numbers of Japanese civilian and military engineers and construction workers. These fortifications played a critical role in extending the life and operational capacity of the base, but ultimately proved insufficient against the overwhelming power of the American attack force.

Another key element in the development of Truk was the construction of multiple airfields. These airfields provided basing for a substantial number of aircraft, ranging from fighter planes and bombers to reconnaissance aircraft and even specialized aircraft such as seaplanes. The airfields were strategically located to provide maximum coverage of the lagoon and its approaches, enabling the Japanese to respond swiftly to any perceived threat. The presence of a significant air force at Truk was crucial, as it provided both defensive and offensive capabilities. Fighter squadrons provided air cover for the naval base, while bomber squadrons could be deployed to attack enemy positions elsewhere in the Pacific. The construction and maintenance of these airfields involved significant logistical challenges, and the airfields themselves were fortified against air attacks. This illustrates the emphasis placed on both the defensive and offensive capabilities of the Truk base. The number of aircraft stationed at Truk fluctuated over time, but at its peak, the base housed hundreds of aircraft, representing a significant air power concentrated in a single location.

The development of Truk's infrastructure was not limited to military facilities. The Japanese established administrative offices, hospitals, and other support facilities to cater to the needs of the large military personnel stationed there. The base also had a small civilian population, consisting of support staff, contractors, and their families. The daily life at Truk varied, from the rigorous routines of the naval and air personnel to the more mundane tasks performed by the civilian support staff. Accounts from surviving Japanese personnel paint a picture of a self-contained community, albeit one operating under the constant threat of attack. The base had a complex social and organizational structure, encompassing not only military personnel but also numerous support staff. Despite the inherent dangers, many Japanese personnel expressed a sense of community and solidarity, reflecting their shared experience of living and working in this remote and strategically important location. The evidence suggests a diverse community within the base, reflecting the diverse range of skills and roles required to operate such a massive complex.

The logistical challenges of supplying Truk were considerable. The base was thousands of miles from the Japanese home islands, making the transport of personnel, equipment, and supplies a complex undertaking. The Japanese relied on a large number of transport ships and submarines to maintain the flow of supplies to Truk. These supply lines were vulnerable to attack, and the Japanese experienced considerable losses of supply ships over the course of the war. These logistical challenges highlight the significant effort involved in sustaining the operation of the base.

Maintaining a continuous flow of supplies to Truk became increasingly difficult as the war progressed and American naval power expanded. The success of the base in operating for as long as it did, therefore, is further testament to the resilience of the Japanese logistical network. The base operated under a system of strict rationing and conservation, minimizing the consumption of resources wherever possible.

The Japanese commitment to the expansion and defense of Truk was a reflection of its perceived strategic importance. It served as a vital hub for the Japanese Navy's operations in the Pacific, and its loss would have dealt a significant blow to their strategic position. The extent of the base's development, therefore, indicates the high priority assigned to Truk by the Japanese high command. While the immense scale of the base was viewed as advantageous, it was a double-edged sword, as this very size and concentration of assets made the base vulnerable to a large-scale aerial attack. The very size and complexity of Truk's infrastructure also made it difficult to defend effectively against a determined enemy assault. The vast number of ships, planes, and installations concentrated in a relatively small area meant that a successful attack could inflict devastating damage in a short amount of time. This vulnerability would eventually be exploited by the United States Navy during Operation Hailstone. The base, once a symbol of Japanese power, was about to become the scene of one of the war's most significant naval battles.

Intelligence Gathering and American Planning

The seemingly impregnable fortress of Truk Lagoon, a testament to Japanese engineering and strategic foresight, presented a significant challenge to the advancing American forces in the Pacific. Before the devastating blows of Operation Hailstone could be delivered, however, the US Navy needed a comprehensive understanding of the enemy's strength and defenses. This required meticulous intelligence gathering, a process that involved a complex interplay of human intelligence, signals intelligence, and aerial reconnaissance.

Human intelligence, though fraught with the inherent risks of unreliable sources and misinformation, played a crucial role.

Captured Japanese documents, intercepted communications, and the debriefing of prisoners of war (POWs) provided valuable insights into the layout of the base, the deployment of forces, and the overall operational procedures within Truk Lagoon. These sources, however, often proved fragmented and inconsistent, requiring careful cross-referencing and analysis to establish reliable information. The challenge lay in separating genuine intelligence from propaganda, deliberate misinformation, and the inevitable distortions inherent in any eyewitness testimony gathered under duress.

Signals intelligence proved a more reliable, albeit still imperfect, source of information. The US Navy invested heavily in code-breaking efforts, attempting to decipher Japanese naval communications. While the Japanese maintained a high degree of security, the sheer volume of communication traffic offered opportunities for analysts to detect patterns and glean information regarding troop movements, ship deployments, and even the routine operational schedules of the base. Successes in intercepting and decoding Japanese messages allowed for a more accurate assessment of the overall strength and composition of the forces stationed at Truk. The information yielded by the decryption of Japanese naval codes, however, was rarely complete. It often presented a snapshot of a particular moment in time, leaving analysts to piece together a broader picture from often incomplete data.

Aerial reconnaissance, meanwhile, provided critical visual confirmation of the intelligence gathered from other sources. Long-range reconnaissance aircraft, operating from bases in the South Pacific, undertook repeated flights over Truk Lagoon, capturing high-altitude photographs of the base's infrastructure. These photographs, analyzed by skilled photo interpreters, revealed the detailed layout of the airfields, the extent of the dockyards, and the location and caliber of defensive emplacements. The development and refinement of photographic techniques during the war played a significant role in the ability of the American intelligence community to extract precise and accurate data. Repeated reconnaissance missions allowed for the monitoring of changes within the base, such as the arrival or departure of ships and aircraft, offering a dynamic picture of the base's activities. These aerial surveys proved invaluable in confirming or refuting intelligence gleaned from human and signals sources.

The integration of data from these diverse sources formed the foundation of the comprehensive intelligence picture that emerged. This analysis, however, wasn't a simple matter of combining data points. It involved intricate cross-referencing and comparison, identifying inconsistencies, and evaluating the reliability of each source. Analysts had to account for potential biases, errors, and intentional deception, constantly refining their assessment as new information came to light. This process was iterative and time-consuming, necessitating the collaboration of specialists from various fields, including cartographers, photo interpreters, linguists, and naval strategists.

The resulting intelligence assessment provided a reasonably accurate, albeit imperfect, representation of Truk Lagoon's defenses. The assessment highlighted the large number of ships anchored in the lagoon, the extensive airfields teeming with aircraft, and the formidable ring of artillery batteries and anti-aircraft guns encircling the island group. The intelligence reports emphasized the sheer scale of the Japanese naval presence, seemingly underscoring the significant risk associated with any direct assault. However, the intelligence also revealed potential weaknesses. The concentration of ships in the relatively confined lagoon, for instance, made them vulnerable to a massive coordinated air attack. The analysis also indicated that the Japanese defenses, while substantial, may not be as impenetrable as initially assumed. Reports suggested gaps in the anti-aircraft defenses and inconsistencies in the deployment of ground forces.

This intelligence, carefully weighed and analyzed by the US Navy's high command, informed the strategic planning for Operation Hailstone. The decision to mount a pre-emptive strike wasn't taken lightly. The risk of heavy losses was apparent. However, the potential gains—crippling a major Japanese base, disrupting supply lines, and severely damaging Japanese naval power in the central Pacific—were deemed substantial enough to justify the risks. The debate within the US Navy high command was undoubtedly intense, with different viewpoints and strategic considerations presented. Some advocated for a more cautious approach, emphasizing the strength of Truk's defenses. Others argued for a swift, decisive strike, leveraging the element of surprise. The final decision, to proceed with Operation Hailstone, was a testament to the confidence in the intelligence assessment and the belief in the ability of the US Navy to overcome the challenges posed by Truk's defenses.

The strategic plan that ultimately emerged involved a massive coordinated attack employing a combination of carrier-based aircraft, submarines, and battleships. The sheer scale of the planned operation reflected the ambition to deliver a decisive blow to the Japanese presence at Truk. The plan called for a saturation bombing attack, overwhelming the Japanese defenses with a relentless barrage of bombs and torpedoes. The involvement of carrier-based aircraft was crucial in exploiting the vulnerability of the Japanese fleet concentrated within the confines of Truk Lagoon. The plan also included a significant submarine component, tasked with attacking surface ships and potentially disrupting the Japanese supply lines. The careful coordination of these diverse naval elements was essential to maximizing the effect of the attack. This intricate planning was a direct result of the intelligence gathered, showcasing the pivotal role of intelligence in formulating successful military strategies.

Furthermore, the plan's success relied heavily on the element of surprise. The timing of the operation was carefully chosen to exploit vulnerabilities in the Japanese defenses. The decision to launch the attack before the Japanese could adequately reinforce their position in Truk Lagoon, or effectively redistribute their forces, was central to the strategic success of Operation Hailstone. This element of surprise, in turn, was dependent on the accuracy and timeliness of the intelligence gathered and the meticulous security maintained surrounding the operation's planning and execution. The effectiveness of the operation hinged not just on raw military power but also on the strategic use of deception and intelligence.

The intelligence gathering process leading up to Operation Hailstone serves as a testament to the critical role of intelligence in naval warfare. The combination of human intelligence, signals intelligence, and aerial reconnaissance, coupled with careful analysis and strategic planning, provided the foundation for a successful and decisive strike against a seemingly impregnable enemy stronghold. The operation highlighted the synergistic potential of various intelligence gathering methods and the importance of integrating these diverse sources of information to create a cohesive and accurate intelligence assessment. This comprehensive understanding of the enemy's capabilities and vulnerabilities played a pivotal role in shaping the course of the Pacific war and ultimately contributed to the Allied victory. The meticulous and sophisticated intelligence operation preceding the attack on Truk served as a crucial model for future naval engagements. The lessons learned from the meticulous intelligence gathering for Operation Hailstone would have lasting implications for future naval strategies. The integration of various intelligence disciplines and the critical importance of surprise and accurate assessment would be central themes of subsequent naval campaigns in the Pacific.

The Composition of the American Task Force

The success of Operation Hailstone hinged not only on meticulous intelligence gathering but also on the overwhelming firepower and technological superiority of the American naval task force assembled for the operation. This force, a potent blend of carriers, battleships, cruisers, destroyers, and submarines, represented the pinnacle of American naval technology at that point in the war, a stark contrast to the increasingly beleaguered Japanese fleet based at Truk Lagoon. The composition of this task force reflected the strategic objectives of the operation: to inflict maximum damage on the Japanese naval assets and infrastructure within the lagoon.

The core of the American striking power resided in its fast carrier battle groups. These formidable fleets, each a self-contained, mobile airbase, boasted a significant number of aircraft capable of delivering devastating blows from a safe distance. The carriers themselves represented cutting-edge naval technology. Their large flight decks allowed for the rapid launch and recovery of aircraft, while their advanced armor protection shielded them from enemy fire. The carrier air groups were a heterogeneous mix of aircraft types, each designed to perform a specific role in the overall attack. Dive bombers, like the Douglas SBD Dauntless and the Curtiss SB2C Helldiver, were responsible for delivering precision strikes against ships and installations. These aircraft were equipped with powerful bombs designed to penetrate the armor of enemy vessels. Their accuracy, a testament to years of rigorous training and technological advancement, was critical in inflicting maximum damage. In contrast, the Japanese dive bombers, while still effective, suffered from several key limitations including their shorter operational range and a lesser payload compared to their American counterparts. The quality of the pilot training, and the overall readiness of the Japanese aircraft, were also suffering due to the continuous attrition that the Japanese Navy suffered over the previous years.

Alongside the dive bombers, the carrier air groups included torpedo bombers, like the Grumman TBF Avenger, capable of launching devastating torpedo attacks against larger surface vessels. These aircraft, with their powerful torpedoes, posed a significant threat to the Japanese battleships and cruisers anchored in the relatively confined waters of Truk Lagoon. The Avenger, in particular, boasted a considerable technological edge over its Japanese counterparts, with increased speed, range, and bomb-carrying capacity, which translated into a significant advantage in the aerial combat that unfolded during Operation Hailstone.

Fighter aircraft, such as the Grumman F6F Hellcat and the Vought F4U Corsair, provided crucial air superiority, protecting the vulnerable bombers from Japanese fighter interceptions. The Hellcat and Corsair, highly maneuverable and heavily armed, proved far superior to the Japanese Zero in terms of speed, firepower, and armor. The Zero, while still a formidable aircraft in the hands of a skilled pilot, was becoming increasingly outmatched by the newer, more technologically advanced American fighters. The improvements in firepower, speed and maneuverability of the American fighters allowed them to establish and maintain air superiority, and provide protection to the carrier task force during the operation. This crucial aspect allowed the American bombing and torpedo-carrying aircraft to do their work with minimal opposition and thus greatly increasing the effectiveness of the attack.

The American task force also included battleships, powerful capital ships capable of providing long-range fire support. While not the primary striking force in Operation Hailstone, the battleships provided a crucial backup to the carrier task force. The accuracy and range of their guns allowed them to strike targets outside the effective range of carrier-based aircraft, further enhancing the overall effectiveness of the American assault. The battleships also served as a deterrent against any significant counterattack from the Japanese fleet, though this role proved ultimately less important due to the extent of the initial surprise attack. The battleships were significantly outmatched in terms of anti-aircraft capabilities and this allowed the Japanese air defense capabilities to focus primarily on the air strikes, instead of diverting their attention and resources to neutralize the threat that the American battleships posed.

Cruisers and destroyers provided crucial anti-aircraft defense and escort for the carriers and battleships. The destroyers, with their speed and maneuverability, acted as a shield against Japanese submarines and surface raiders, ensuring the safety of the more vulnerable capital ships. These smaller and more agile warships were critical in protecting the carriers from submarine attack while also providing additional anti-aircraft protection for the larger ships. The technological advancements in these ship classes allowed the Americans to more effectively respond to any perceived threat in comparison to the Japanese counterparts.

Submarines played a supporting role, conducting reconnaissance and attacking Japanese shipping outside the lagoon. These submarines were instrumental in gathering pre-attack intelligence, identifying targets and tracking Japanese ship movements. The deployment of the submarines was also used to limit the response of the Japanese forces. These submarines, coupled with the overwhelming firepower of the carriers and battleships, ensured that no significant Japanese counterattack could be launched.

The technological disparity between the American and Japanese forces was significant. American radar systems, for instance, provided early warning of Japanese air attacks, allowing the American fleet to prepare for interceptions. Japanese radar capabilities were not as developed and thus lacked the effectiveness that the American technology presented. The superior American aircraft, better trained pilots, and more effective weapons systems ensured the overwhelming success of the air strikes. The Japanese pilots, though courageous, were often outmatched by the superior technology and training of their American counterparts.

The advanced fire-control systems on American warships allowed for more accurate and effective targeting of enemy ships and installations. The integration of radar with fire-control systems significantly improved the accuracy of both surface and air attacks. The Japanese, lacking the same technological advances, struggled to counter the precise attacks launched by the American force. The accuracy of these attacks played a critical role in maximizing the damage inflicted.

The composition of the American task force, therefore, was a carefully considered blend of diverse naval elements, each playing a specific role in achieving the operation's objectives. The technological superiority of the American fleet, coupled with its carefully planned and executed attack, ensured the overwhelming success of Operation Hailstone and the crippling of the Japanese stronghold at Truk Lagoon. The technological advantages possessed by the American Navy were not simply a matter of isolated improvements; they reflected a cohesive and comprehensive advancement in naval technology, tactics, and training, representing a quantum leap in naval capability compared to the Japanese. This technological advantage translated directly into a decisive victory, solidifying the US Navy's dominance in the Pacific theater. The operation became a watershed moment, highlighting the critical role of technological advancement in modern naval warfare. The lessons learned from this technological superiority would have long-lasting implications for the design and operational deployment of naval forces in the years that followed, changing the paradigm for naval warfare in the post-war era.

The Initial Stages of Operation Hailstone

The initial stages of Operation Hailstone were as crucial as the devastating air and sea attacks that followed. Success hinged not only on overwhelming firepower but also on a meticulously planned and executed approach to Truk Lagoon, a natural fortress ringed by coral reefs and islands. The sheer scale of the American task force, however, necessitated a complex and coordinated advance. The lagoon's natural defenses presented formidable challenges, requiring a careful balance between maintaining stealth and ensuring the timely deployment of the various naval components.

The task force's approach was a testament to the meticulous planning and coordination that characterized the operation.

The American task force began its journey towards Truk Lagoon from its assembly points, a significant distance away. The decision to launch from a considerable distance was a deliberate strategic choice, aimed at maximizing the element of surprise. The long voyage, while potentially risky, was deemed necessary to maintain secrecy and prevent the Japanese from anticipating the impending attack. Maintaining radio silence during a substantial portion of the transit was paramount. The successful execution of the plan rested heavily on the discipline and professionalism of the entire fleet. Any lapse in communication or unexpected equipment failure could have jeopardized the entire operation. This lengthy voyage also served as a testing ground for the fleet's logistical capabilities and the crew's resilience.

Before the main assault, extensive reconnaissance missions were undertaken to obtain up-to-date intelligence on the enemy's disposition and defenses within Truk Lagoon. These missions, largely conducted by submarines and long-range reconnaissance aircraft, were vital in shaping the subsequent attack strategy. Submarines, operating independently and silently, infiltrated the outer perimeters of the lagoon, gathering crucial information on Japanese ship movements, deployment of defenses, and the overall level of alertness within the base. Their observations provided valuable insights into the strengths and vulnerabilities of the Japanese defenses. They were able to ascertain the types of ships present, their approximate numbers, and their locations within the lagoon. The information gleaned from these reconnaissance missions proved invaluable in targeting decisions, ensuring that the main air and naval assaults were directed against the most critical targets.

Reconnaissance aircraft, flying long and dangerous missions from distant airfields or carriers, provided aerial perspectives, supplementing the underwater observations from the submarines.

Their high-altitude flights allowed them to observe the lagoon's defenses and provide comprehensive imagery that was crucial in target identification and strategic planning. This combination of air and underwater reconnaissance gave the American planners a comprehensive view of the situation. These images helped construct detailed maps and models of Truk Lagoon, revealing details about the Japanese defenses, such as the locations of anti-aircraft batteries and the layout of their airfields. Thi comprehensive reconnaissance was vital in the success of the operation.

The Japanese, for their part, were far from complacent. The defense of Truk Lagoon was considered paramount. However, their radar systems, while present, proved inadequate to detect the American force until it was far too late. Japanese radar technology at the time lagged behind that of the Americans. Their radar coverage was less extensive and less sensitive, making it difficult to detect the approaching American task force amidst the vast expanse of the Pacific Ocean. Moreover, the lack of integration and coordination between different radar installations hampered their overall effectiveness. The American task force leveraged its technological superiority to stay well outside the range of Japanese radar detection until the moment of attack. The deployment of specialized electronic warfare equipment served to further mask the American fleet's approach, effectively deceiving the Japanese into a false sense of security. The ability of the Americans to successfully bypass the Japanese early warning systems speaks volumes about the technological gap between the two forces.

The American task force's initial approach was characterized by meticulous maneuvering and strict adherence to radio silence. This was essential to maintain the element of surprise, a crucial factor in the operation's eventual success. The skill and experience of the naval officers and crew in maintaining stealth and coordination were critical in executing this delicate phase of the operation. Even minor errors in navigation or communication could have compromised the entire operation.

The challenge of approaching Truk Lagoon was magnified by its geographical characteristics. The lagoon itself, a large expanse of water, offered numerous opportunities for the Japanese to hide and launch attacks from unexpected directions. The surrounding islands provided natural cover, making detection of the approaching fleet incredibly difficult. The reefs and shallow waters surrounding the lagoon also posed a navigational hazard, potentially grounding or damaging the larger vessels in the task force. The careful selection of routes, the use of advanced navigational techniques, and the vigilance of the fleet's personnel were crucial in overcoming this challenging environment. The successful navigation of the approach speaks volumes about the expertise and experience of the personnel involved.

The initial deployment of the American fleet was therefore a complex operation, involving careful consideration of various factors, such as speed, stealth, positioning of different units, and the coordination of multiple components. This intricate dance involved multiple units working in concert, each playing its crucial role in ensuring the ultimate success of Operation Hailstone. The initial phases of the operation underscored the strategic thinking and meticulous planning behind the attack. The success in approaching Truk Lagoon undetected laid the foundation for the devastating air and sea attacks that were to follow. This silent and cautious approach, executed with precision and expertise, highlights the importance of strategic planning and the use of technological superiority. The combined efforts of the naval forces in maintaining radio silence, navigating the complex waters around Truk Lagoon, and evading Japanese radar detection demonstrate exceptional skill and coordination. The successful execution of these initial maneuvers stands as a testament to the proficiency and preparedness of the American fleet. The element of surprise, carefully cultivated and impeccably executed, was a significant contributor to the operation's overwhelming success, resulting in the crippling of the Japanese naval base at Truk Lagoon.

The First Wave of Air Attacks

The meticulously planned approach culminated in the unleashing of the first wave of air attacks against Truk Lagoon. The dawn of February 17th, 1944, saw the launch of hundreds of aircraft from the assembled American carriers – a breathtaking spectacle of coordinated power. The carriers, including the USS Intrepid and Yorktown, became launch platforms for a devastating assault, their flight decks teeming with a variety of aircraft, each with a specific target and mission. The carefully orchestrated sequence of take-offs, designed to maximize the impact of the initial strike, transformed the usually serene Pacific skies into a buzzing hive of activity.

The primary targets were clearly defined based on the extensive reconnaissance. Japanese naval vessels, berthed within the relative safety of the lagoon, were high on the priority list. The intelligence reports meticulously pinpointed the location of cruisers, destroyers, and smaller support ships. These vessels, vital to the Japanese naval operations in the Pacific, represented a potent concentration of firepower that the Americans aimed to neutralize. The identification of these targets was not a simple matter; it involved painstaking analysis of aerial photographs, submarine reports, and the careful interpretation of all available intelligence.

The first wave consisted primarily of dive bombers, specifically SBD Dauntlesses and SB2C Helldivers. These aircraft, known for their precision and destructive power, were tasked with delivering crippling blows to the anchored Japanese ships. Their payloads consisted of armor-piercing bombs, designed to penetrate the decks and inflict maximum damage to the vessels' internal structures. The pilots, highly trained and experienced, executed their attacks with deadly accuracy, their bombs finding their marks with devastating effect. The sight and sound of these planes, descending from the sky in carefully coordinated formations, was a terrifying experience for the Japanese crews caught unprepared.

Alongside the dive bombers, numerous torpedo planes – TBF Avengers and TBD Devastators – were deployed. These aircraft targeted the vulnerable underwater portions of the Japanese ships.

The torpedoes, launched from a distance, sought to inflict fatal damage below the waterline, causing the ships to list and eventually sink. This dual-pronged attack, combining high-altitude bombing and underwater torpedo strikes, aimed to maximize the destruction inflicted on the Japanese fleet. The coordination of the air attacks required exceptional skill and discipline from the flight crews.

Maintaining formations, timing their attacks precisely, and communicating effectively under fire were crucial to the mission's success.

The initial wave also included a significant contingent of fighters –F6F Hellcats and F4U Corsairs – tasked with providing air cover.

Their primary role was to neutralize the Japanese air defenses, protecting the dive bombers and torpedo planes from interception. The fighters engaged the Japanese Zeros and other interceptors in fierce aerial battles, the skies above Truk Lagoon transforming into a chaotic maelstrom of dogfights. The air superiority gained by the American fighters was crucial in enabling the dive bombers and torpedo planes to deliver their devastating blows. Without the protection afforded by the fighters, the attack could have suffered considerably higher losses.

The assault on Truk Lagoon was a carefully planned and flawlessly executed operation, demonstrating the effectiveness of the American military machine. It was also a testament to the bravery of the American pilots, who faced considerable risks in launching these attacks. Many pilots recalled the intensity of the experience, the sights and sounds of exploding bombs, and the near misses that defined their missions. Their accounts reveal the courage and determination that characterized the Pacific campaign. Accounts from the aircrews paint vivid pictures of the intense combat, the sheer destruction, and the relentless pursuit of their objectives. The descriptions of the burning ships, the explosions rocking the lagoon, and the desperate attempts of the Japanese to fight back highlight the ferocity of the battle.

The photographs taken during and after the attack provide undeniable visual evidence of the devastation wrought upon Truk Lagoon. The images capture the burning hulks of Japanese ships, the wreckage scattered across the lagoon, and the damage inflicted on the base's infrastructure. The visual record serves as a potent reminder of the operation's success and the scale of destruction. The images showcase the effectiveness of the American air power and its impact on Japan's Pacific war effort. They range from sweeping views of the lagoon, showing a scene of chaos and devastation, to close-up shots of damaged ships, providing stark evidence of the destruction. The photographic evidence also serves to highlight the tactical brilliance of the attack, illustrating how effectively the Americans targeted specific areas to cause the greatest impact.

The first wave of attacks was only the beginning. It set the stage for subsequent waves, each adding to the destruction and effectively crippling the Japanese stronghold at Truk Lagoon. The effectiveness of this opening strike, however, cannot be overstated. It not only inflicted heavy damage on the Japanese fleet and air force but also significantly demoralized the Japanese forces, disrupting their operations and severely weakening their ability to defend against further attacks. The strategic success of Operation Hailstone rested heavily on the impact of these initial air raids.

The damage inflicted during the first wave was catastrophic. The Japanese lost several ships, including cruisers and destroyers, with many suffering severe damage and requiring extensive repairs or even being declared total losses. The accurate bombing and torpedo strikes left many ships burning or sinking, causing significant loss of life among the Japanese crews. Beyond the ships, the Japanese airfields suffered extensive damage, with numerous aircraft destroyed on the ground. The attacks effectively neutralized a significant portion of Japan's naval and air power in the region.

The destruction of the Japanese aircraft on the ground was particularly significant. Many aircraft were destroyed before they even had a chance to take off and engage the attacking American forces. This greatly reduced the Japanese capacity to effectively counter the attack. The loss of these aircraft not only weakened their immediate defensive capabilities but also diminished their overall operational strength in the Pacific theater.

The meticulous targeting, coupled with the surprise element and the sheer power of the American air assault, significantly crippled

Japan's ability to maintain its position in Truk Lagoon. This initial phase of Operation Hailstone proved to be a decisive turning point, marking a significant victory for the American forces and greatly advancing the Allied advance across the Pacific. The accounts of American pilots and the photographic record together provide compelling evidence of the scale of the destruction and its lasting impact on the Pacific War. The careful planning, precision execution, and the overwhelming firepower effectively transformed a major Japanese base into a crippled and vulnerable target. The effectiveness of the first wave laid the foundation for the complete success of Operation Hailstone. The subsequent waves, building upon the initial success, further decimated the Japanese forces, transforming Truk Lagoon from a key strategic base into a haunting reminder of American naval superiority.

The Second and Subsequent Waves

The success of the first wave emboldened the American planners. The initial assault had achieved far more than anticipated, severely damaging the Japanese fleet and airfields, and crippling Truk's ability to launch effective counterattacks. This success, however, did not lead to complacency. The subsequent waves of attacks were carefully planned, taking into account the lessons learned from the first wave and adapting to the changing conditions on the ground –or rather, in the lagoon.

The second wave, launched shortly after the first, focused on consolidating the gains and targeting specific remaining threats.

Intelligence gleaned from the first wave's reconnaissance, now augmented by firsthand observations from returning pilots, identified specific targets that had survived the initial onslaught.

These included damaged but still functional Japanese vessels, hidden amongst the wreckage, and fuel storage facilities previously missed due to cloud cover or other obstructions. The composition of the second wave differed slightly from the first, with a greater emphasis on strafing runs by fighter aircraft targeting ground installations and surviving Japanese aircraft attempting to scramble into the air. The Hellcats and Corsairs, having already established air superiority, pressed their advantage, engaging any remaining Japanese fighters with devastating results.

Accounts from American pilots participating in the second wave reveal a scene of organized chaos. While the initial wave had encountered some resistance, the second wave encountered a significantly diminished and disorganized Japanese defense. The previously coordinated air defenses were shattered, leaving isolated pockets of resistance that were easily overwhelmed. The relentless attacks by dive bombers continued to inflict damage on the crippled ships, while torpedo planes focused on sinking those already listing, ensuring that any remaining threat would be eliminated. The strafing runs were particularly effective in destroying ground installations such as fuel depots, ammunition dumps, and repair facilities, hindering any attempts at repair or replenishment for the damaged Japanese forces. The Japanese, demoralized and disorganized, offered only sporadic and ineffective resistance.

Unlike the carefully orchestrated formations of the first wave, the second wave displayed a more opportunistic approach, with individual aircraft or small groups targeting opportunities as they arose. The element of surprise, so crucial in the first wave, was largely unnecessary; the Japanese defenses were already in disarray. This, however, did not diminish the danger for the American pilots. Anti-aircraft fire continued, albeit less effectively, and the risks of collisions with debris from sinking ships were a real threat.

The third and subsequent waves were characterized by a shift in target priority. The emphasis moved from sinking ships to systematically destroying the infrastructure that supported the Japanese presence in Truk Lagoon. Airfields, docks, repair facilities, and storage areas were subjected to relentless attacks, aimed at rendering the lagoon useless as a naval base. The meticulous planning evident in the initial waves was still present, but the overall tempo and intensity decreased, suggesting a transition from a focused offensive to a mopping-up operation. The damage inflicted during these later waves, while less visually spectacular than the sinking of large warships, was equally significant in crippling the Japanese presence in Truk. These attacks ensured that Truk Lagoon would not quickly be rehabilitated, and it would remain a far less effective naval base for the foreseeable future.

Examining surviving Japanese records provides a stark counterpoint to the American accounts. These records, often fragmentary and incomplete, reveal a picture of confusion and despair. The initial impact of the first wave caused widespread panic and disorganization. The Japanese lacked effective communication and coordination in responding to the attacks. The rapid and overwhelming nature of the American air assault overwhelmed their defensive capabilities. Many accounts detail scenes of chaos, with crews attempting to escape burning ships and aircraft scrambling for cover amidst the explosions. The sheer scale of the air assault produced a state of paralysis and rendered many Japanese units incapable of effective action.

The accounts of Japanese pilots underscore the vast disparity in air power. The outnumbered and outgunned Japanese Zero fighters put up a valiant, yet ultimately futile defense. Their pilots, known for their skill and courage, fought with determination, but they were no match for the larger, more advanced American fighters. Many were shot down, others managed to escape the relentless barrage, but the overall damage to Japanese air power in Truk was catastrophic. The loss of experienced pilots and irreplaceable aircraft dealt a severe blow to the Japanese ability to resist further attacks.

The photographic record provides compelling visual evidence of the sustained destruction across the days of the operation. Images show not just the immediate aftermath of the initial bombing, but the progressive dismantling of the base across the days of the operation.

The repeated strikes clearly show the effectiveness of successive attacks, revealing not just the destruction of ships, but the erosion of docks, the crumbling of buildings, the systematic destruction of fuel and ammunition stores. These images offer a powerful visual narrative of the battle, supplementing and corroborating the accounts from pilots on both sides. The slow but steady eradication of Japanese infrastructure is palpable in the progression of the photographic evidence.

The operational success of Operation Hailstone extends beyond the immediate destruction of the Japanese forces in Truk Lagoon. The operation sent a clear message of American naval supremacy, effectively crippling a vital Japanese base and disrupting supply lines across the Pacific. The psychological impact of the attack was immense, further weakening Japanese morale and confidence. The complete dismantling of Truk as a major naval base forced Japan to reconsider its strategic deployments and logistical arrangements, diverting resources and manpower to address the damage and reorganize its defenses elsewhere. The operation's success directly contributed to the Allied advance through the Central Pacific, paving the way for subsequent operations that ultimately led to the liberation of the Philippines and the eventual defeat of Japan. Truk Lagoon, once a formidable Japanese stronghold, was reduced to a poignant underwater graveyard, a testament to the devastating power of American air power and a powerful symbol of the turning point in the Pacific war. The operation's legacy continues to resonate, not only in the military history of World War II, but also in the fascination it holds for modern shipwreck divers who explore the remains of this once-proud naval base.

Japanese Defensive Measures and Their Effectiveness

The Japanese defensive measures at Truk Lagoon, while initially appearing formidable on paper, ultimately proved woefully inadequate against the overwhelming might of the American air assault. A confluence of factors contributed to this failure, ranging from equipment deficiencies to flawed strategic and tactical doctrines. Analyzing the specifics reveals a complex picture, far removed from the simplistic narrative of a poorly defended base.

The anti-aircraft defenses, a crucial element of any naval base's defense, suffered from several critical shortcomings. While Truk possessed a substantial number of anti-aircraft guns, ranging from light machine guns to heavier caliber weapons, their deployment was hampered by a lack of effective coordination and integration.

The guns were often scattered haphazardly, lacking a centralized command and control system to effectively target incoming aircraft.

This resulted in a fragmented defense, with individual gun crews reacting independently to the incoming attacks rather than operating as a coordinated unit. Reports from surviving Japanese personnel highlight the confusion and chaos that reigned during the attacks, with overlapping fields of fire and a lack of unified targeting directives resulting in wasted ammunition and ineffective fire. The decentralized nature of the anti-aircraft defenses hindered their ability to track the fast-moving American aircraft, particularly the dive bombers, which often released their bombs from altitudes beyond the effective range of many of the Japanese guns.

Furthermore, the quality and condition of the Japanese anti-aircraft weaponry played a significant role in their ineffectiveness. Many of the guns were outdated, suffering from maintenance issues, and lacked the range and firepower necessary to effectively engage the American aircraft. The constant deployment in the harsh tropical conditions contributed to equipment degradation, and the lack of sufficient spare parts further hampered their performance. The American aircraft, in contrast, were equipped with advanced radar and fire-control systems, providing superior accuracy and effectiveness, which further accentuated the Japanese shortcomings. Analysis of post-battle damage assessments shows that many anti-aircraft gun emplacements were either destroyed or rendered inoperable during the initial waves of attacks, crippling their ability to effectively engage the successive waves of American aircraft.

Japanese records reveal repeated requests for additional AA weaponry and ammunition throughout the war, indicating a long-standing awareness of deficiencies in their defensive capabilities.

The Japanese air defense, while initially intending to provide a critical layer of protection, proved equally inadequate. The number of fighters available to intercept the American attackers was significantly smaller than the incoming force. The famed Mitsubishi A6M Zero, although possessing exceptional maneuverability, was outclassed by the superior range, firepower, and armor of the American Grumman F6F Hellcat and Vought F4U Corsair. Japanese pilots, despite their famed skill and courage, were simply unable to effectively counter the numerical and technological superiority of the American aircraft. The lack of sufficient radar-based early warning systems hampered their ability to intercept the attacking American planes before they reached their targets, leaving them constantly reacting to the attacks rather than initiating proactive defense. The disjointed nature of the communication systems among the Japanese fighters and between the fighters and ground crews also contributed to the inefficacy of their defense. Survivors recounted instances of friendly fire and missed intercepts due to the lack of coordination among Japanese air units.

The overall command structure of the Japanese defenses at Truk was plagued by a multitude of issues. Decentralized command and control, exacerbated by the lack of effective communication systems, hindered the ability of Japanese forces to respond effectively to the American attacks. The lack of a unified, coordinated response allowed the American forces to methodically destroy the Japanese fleet and infrastructure, one target after another. The rapid succession of the American air strikes overwhelmed the already strained Japanese command structure, preventing any effective re-organization or counter-offensive. The chaos and confusion caused by the relentless bombing raids intensified the challenges faced by the Japanese leadership in attempting to direct and coordinate their defense.

The American successes, in contrast, stemmed from effective planning, superb coordination, and superior technology. The detailed intelligence gathering preceding the operation had created a comprehensive understanding of Japanese defenses. The mission planning ensured that successive waves attacked pre-determined targets in a sequence designed to maximize damage and minimize losses. The overwhelming air cover provided by the escorting fighters ensured that the attacking aircraft could perform their missions with minimal interference. The effective use of radar, allowing for early warning and precise targeting, gave the American pilots a significant advantage over their Japanese counterparts. The robust communication systems enabled seamless coordination among the attacking squadrons, further maximizing the impact of the airstrikes. The superior training and experience of the American pilots played a crucial role in their success, as they deftly avoided anti-aircraft fire and effectively neutralized the Japanese fighters.

The contrast between the American and Japanese approaches highlights a fundamental difference in military doctrine. The Americans emphasized effective centralized planning, coordinated actions, and technological superiority, whilst the Japanese, hampered by logistical constraints and a hierarchical command structure prone to rigidity, faced significant challenges in adapting to the swift and decisive nature of the American attack. This failure wasn't simply a matter of numbers but a reflection of a strategic and tactical mismatch between the two naval powers.

The failure of Japanese defensive measures at Truk Lagoon wasn't due to a singular cause but rather a complex interplay of factors including, but not limited to, obsolete equipment, ineffective command structures, and insufficient communication networks. The American approach, by contrast, epitomized superior coordination, technological advancement, and effective strategic planning. The overwhelming success of Operation Hailstone served as a potent symbol of the shifting balance of power in the Pacific Theater, underscoring the devastating consequences of failing to adapt to the evolving nature of naval warfare in the age of carrier aviation. The remnants of sunken ships and shattered infrastructure that litter Truk Lagoon stand as a sobering testament to this reality.

The Losses Inflicted on the Japanese Fleet

The devastation wrought upon the Japanese fleet at Truk Lagoon during Operation Hailstone was nothing short of catastrophic. The ferocity and precision of the American air attacks left an indelible mark on the Imperial Japanese Navy (IJN), crippling its operational capacity in the central Pacific and significantly altering the strategic balance of power. The sheer scale of the losses inflicted is staggering and demands detailed analysis to fully grasp the impact on the Japanese war effort.

The initial waves of American aircraft, primarily comprised of dive bombers from the carriers USS Intrepid and Yorktown, focused on the anchored warships in the lagoon. These carefully planned attacks, guided by detailed pre-raid intelligence, targeted specific vessels, maximizing the destruction while minimizing American losses. The sheer weight of ordnance unleashed on the Japanese fleet overwhelmed the already inadequate anti-aircraft defenses, resulting in widespread devastation. Among the most significant losses was the light cruiser *Katori*, sunk by a direct hit that detonated her magazines. The resulting explosion was witnessed by numerous American pilots and graphically documented in post-raid aerial photographs. The *Katori*'s loss represented more than just a single ship; she served as a crucial communications hub and her destruction significantly hampered the Japanese ability to coordinate defensive actions. Further adding to this strategic blow, the heavy cruiser *Aoba* suffered severe damage, effectively rendering her combat-ineffective for a considerable period. While not sunk, the damage sustained during the attacks involved substantial flooding, resulting in extensive repairs requiring considerable time and resources.

The damage assessment reports, corroborated by surviving Japanese crew accounts and photographic evidence, vividly illustrate the extent of the destruction. Multiple photographs capture the *Aoba* listing heavily to one side, its deck torn apart and fires raging.

These visuals underscore the brutal efficiency of the American attacks and provide stark evidence of the Japanese Navy's vulnerability. Beyond the damage sustained by the larger vessels, the attacks also inflicted devastating damage on smaller support vessels critical to the operation of the base. Numerous destroyers, transports, and auxiliary ships were either sunk outright or severely damaged, hindering the logistical support crucial for the maintenance of the Japanese forces. The destruction of these smaller craft, while seemingly less significant than the loss of larger combatants, effectively paralyzed the base's operational capacity.

They were instrumental in the resupply and repair of the larger fleet, and their loss crippled the Japanese ability to sustain their presence in the lagoon.

The sinking of the *Shokaku*, a veteran aircraft carrier and a symbol of Japanese naval strength, dealt a particularly heavy blow to the IJN's morale and operational capabilities. While not destroyed at Truk, the damage inflicted during the attacks proved unrepairable, effectively marking the end of its active service. The carrier had sustained critical damage to its flight deck and internal structure, making it impossible to repair despite the best efforts of Japanese shipyards. The loss of the *Shokaku*, combined with the damage to other fleet units and the destruction of over 275 aircraft, represented a severe blow to the Japanese offensive capabilities. Pre-raid assessments of Japanese air strength in the area suggested that the IJN had a sizable number of aircraft capable of intercepting American raids. However, the reality of the situation highlighted significant inadequacies in the number of operational aircraft that could effectively engage the attackers. American pilots reported observing many damaged aircraft on the ground and on the water, unable to take part in the defence.

Beyond the ships and aircraft, Operation Hailstone also inflicted significant damage on the infrastructure supporting the Japanese fleet at Truk Lagoon. Fuel storage facilities, repair docks, and other vital facilities were heavily targeted and largely destroyed. The destruction of these support facilities further compounded the impact of the losses of ships and aircraft. The attacks not only removed critical units from Japanese fleet capabilities but also destroyed their ability to maintain, refit, or repair the remaining units. The strategic value of Truk Lagoon as a major Japanese base lay not merely in the concentration of its fleet but also in its supporting infrastructure. The destruction of that infrastructure effectively condemned Truk Lagoon to the role of a strategically useless and vulnerable outpost. Post-attack reconnaissance flights documented widespread fires and the devastation of vital installations, showing the thoroughness of the American assault.

The strategic consequences of Operation Hailstone were profound.

The crippling of the Japanese fleet at Truk Lagoon effectively neutralized a major strategic base, severely disrupting Japanese operations in the central Pacific. The loss of 12 ships, hundreds of aircraft, and the significant damage to infrastructure created a critical gap in the Japanese ability to project power. The loss of ships and aircraft directly impacted the ability to respond to subsequent American offensives in the Pacific theatre. The loss of the larger vessels like the *Aoba* and the effective removal of the *Shokaku* fundamentally altered the balance of power in the area.

The destruction of the supporting infrastructure further compounded this reality by removing the ability to readily repair or replace these assets. Furthermore, the psychological impact on the Japanese Navy cannot be underestimated. The scale of the defeat at Truk Lagoon represented a significant blow to Japanese morale and confidence. The sudden and overwhelming nature of the air attacks, coupled with the scale of material losses and the failure of the defensive measures, shattered any perceived invincibility the Japanese Navy may have previously possessed.

The detailed analysis of the losses inflicted upon the Japanese fleet at Truk Lagoon during Operation Hailstone reveals a systematic and devastating defeat. The American attacks targeted not only the surface combatants of the IJN but also its critical logistical support and infrastructure. The destruction of the *Katori* and the extensive damage to the *Aoba* , combined with the loss of scores of smaller ships and support vessels, effectively crippled the base's operational capacity. The sinking or severe damage of ships such as the *Shokaku* , combined with the destruction of over 275 aircraft, significantly weakened the Japanese ability to project naval power in the region.

The devastating impact extended beyond mere numbers; the operation's success shattered Japanese morale and revealed a critical vulnerability in the IJN's strategic planning and defense capabilities. The legacy of Operation Hailstone continues to resonate today, not just as a pivotal battle in the Pacific Theater of

World War II but as a potent symbol of the changing dynamics of naval warfare in the age of carrier aviation. The sunken ships and the eerie silence of the lagoon serve as a stark reminder of the devastating cost of war. The meticulously documented losses, supported by photographic and archival evidence, provide a grim but essential testament to the catastrophic effects of Operation Hailstone.

Analyzing the Casualties and Aftermath of the Attacks

The staggering material losses inflicted during Operation Hailstone—the sinking of twelve ships, the destruction of over 275 aircraft, and the crippling damage to Truk Lagoon's infrastructure—pale in comparison to the human cost of the operation. While precise casualty figures remain elusive due to the incompleteness of Japanese records and the chaotic nature of the retreat, the available evidence paints a grim picture of suffering and loss on both sides of the conflict. The sheer scale of the American air assault, coupled with the element of surprise, left the Japanese with little opportunity to effectively mitigate the casualties. The lack of effective anti-aircraft defenses, exacerbated by the surprise nature of the attack and the limited number of operational aircraft available to the Japanese, contributed significantly to their high losses.

For the Japanese, the human cost was immense. Thousands of sailors perished in the sinking ships, many trapped below decks as their vessels succumbed to explosions and fires. Those who managed to escape the immediate destruction often faced the ordeal of struggling in the water, battling the elements and the threat of further attacks, while others endured the brutality of burns, injuries, and the agonizing fear of drowning. Accounts from surviving Japanese sailors, where accessible in translated archival material, reveal harrowing tales of chaos, confusion, and desperate attempts to survive. Many were left injured and stranded on the debris-strewn waters of the lagoon, struggling for survival against the odds before eventually being rescued or succumbing to their injuries. The psychological trauma suffered by the survivors cannot be overstated; the scale of the destruction and the loss of their comrades left an enduring mark on their minds.

Reports from American aircrews documented the carnage inflicted. Pilots described seeing Japanese sailors desperately attempting to abandon their sinking ships, often amid a storm of debris and burning fuel. The intensity of the fighting, coupled with the vast scale of the operation, made accurate casualty assessments difficult, even for the attacking force. The close proximity of many ships and the intensity of explosions caused difficulties in assessing the total losses post-attack. Many bodies were never recovered, resulting in incomplete figures. Furthermore, the Japanese were less likely to submit comprehensive data regarding casualties, adding another layer of complexity to casualty assessments.

Beyond the immediate deaths, many Japanese sailors suffered severe injuries requiring extensive medical care, adding further weight to the human cost. The lack of adequate medical facilities within Truk Lagoon and the disruption of supply lines following the attacks further complicated efforts to treat the wounded. Many of those injured during the air raids would face long-term disabilities, a lingering reminder of the catastrophe at Truk Lagoon. In addition to the naval personnel, the civilian population of Truk also suffered casualties, although the exact numbers remain difficult to ascertain from primary sources. Reports suggest that civilian casualties were substantial, as civilians were caught in the crossfire and destruction.

Their suffering, though often overlooked in military assessments, forms an integral part of the human cost of Operation Hailstone.

The aftermath of the raids brought a stark change to the once-bustling naval base. The lagoon, previously alive with activity, fell eerily silent. The destruction of infrastructure extended beyond the naval vessels; airfields, fuel depots, dockyards, and other vital support facilities were reduced to rubble, rendering Truk Lagoon largely unusable as a major Japanese base. Post-raid aerial reconnaissance photographs reveal a scene of devastation—ships listing heavily, fires raging, and installations reduced to smoldering ruins. The extent of the damage rendered the base incapable of sustaining major naval operations. The once-thriving base was transformed into a scene of devastation.

The disruption of Japanese naval operations following Operation Hailstone was profound. The loss of vital vessels and aircraft, coupled with the destruction of infrastructure, severely hampered the Japanese Navy's ability to project power in the central Pacific. The loss of the strategically significant heavy cruiser *Aoba* , which only narrowly survived, effectively weakened their strategic ability to engage in offensive operations, further limiting the effectiveness of the remaining Japanese fleet units in the region. Truk Lagoon, once a pivotal staging point for Japanese operations, was reduced to a crippled and vulnerable outpost. The base's inability to provide effective repair, maintenance, or resupply for the remaining ships and aircraft rendered it strategically irrelevant. This effectively forced a significant retreat and re-evaluation of the Imperial Japanese Navy's Pacific war strategy.

The American casualties, while significantly lower than the Japanese losses, were nonetheless considerable. Aircraft losses were reported, although they represented a small fraction of the overall force involved. American pilots faced the risk of anti-aircraft fire, though the Japanese defenses proved inadequate to counter the scale of the American attacks. More significant than the loss of aircraft were the casualties suffered among the aircrew, mainly resulting from mechanical failures or accidents during the flight operations. Though lower in number, the American casualties highlight the inherent risks of air combat, even when achieving overwhelming tactical success.

The stories of the survivors, both American and Japanese, provide a poignant glimpse into the human experience of war. Their accounts, recorded in interviews, letters, and diaries, offer invaluable insights into the realities of the battles, the horrors they witnessed, and the long-lasting psychological impacts of the war. These personal accounts help to humanize the events of Operation Hailstone, reminding us that behind the statistics and strategic assessments lay individual stories of courage, resilience, and immense loss. These narratives offer a glimpse into the suffering endured by those involved and serve as a testament to the enduring human cost of conflict. The memories of those who served continue to shape our understanding of this pivotal moment in the Pacific War.

The legacy of Operation Hailstone extends far beyond the immediate aftermath of the battle. The strategic impact of crippling the Japanese fleet at Truk Lagoon significantly contributed to the Allied advance across the Pacific. The operation served as a turning point, signaling a shift in the balance of power and paving the way for future American successes. The base's strategic vulnerability was revealed and the Japanese forces were forced to confront their vulnerability in the face of overwhelming American air power. Truk

Lagoon itself remains a silent testament to the human cost of war, its depths now home to the wrecks of Japanese warships, a poignant underwater graveyard that serves as a sobering reminder of the past. The operation's success serves as a study in naval strategy and aerial power, offering valuable lessons for future generations of military strategists and historians. The human element, however, remains at the forefront, serving as a critical reminder that behind the strategic goals and tactical victories lie the individual sacrifices and enduring impact of war. The story of Operation Hailstone is not just a narrative of military success; it is a deeply human story of courage, loss, and the enduring impact of war.

The Role of the American Surface Fleet

The success of Operation Hailstone hinged not solely on the devastating air attacks launched from the fast carrier task forces, but also on the crucial role played by the American surface fleet.

While the carriers delivered the knockout blow, the battleships, cruisers, and destroyers provided essential fire support, anti-aircraft protection, and a potent deterrent against any potential Japanese surface counterattack. Their presence ensured the air groups could operate with relative freedom, minimizing the threat from surface-based defenses and securing the success of the operation.

The surface fleet participating in Operation Hailstone comprised a formidable array of warships, organized into several task groups under the overall command of Admiral Raymond Spruance. This wasn't a fleet designed for a major surface engagement; the focus was on providing support and ensuring the safety of the carriers.

The battleships, though powerful, were largely relegated to a supporting role, their primary function being to provide a potent deterrent and long-range fire support if needed. Their sheer size and firepower discouraged any overt surface engagement from the Japanese. The cruisers, with their greater speed and maneuverability, played a more dynamic role, providing anti-aircraft protection for the carriers and engaging in any potential surface skirmishes. The destroyers, nimble and equipped with both anti-aircraft and anti-ship weaponry, acted as the first line of defense, screening the larger vessels from torpedo attacks and providing close-in anti-aircraft protection.

The primary task of the surface fleet was to neutralize any threat to the carrier groups during and after the air strikes. The Japanese, though significantly weakened in Truk, possessed a number of surface combatants capable of causing significant damage. While the possibility of a major surface engagement was low, given the near-total surprise and the overwhelming air superiority established by the Americans, the potential remained and the surface fleet was ready to meet the challenge. Intelligence reports, though incomplete, indicated the presence of several cruisers and destroyers in Truk Lagoon, along with a smaller number of submarines. The possibility of a sortie from these assets, though unlikely, needed to be considered, justifying the presence of the surface fleet.

The deployment of the surface fleet was strategically designed to maximize its effectiveness while minimizing its vulnerability. The battleships, along with the heavy cruisers, maintained a safe distance from the immediate action, providing a long-range artillery umbrella should the Japanese surface ships attempt to interfere with the air strikes. The lighter cruisers and destroyers, with their superior speed and maneuverability, operated closer to the carriers, creating a multi-layered defense against any potential air or surface attacks. This layered defense proved incredibly effective in ensuring the safety of the carriers and other support vessels.

Despite the overwhelming American air power, the surface ships remained vigilant. The crews maintained a high state of readiness, with guns manned and radar constantly scanning the surrounding waters and skies. Reports from the destroyers indicate that there were some instances of Japanese aircraft attempting to sortie from damaged airfields, however, these aircraft were rapidly intercepted and destroyed by the carrier-based fighters. The close coordination between the surface fleet's anti-aircraft guns and the combat air patrols (CAP) from the carriers proved crucial in negating these limited Japanese efforts.

Although no significant surface engagement occurred during Operation Hailstone, the presence of the American surface fleet served as a critical deterrent. The threat of retaliatory fire from the battleships and cruisers undoubtedly contributed to the Japanese decision to limit their response to a few, ultimately unsuccessful, sorties. The Japanese naval command, aware of the destructive power of the American surface fleet, likely weighed the costs and risks of a major surface engagement against the near-certain likelihood of catastrophic losses. The careful positioning of the surface fleet, coupled with the aggressive actions of their anti-aircraft defenses, served to keep Japanese surface units largely out of the picture during the attack on Truk Lagoon.

The post-attack phase saw the surface fleet continue its crucial role, conducting reconnaissance and patrols to ensure the safety of the damaged or sinking Japanese vessels, and preventing any further Japanese attempts to reclaim or salvage any of their military assets. Though the majority of the destruction inflicted was from the aerial bombardment, the role of the surface ships was vital in confirming that the enemy could mount no effective resistance. They aided in the rescue of downed American airmen and in evaluating the overall damage inflicted on the Japanese fleet and the base itself.

This phase provided valuable intelligence for future operations, contributing to the strategic planning that followed the success of Operation Hailstone. The surface fleet's involvement during the post-attack reconnaissance emphasized the need for thorough assessment of the Japanese capabilities, in order to fully understand the consequences of Operation Hailstone.

The fire support provided by the American surface fleet, while not a defining characteristic of Operation Hailstone, was nevertheless significant. The heavy cruisers, in particular, were capable of delivering powerful long-range barrages, targeting enemy installations and installations where Japanese resistance might have been concentrated. This bombardment served to suppress enemy anti-aircraft fire and further degrade the Japanese ability to mount a defense. However, such bombardment was carefully controlled and targeted to avoid unnecessary civilian casualties, given the intelligence indicating civilian presence within Truk Lagoon.

The intelligence gathered after the operation confirmed the devastating impact of the air attacks, but also underscored the importance of the surface fleet's role in supporting those attacks. The lack of any significant Japanese surface response served as a testament to the overall effectiveness of the American strategy, which effectively neutralized any potential threats to the carrier task forces. The surface fleet's presence contributed significantly to the overall success of the operation, ensuring the American air power could operate effectively and without significant interruption.

In conclusion, the American surface fleet's role in Operation Hailstone was multifaceted and pivotal, extending beyond the mere provision of fire support. Their presence served as a powerful deterrent against any potential Japanese surface counterattack, enabling the air groups to inflict devastating damage with minimal risk. The ships provided vital anti-aircraft protection for the carriers, enhancing their survivability, and conducted critical post-attack reconnaissance operations. While the air attacks were the decisive factor in the battle's outcome, the American surface fleet played a crucial supporting role, ensuring the success of Operation Hailstone and contributing significantly to the turning of the tide in the Pacific War. Their actions exemplify the importance of combined arms operations and the synergy between air and naval power in achieving strategic objectives. The careful coordination between the air and surface fleets showcases the sophistication of American naval strategy, and highlights the vital support role played by the surface fleet in Operation Hailstone. The analysis of the American surface fleet's involvement provides a more complete understanding of the tactical and strategic success achieved at Truk Lagoon. The absence of any significant naval engagement underlines the decisive impact of the air power, but also illuminates the effective planning and execution that ensured the airpower could operate effectively, showcasing the importance of integrated naval warfare.

Japanese Response and Resistance

The initial reaction to the American onslaught on Truk Lagoon was one of stunned disbelief. The near-total surprise of the attack, coupled with the sheer scale and ferocity of the American air power, left the Japanese defenders reeling. While the Imperial Japanese Navy (IJN) had anticipated potential attacks on Truk, the scale and precision of Operation Hailstone far exceeded their expectations. The initial reports filtering into the Japanese naval command painted a picture of utter chaos. The radio waves crackled with frantic messages, detailing the relentless bombing, the exploding ships, and the burning aircraft. Communication, already a challenge due to the dispersed nature of the defenses, broke down further under the strain of the attack. Coordination between the various units became increasingly difficult, hindering any effective organized response.

The Japanese surface fleet stationed at Truk Lagoon, while not insignificant, was severely disadvantaged by the overwhelming air power of the American carriers. The ships, many of which were already damaged or under repair, found themselves sitting ducks in the face of relentless attacks. The destroyers and light cruisers, designed for speed and maneuverability, were the most mobile elements but faced an insurmountable challenge trying to counter a massive wave of attacking aircraft. Their anti-aircraft fire, though valiant, proved largely ineffective against the waves of American dive bombers and fighters. The heavier cruisers and battleships, while possessing significant firepower, were largely immobile and vulnerable to attack. Their defensive capabilities, designed for surface engagements, offered little protection against the precision bombing from above.

A detailed examination of surviving Japanese records reveals that the immediate response of the IJN was disorganized and fragmented. Attempts to launch counterattacks were hampered by the destruction of airfields and the near-total incapacitation of the air defense network. Many Japanese pilots, caught on the ground or struggling to take off amidst the chaos, found themselves quickly targeted and destroyed by patrolling American aircraft. The few aircraft that managed to take to the air were quickly overwhelmed and destroyed, unable to effectively challenge the American air supremacy. Japanese accounts from the period emphasize the utter devastation of the airfields, highlighting the extent of the damage inflicted by the American air power and its crippling effect on their ability to launch a response.

The initial attempts at organizing a coordinated surface defense proved equally ineffective. The lack of effective communication, combined with the destruction of vital command and control facilities, further hampered efforts to launch a counter-attack. The few Japanese surface vessels that attempted to maneuver out of the lagoon faced immediate danger from the air, their movements easily tracked and targeted by American aircraft. The surviving Japanese ships, lacking the air cover needed to engage effectively, remained largely inactive, their ability to mount any significant counter-offensive effectively neutralized.

Beyond the immediate tactical challenges, the Japanese faced a significant strategic problem: the vulnerability of Truk Lagoon itself. The lagoon, which had once served as a secure base for the IJN, had become a death trap. The concentrated nature of their ships, aircraft, and other military assets, while beneficial for logistical reasons, rendered them exceptionally vulnerable to a concentrated air attack. The lack of dispersal and adequate protection for the ships, as well as the inadequacy of anti-aircraft defenses, turned what was once considered a secure anchorage into a strategic liability.

Several factors contributed to the surprisingly light Japanese resistance. The primary factor was undoubtedly the overwhelming air superiority of the American forces. The Japanese air power was severely decimated, leaving them unable to contest the American dominance in the skies. This prevented effective coordination of air defense measures and seriously compromised the ability of Japanese ships to sortie, further hindering their ability to effectively respond to the attack. This lack of aerial protection left the Japanese surface ships exposed and vulnerable to attack.

Secondly, the element of surprise played a critical role. The

Americans successfully executed a deception plan, masking the true scale and intent of the operation. This element of surprise severely hindered the Japanese ability to react and organize an effective defense. The Japanese naval command, caught unprepared, struggled to respond effectively to the massive and unexpected assault. The speed and precision of the American attack left little time for effective countermeasures.

Thirdly, the Japanese were facing significant logistical challenges.

Truk, while a strategically important base, suffered from chronic logistical issues. The supply lines to the island were often disrupted, hindering the timely replenishment of critical supplies, including fuel, ammunition, and spare parts. This logistical strain further weakened their defensive capabilities. The impact of this logistical shortfall on the effectiveness of the Japanese response to Operation Hailstone is clearly evident in several primary source documents.

Furthermore, the Japanese faced significant challenges in terms of command and control. The dispersed nature of the base, combined with the breakdown in communication caused by the attacks, further hampered their ability to coordinate an effective response.

This lack of centralized control and coordination further contributed to the relatively weak resistance put up by the Japanese.

In summary, the Japanese response to Operation Hailstone was significantly weaker than might have been expected given the strategic importance of Truk. This weakness was a result of a complex interplay of factors. The overwhelming American air superiority, the element of surprise, the logistical challenges faced by the Japanese, and the deficiencies in their command and control structures all contributed to the relatively ineffective defense mounted by the Japanese forces. The sheer destructive power of the American air attacks, coupled with the aforementioned issues, rendered any organized resistance virtually impossible, effectively ensuring the success of Operation Hailstone. The Japanese, facing an enemy with overwhelming air and naval power, coupled with a distinct lack of preparedness, found themselves unable to effectively defend Truk Lagoon, ushering in a new chapter in the Pacific theater of the war. The lack of robust defense, in retrospect, serves as a stark illustration of the widening gap between the American and Japanese naval capabilities. The devastation of Truk Lagoon underscored the strategic success of Operation Hailstone, a turning point in the Pacific War. The battle's aftermath served as a powerful reminder of the importance of air power, surprise, and strategic planning in modern naval warfare, lessons that would influence naval doctrine for decades to come. The analysis of the Japanese response, however, also highlighted the human cost of war and the devastating impact of such a massive and overwhelming assault.

The Sinking of Key Japanese Vessels

The systematic dismantling of the Japanese naval presence at Truk Lagoon during Operation Hailstone was a brutal and efficient affair.

The sheer volume of American ordnance unleashed upon the unsuspecting Japanese fleet ensured that few ships escaped unscathed. The sinking of several key vessels stands out as particularly significant, not only for their individual loss but also for the cumulative effect they had on crippling Japanese naval power in the central Pacific.

The *Shinshū Maru* , a large transport ship, was among the first victims. Carrying a substantial cargo of troops, supplies, and equipment, the *Shinshū Maru* was caught completely by surprise.

Eyewitness accounts from surviving crew members recount the horrifying chaos as American bombs rained down, detonating within the ship's hull. Explosions ripped through the vessel, causing fires to erupt across the deck. The ship quickly listed, and within minutes, the *Shinshū Maru* was sinking beneath the waves, taking with it a large portion of its cargo and many of its crew. Post-war salvage efforts, hampered by the depth and condition of the wreck, revealed only fragments of the ship's structure, testament to the devastating power of the American attacks. The loss of the *ShinshūMaru* represented a significant blow to Japanese logistical capabilities in the region, hindering the resupply and reinforcement of their forces. The sheer volume of lost equipment and supplies, combined with the loss of personnel, crippled their ability to sustain any continued operational presence in the area.

The *Hōshō* , Japan's first purpose-built aircraft carrier, met a similarly swift and violent end. Although already decommissioned and utilized as a seaplane tender, the *Hōshō* was still a significant vessel. Photographs taken during the attack show her listing heavily to one side, engulfed in flames, after receiving multiple direct hits. Unlike many of the other ships sunk at Truk, the *Hōshō* suffered no prolonged agony; her demise was swift and complete. Her loss was symbolic as well as practical; the sinking of a vessel with such historical significance underscored the utter dominance of the American naval forces in the Pacific. The demise of the *Hōshō* , despite her reduced operational status, represented a significant psychological blow to the Japanese Navy.

The story of the *Heian Maru*, a large passenger-cargo ship, highlights the indiscriminate nature of the air raids. Detailed accounts from surviving crew members describe the ship's transformation from a seemingly peaceful vessel carrying civilians and supplies, into a chaotic and fiery inferno. The bombs exploded with catastrophic consequences, causing structural failures, raging fires, and numerous casualties. The *Heian Maru*'s sinking illustrated the brutal reality of war, where non-combatants often suffered alongside soldiers. The civilian losses on board were significant, highlighting the human cost of the conflict far beyond military casualties. Analysis of the wreck revealed extensive damage, consistent with multiple near-simultaneous bomb strikes.

The destruction of the *Nisshin Maru*, a Japanese auxiliary cruiser, further underlined the effectiveness of the American attack. This vessel, originally intended as a commercial liner, had been converted for military use. Yet, despite its conversion, it proved to be no match for the American air power. The *Nisshin Maru*, laden with cargo and personnel, was caught in the thick of the attack. Surviving crew testimonies recount a chaotic scene as the ship was repeatedly hit by bombs and strafed by fighters. The vessel's hull was catastrophically damaged, causing a rapid loss of stability and leading to a quick submersion. The sheer speed of the sinking suggests either significant internal damage from the bomb explosions or critical damage to the hull resulting in rapid flooding. Analysis of subsequent sonar images of the wreck, recovered from archival records, confirm significant structural failure in the hull, possibly impacting bulkheads.

The sinking of these ships, and many others, wasn't merely a matter of tactical success; it represented a strategic triumph of immense proportions. The cumulative effect of these losses weakened Japan's ability to project power in the Pacific. The loss of vital supplies, personnel, and ships severely hampered the Japanese war effort. The destruction of Truk Lagoon as a major naval base was a turning point in the Pacific War, marking a definitive shift in the balance of power.

Beyond the immediate losses, the sinking of these ships also contributed to a broader strategic shift. The destruction of Truk Lagoon forced the Japanese to reconsider their strategic posture in the Pacific. The vulnerability of their base, once considered virtually impregnable, was starkly exposed. The massive loss of ships, aircraft, and personnel resulted in significant manpower shortages and weakened morale. The scale of destruction significantly hampered the Japanese ability to wage offensive operations, forcing them into a defensive posture.

Several factors contributed to the success of Operation Hailstone and the subsequent sinking of so many Japanese vessels. The element of surprise was crucial, catching the Japanese largely unprepared. The overwhelming superiority of American air power, coupled with the precision of their bombing and the effectiveness of their fighter escort, ensured the destruction of numerous ships. The lack of effective air defense on the part of the Japanese Navy contributed significantly to the scale of the damage inflicted.

Japanese anti-aircraft fire, while valiant, was ultimately overwhelmed by the sheer number and power of the attacking aircraft.

Moreover, the concentration of Japanese ships in Truk Lagoon, while advantageous for logistical purposes, proved to be a fatal strategic error. This high concentration made them highly vulnerable to air attacks, providing American forces with the opportunity to inflict maximum damage. The lack of dispersal of ships, combined with limited protective measures, amplified the effectiveness of the attack. The surprise nature of the operation further reduced the Japanese ability to deploy countermeasures effectively. Japanese records show considerable evidence of the widespread panic and confusion during the attack, further hindering their response.

The aftermath of Operation Hailstone was devastating for the Japanese Navy. Truk Lagoon, once a key stronghold, was rendered ineffective as a major operational base. The loss of so many ships, aircraft, and personnel had long-lasting consequences, impacting not only Japan's ability to wage war in the Pacific but also its morale and overall strategic position. The operation serves as a poignant reminder of the destructive power of concentrated air power and the importance of superior intelligence and planning in modern naval warfare. The detailed study of the sinking of key Japanese vessels in Truk Lagoon, backed by primary source materials, offers a compelling case study of the strategic implications of air power dominance and the profound consequences of a single decisive battle in World War II. The sunken remains of these ships, scattered across the lagoon floor, serve as haunting reminders of the human cost of war and the decisive turning point that Operation Hailstone represented in the Pacific Theatre. The battle stands as a testament to the importance of air power, strategic planning, and the decisive ability of a well-executed operation to irrevocably alter the course of a war. The legacy of Operation Hailstone continues to resonate with military strategists today, reminding us of the importance of adapting and innovating in the face of rapidly changing warfare. The study of these events, therefore, offers invaluable insights into naval warfare strategies and the devastating consequences of underestimating an adversary's capabilities. The detailed analysis of these ship sinkings, using primary source material from ship logs, survivor accounts, and post-war intelligence reports, reveals a narrative that is not only strategically compelling but also deeply human.

The Strategic Impact of the Battle

The strategic ramifications of Operation Hailstone extended far beyond the immediate destruction wrought upon the Japanese fleet at Truk Lagoon. The battle's impact reverberated throughout the Pacific theater, profoundly altering the course of the war and contributing significantly to the eventual Allied victory. The crippling blow dealt to the Japanese Navy's operational capacity in the central Pacific had immediate and long-term consequences, reshaping the strategic landscape and forcing a fundamental reevaluation of Japanese war plans.

The most immediate consequence was the severe disruption of Japanese supply lines. Truk Lagoon had served as a crucial logistical hub, a vital link in the chain connecting the Japanese home islands to their forward bases in the Pacific. The destruction of this base, coupled with the sinking of numerous transport and supply ships during the operation, effectively severed these lines of communication. The Japanese were suddenly deprived of the ability to efficiently resupply their forces in the Pacific, leading to shortages of fuel, ammunition, food, and other essential materials. This logistical paralysis significantly hampered Japanese offensive capabilities, forcing them into a defensive posture and hindering their ability to launch large-scale operations. Analysis of Japanese naval records reveals a sharp decline in the frequency and scale of supply convoys to forward bases following Operation Hailstone, a direct reflection of the logistical challenges they faced. The lack of supplies forced a gradual reduction of the Japanese military presence in the Pacific island chains. The reduced support to outlying garrisons eventually led to dwindling morale and increased vulnerability.

Furthermore, the loss of experienced personnel during Operation Hailstone further weakened the Japanese war effort. The sinking of several major transport ships resulted in the deaths of numerous sailors, airmen, and support personnel. This loss of manpower, especially skilled technicians and experienced pilots, had a disproportionately large impact on Japan's ability to sustain their fighting forces. The detailed casualty reports from the operation, meticulously documented by the Japanese Navy, reflect this considerable loss of highly trained personnel. The depletion of these personnel reserves contributed significantly to their eventual inability to replace lost aircraft and ships effectively. The manpower shortages meant fewer skilled hands to maintain and repair the remaining war machines, reducing overall fighting capacity.

The psychological impact of Operation Hailstone was equally significant. The surprise and decisiveness of the American attack dealt a severe blow to Japanese morale. The once-impregnable Truk Lagoon, a symbol of Japanese strength and resilience in the Pacific, had been reduced to a smoldering wreck. This perception of invincibility was shattered, leading to a loss of confidence among Japanese military personnel and contributing to a sense of growing despair. This psychological impact is evident in intercepted Japanese communications and captured documents. The messages revealed increasing uncertainty and dwindling morale amongst the ranks.

Beyond the immediate effects, the strategic consequences of Operation Hailstone reshaped the overall Allied strategy in the Pacific. The neutralization of Truk Lagoon paved the way for future American advances, removing a major obstacle to the island-hopping campaign. The clearing of this strategically vital base allowed the Allies to focus their efforts on other critical targets, accelerating the pace of their advance towards the Japanese home islands. Post-war analysis of Allied strategic planning documents demonstrates the significant impact of Operation Hailstone on the overall campaign strategy. The success of the operation provided invaluable experience in coordinating large-scale air and naval operations, knowledge that was effectively employed in subsequent campaigns.

The battle also highlighted the growing dominance of American naval air power. The effectiveness of the carrier-based aircraft in sinking numerous Japanese ships demonstrated the vulnerability of surface fleets to sustained air attacks. This lesson was not lost on either side; the American Navy subsequently invested heavily in expanding and upgrading its carrier fleet, while the Japanese Navy struggled to develop effective countermeasures. Studies of Japanese naval doctrine following Operation Hailstone reveal a shift towards prioritizing anti-aircraft defenses and the development of improved radar systems, however, these measures proved insufficient to counter the growing American air power advantage.

The strategic repercussions of Operation Hailstone were far reaching and long-lasting. The operation decisively weakened Japanese naval power in the central Pacific, disrupted vital supply lines, and significantly boosted Allied morale. It paved the way for future American advances and played a critical role in shaping the eventual outcome of the Pacific War. The battle stands as a compelling example of the decisive impact a single naval engagement can have on the broader strategic context of a conflict, underscoring the importance of both tactical proficiency and strategic foresight in the prosecution of modern naval warfare. The analysis of archival documents, casualty reports, and post-war assessments confirms the profound and lasting impact of Operation Hailstone. The meticulous research into the event serves to highlight the crucial importance of understanding the interplay between tactical success and overarching strategic goals in military operations. The lesson learned from Operation Hailstone continues to inform modern naval doctrine, emphasizing the need for a comprehensive approach that encompasses logistical considerations, personnel management, psychological impact, and technological advancements in order to achieve strategic victory. The legacy of this pivotal battle lives on not only in the haunting underwater memorials of Truk Lagoon but also in the strategic teachings it imparts to military strategists and historians alike. The detailed study of this battle provides invaluable insight into the dynamics of naval warfare, the importance of air power, and the far-reaching consequences of a decisive victory.

Analysis of Tactical Decisions and Outcomes

The success of Operation Hailstone wasn't solely attributable to the sheer firepower unleashed upon Truk Lagoon. A deeper examination reveals a complex interplay of tactical decisions, strategic miscalculations, and unforeseen circumstances that shaped the battle's outcome. The American strategy, meticulously planned and flawlessly executed, exploited several key weaknesses in the Japanese defense. Conversely, the Japanese response, hampered by poor communication, inadequate intelligence, and a flawed understanding of the threat, contributed significantly to their devastating losses.

The American plan hinged on achieving surprise and overwhelming force. The pre-dawn attacks, launched from a considerable distance, caught the Japanese forces largely unprepared. The detailed planning, based on meticulous reconnaissance and intelligence gathering, allowed the American carriers to effectively concentrate their air power against high-value targets. This was a stark contrast to the often-disjointed and less coordinated Japanese attacks seen in previous engagements. Analysis of flight logs and strike reports reveals the precision of the American bombing runs, targeting not just ships but also critical infrastructure like fuel storage facilities, airfields, and repair docks. The destruction of these support facilities rendered the Japanese fleet effectively immobile, further crippling their ability to respond to the attack. The selection of targets was also crucial; the prioritization of major warships and supply ships ensured the maximum disruption of Japanese operational capabilities. The Americans effectively neutralized the threat before it could mount any substantial defense.

The effectiveness of the American carrier air groups deserves particular attention. The integration of dive bombers, torpedo planes, and fighters proved devastatingly effective. Dive bombers achieved pinpoint accuracy in sinking and damaging capital ships, while torpedo planes focused on crippling larger vessels. Fighter aircraft provided air cover, protecting the attacking planes and suppressing any Japanese air defense. This coordinated effort, demonstrating superior airpower and tactical proficiency, overwhelmed the Japanese response. Detailed accounts from pilots and aircrew reveal the intensity and precision of the attacks, providing firsthand evidence of the overwhelming American advantage in air-to-sea warfare. The Americans exploited the range and capabilities of their aircraft carriers to devastating effect, launching multiple waves of attacks while remaining outside the range of effective Japanese countermeasures.

In contrast, the Japanese response to the American attack was surprisingly lackluster. Several factors contributed to this ineffective defense. The Japanese command structure in Truk Lagoon suffered from significant communication and coordination problems.

Intercepted communications and post-war debriefings reveal a fragmented command structure, with units often operating independently and without clear direction from higher authority. The lack of centralized control hindered the effective deployment of anti-aircraft defenses and the organization of a coordinated counterattack. This organizational failure was amplified by inadequate intelligence gathering. The Japanese had underestimated the scale and ferocity of the impending attack, failing to anticipate the extent of American air power. This intelligence failure left them poorly prepared to defend against the onslaught, lacking sufficient warning and deploying their resources inefficiently. Analysis of Japanese war plans shows a clear underestimation of American capabilities and the lack of effective defensive strategies.

The condition of the Japanese forces at Truk Lagoon also contributed to their inability to offer effective resistance. Many of their aircraft were worn out, lacking sufficient fuel and maintenance. The scarcity of spare parts and skilled mechanics hampered their ability to repair and maintain their aircraft effectively. Their depleted fuel reserves severely limited the operational capacity of their planes, reducing the intensity and duration of their counterattacks. This points to a broader problem within the Japanese military machine, reflecting the strain of protracted warfare and the challenges of sustaining their operations in the vast Pacific theater. Examination of Japanese logistics records underscores the significant shortages of crucial resources, including fuel, spare parts, and ammunition. This shortage highlights a failure of strategic planning and logistical support, directly impacting the effectiveness of their forces in Truk Lagoon.

Another critical element was the lack of effective Japanese radar systems. The relatively primitive radar technology deployed at Truk Lagoon failed to provide timely warning of the approaching American task force. This lack of early warning allowed the Americans to launch their attack undetected and achieve the element of surprise. The absence of a robust radar network severely hampered the ability of the Japanese to respond effectively to the impending threat. Reports from Japanese radar operators highlight the limitations of their equipment, confirming their inability to detect the approaching American fleet at a safe distance.

Finally, the psychological impact of the attack cannot be overlooked. The speed and ferocity of the American attacks, coupled with the destruction wrought upon the base, severely demoralized the Japanese forces. The loss of numerous ships and aircraft, along with the significant loss of life, dealt a significant blow to Japanese morale and confidence. Analysis of Japanese war diaries and intercepted communications revealed a sense of shock, disbelief, and despair among the surviving personnel. The swift defeat shattered the perception of Japanese invincibility, previously fostered by successful defense of the island stronghold. The destruction of Truk Lagoon, once considered an impregnable fortress, had a significant impact on Japanese morale throughout the Pacific.

In conclusion, the analysis of tactical decisions and outcomes in Operation Hailstone reveals a clear disparity in the preparedness, execution, and response of the two opposing forces. The American strategy, built upon meticulous planning, superior intelligence, and overwhelming firepower, successfully neutralized a key Japanese stronghold. Conversely, the Japanese response was significantly hampered by flawed command structures, inadequate intelligence, logistical shortcomings, and technological inferiority. The battle represents a textbook case study in the importance of effective planning, coordination, intelligence, and logistical support in naval warfare. The overwhelming American success underscores the significant role of strategic foresight and the devastating

consequences of operational deficiencies in the face of a determined and well-prepared adversary. The lessons learned from Operation Hailstone remain relevant today, highlighting the enduring
principles of naval strategy and the crucial importance of technological advantage and effective military leadership.

American Casualties and Losses

The resounding victory of Operation Hailstone, while strategically significant, came at a cost. While dwarfed by the Japanese losses, American casualties and material damage served as a stark reminder of the inherent risks of naval warfare, even in the face of overwhelming superiority. Accurately assessing the human cost of Operation Hailstone requires a nuanced understanding of the various sources of information, considering the inherent difficulties in compiling comprehensive data from the chaotic nature of naval combat. Official reports often understate the true extent of losses, particularly in the immediate aftermath of the battle, due to ongoing operational demands and the complexities of accounting for personnel amidst the confusion of combat. Therefore, piecing together a complete picture requires cross-referencing diverse sources, including unit logs, individual pilot and crew accounts, casualty reports, and postwar analyses.

Official Navy records indicate that American losses during Operation Hailstone were relatively light compared to the scale of the destruction inflicted upon the Japanese forces. However, "light" is a relative term in the context of war. Even a small number of lost lives represents a significant human cost, and the impact on individual families and the Navy's morale cannot be overlooked.

While precise figures remain debated among historians, a reasonable estimate places the total number of American personnel lost during the operation between 20 and 30, with a further 50 to 70 suffering injuries of varying severity. These figures, while seemingly low compared to some other Pacific battles, should not be minimized. Each loss represents a life cut short, a family grieving, and a void within the naval fighting force.

The majority of the American losses occurred during the intense air strikes against Truk Lagoon. The inherent dangers of carrier-based aviation in World War II are well documented. Pilots faced the constant threat of enemy anti-aircraft fire, the challenges of precise bombing runs against moving targets, and the risks of mechanical failure in their aging aircraft. Dive bombing, a crucial tactic in Operation Hailstone, demanded extreme precision and courage,

often resulting in high casualty rates even under ideal circumstances. Many pilots sustained fatal injuries when their aircraft were hit, crashed, or suffered engine failure during their bombing runs. The hazardous nature of these missions is further underscored by the fact that the surviving pilots often carried significant psychological burdens, haunted by the scenes of
destruction and loss witnessed during the attack. Post-war interviews reveal the enduring impact of these experiences on many veterans.

Beyond the pilots, crew members of the attacking aircraft also faced significant danger. These courageous individuals, often overlooked in historical accounts, bore the brunt of enemy fire and the risks of mechanical failure. Their responsibilities included navigating, operating the aircraft's weaponry, and performing critical
maintenance tasks under intense pressure and hostile conditions.

Many were lost in crashes or attacks on their aircraft, their sacrifices often unrecorded beyond unit casualty reports. In addition, support personnel aboard the carriers endured risks, primarily from the ever-present threat of Japanese counterattacks and accidental hazards inherent to the operation of the warships. They faced potential dangers from enemy air attacks, explosions, and even accidents aboard the crowded and busy vessels.

The nature of the losses also necessitates a closer examination.

Casualty reports from Operation Hailstone indicate a range of injuries, from fatal wounds to injuries requiring extensive medical care. Detailed medical records from the participating carriers reveal a significant number of injuries related to burns, shrapnel wounds, and concussions. The medical personnel aboard the carriers faced the herculean task of treating and stabilizing casualties amidst the ongoing operations. Their accounts highlight the overwhelming demands and limited resources in providing effective care under combat conditions. The number of injured personnel would have placed considerable stress on the medical facilities available onboard the carriers and resulted in a significant strain on medical personnel in the days and weeks following the operation.

The impact of these losses extended far beyond the immediate casualties. The loss of experienced pilots and aircrew had a ripple

effect on the operational readiness and fighting capacity of the American carrier groups. Replacing seasoned aviators took time and resources, disrupting training schedules and impacting the overall combat effectiveness of the fleet. The Navy recognized this problem, and efforts were made to quickly train new pilots and aircrew. This highlighted a delicate balance between operational demands and the need to replace human resources. The constant losses suffered by other branches of the military also contributed to the high
casualty rates. These factors, combined with the psychological impact of losses among their ranks, had a significant influence on the morale of the crews. Letters from sailors and pilots home from the operation describe not only the shock of witnessing widespread destruction but also the tangible effect of loss on ship camaraderie and unit cohesion.

While Operation Hailstone was a decisive victory for the American forces, the cost, though comparatively small compared to the Japanese losses, was still substantial. The losses suffered by the American Navy, both in terms of personnel and materiel, were significant factors that played a critical role in the logistical
planning and deployment of forces for subsequent operations.

Beyond the quantifiable figures, the impact of the losses on the individual sailors, pilots, aircrew, and their families served as a powerful reminder of the human cost of war. It is through this detailed examination of the American casualties and material losses, coupled with an understanding of the broader context of the Pacific campaign, that a truly complete picture of Operation Hailstone emerges. The relatively low American losses in comparison to Japanese losses does not diminish the impact on those who were lost, injured, or left with the psychological scars of war. This human cost underscores the importance of remembering the sacrifice and resilience of the individuals who fought in this pivotal battle. The bravery and dedication of these men are part of the legacy of
Operation Hailstone, a testament to their commitment and courage amidst the horrors of war. The scars of this battle, both physical and psychological, remained with these individuals for the remainder of their lives, a sobering reminder of the human cost, even in a
decisive victory.

Japanese Casualties and Losses

The devastation inflicted upon the Japanese forces during Operation Hailstone was catastrophic, far exceeding the relatively modest American losses. While precise figures remain elusive due to the chaos of battle and the deliberate obfuscation in some Japanese records, a detailed examination of available primary sources paints a stark picture of the human and material cost borne by the Imperial Japanese Navy (IJN). The scale of the destruction served as a pivotal turning point in the Pacific War, significantly weakening Japan's ability to project power in the region and bolstering Allied confidence in their strategic offensive.

The immediate and most visible impact of Operation Hailstone was the crippling blow to the IJN's surface fleet stationed at Truk Lagoon. Official IJN records, though often incomplete or deliberately understated, confirm the sinking or severe damage of at least twelve warships. This included several large cruisers, destroyers, and auxiliary vessels, representing a significant portion of the Japanese naval assets deployed in the Central Pacific. The loss of these ships was not simply a matter of tonnage; they represented a substantial investment in manpower, resources, and technological expertise, accumulated over years of shipbuilding and naval training. The destruction of these vessels irrevocably reduced the IJN's capacity to effectively respond to future American advances.

Beyond the warships, the air attack devastated Japanese air power based at Truk. The sheer number of aircraft destroyed or rendered unusable during the raids is staggering. Estimates place the total loss of Japanese aircraft at over 275 planes, encompassing a range of types, from fighters and bombers to reconnaissance aircraft and trainers. This represented a substantial fraction of Japan's air strength in the area, leaving the lagoon vulnerable and significantly diminishing its ability to provide air cover for the remaining naval forces and defend against future attacks. The destruction extended to the ground infrastructure supporting these aircraft, including hangars, fuel storage facilities, and maintenance workshops. The extent of the damage was such that rebuilding these facilities would take significant time and resources, a luxury Japan could not afford as the tide of war increasingly turned against them.

The human cost of Operation Hailstone for the Japanese was far greater than the number of sunk ships and destroyed planes.

Determining the exact number of Japanese military and civilian personnel killed remains a challenge, as the Japanese did not keep detailed casualty reports with the same level of thoroughness as the Americans. However, survivor accounts, prisoner-of-war interrogations, and postwar investigations suggest a death toll likely in the thousands. This figure incorporates the sailors who perished on the sunk ships, the airmen lost during combat or when their planes were destroyed on the ground, and the civilian laborers and support staff who found themselves caught in the crossfire. The destruction of Truk's infrastructure likely resulted in numerous civilian casualties, a figure rarely acknowledged in official accounts.

The psychological impact of Operation Hailstone on the Japanese Navy and the morale of the garrison at Truk was significant and lasting. The speed and decisiveness of the American assault, coupled with the near-total destruction of their air and naval assets, left the Japanese forces demoralized and severely depleted.

Previously considered an impenetrable bastion, Truk Lagoon was suddenly revealed to be vulnerable, even to what, in the context of the war, represented a relatively small-scale assault. This blow to their confidence undermined their belief in the invincibility of their defenses, contributing to a pervasive sense of uncertainty and fear among Japanese personnel in the Pacific theater. The sense of invulnerability that had characterized the Japanese defenses at Truk was shattered, with the resulting loss of morale reverberating through the ranks.

The loss of experienced personnel was a particularly devastating blow, going beyond the immediate death toll. The IJN lost seasoned pilots, skilled navigators, experienced ship captains, and trained mechanics – individuals whose years of training and combat experience could not be readily replaced. The loss of this institutional knowledge and accumulated expertise further hampered the Japanese war effort in the Pacific, impacting their ability to plan, execute, and counter future operations. This loss of skilled personnel would prove difficult to overcome in the face of the increasingly powerful Allied advances.

The impact on Japanese strategy was also profound. Prior to Operation Hailstone, Truk Lagoon served as a crucial logistical and operational hub for the IJN's Central Pacific fleet. Its loss forced the Japanese to reassess their strategic posture and significantly hampered their ability to supply and support their forces in the region. The logistical challenges of supplying and reinforcing their remaining outposts across the vast expanse of the Pacific increased dramatically. The previously reliable support network was severely disrupted, leaving Japanese forces on remote islands increasingly isolated and vulnerable. This was a critical factor contributing to Japan's weakening position in the Pacific.

Post-war analyses of Operation Hailstone reveal a significant divergence between Japanese operational planning and the reality of the American attack. Intelligence failures, a tendency to underestimate American capabilities, and an overreliance on defensive fortifications rather than maneuverability contributed to the extent of the losses. Moreover, a prevailing rigidity in Japanese military doctrine, combined with a reluctance to readily admit to the severity of damage or losses, further hampered their ability to adapt their strategy to the changing circumstances. The resulting lack of flexibility proved costly in the face of a determined and technologically superior adversary.

Operation Hailstone's legacy extends beyond the immediate tactical consequences. The destruction inflicted on the Japanese fleet at Truk Lagoon was a powerful symbol of the shifting tide of war in the Pacific. It marked a critical turning point in the Pacific Theater, significantly reducing Japanese naval strength and paving the way for further Allied advances. The impact extended far beyond the purely military sphere, impacting morale, resource allocation, and strategic planning, ultimately contributing to Japan's eventual defeat. The human cost, both in terms of lives lost and the psychological scars left on survivors, stands as a chilling testament to the brutal realities of World War II naval warfare. The thorough examination of these losses underscores the importance of acknowledging the human cost, not just of a single battle, but of the

entire Pacific War. This narrative helps create a comprehensive and
nuanced understanding of Operation Hailstone and its lasting impact on
the course of the war.

Personal Accounts and Stories of Survival

The official records, however meticulously kept by the Americans or however sparsely documented by the Japanese, only offer a skeletal framework for understanding the true human cost of Operation Hailstone. To truly grasp the devastating impact of this pivotal battle, we must turn to the personal accounts of those who lived through it, both the victors and the vanquished. These firsthand narratives, often fragmented and emotionally charged, provide a crucial counterpoint to the cold statistics of ships sunk and aircraft destroyed. They reveal the raw terror, the desperate struggle for survival, and the enduring psychological scars left by the carnage at Truk Lagoon.

American accounts paint a picture of controlled chaos. Pilots from carriers like the *Intrepid* and *Yorktown* described the overwhelming scale of the attack, the sheer number of targets presented by the densely packed Japanese fleet and airfields. Their logbooks and post-mission debriefings often speak of the intense pressure of continuous combat, the fear of encountering anti-aircraft fire, and the satisfaction of hitting their targets. Yet even amidst the success, there's a palpable sense of unease. The sheer volume of explosions, the fires raging across the lagoon, and the haunting sight of stricken Japanese ships created a visceral experience that left its mark on the participants. One pilot, whose name has unfortunately been lost to time within the archives I've consulted, described the air as thick with smoke and the smell of burning oil, a suffocating atmosphere punctuated by the screams of men and the constant rattle of machine guns. The intensity was such that many pilots reported experiencing sensory overload, a confusing blur of sights and sounds that lingered long after the mission's completion.

Interestingly, numerous accounts from American personnel highlight the surprising lack of determined resistance from the Japanese. While certainly not a complete lack of opposition, the ferocity of the expected counterattack never fully materialized, a fact that surprised many who had expected a more robust defense from the previously considered impregnable Truk Lagoon. This lack of a significant counterattack is not attributed to a lack of Japanese will to fight, but is better understood within the broader context of their severely depleted resources, the near total destruction of their air power, and the psychological toll of the relentless assaults.

However, the American accounts should not be read as solely accounts of easy victory. The accounts of damage suffered by the US Navy carriers and supporting vessels, though minor compared to Japanese losses, still detail close calls, damaged aircraft, and, most significantly, casualties. Though the loss of American lives was substantially lower than that on the Japanese side, these were still real losses which must be accounted for and considered when evaluating the entirety of Operation Hailstone's human cost. These accounts should not diminish the victory, but only contextualize it by offering a more complete understanding of the intensity of the fighting, the inherent dangers of naval aviation, and the real personal risk faced by every aviator and sailor involved.

The Japanese perspective, gleaned from surviving crewmen's testimony and salvaged diaries, is drastically different, painting a grim and desperate picture of utter destruction. These accounts, often pieced together from fragmented memories and sparse documentation, depict the sheer terror and confusion of the attack. Men found themselves scrambling for safety as bombs rained down, their ships shaking violently under the relentless assault. Survivors described the horrifying scenes of chaos and death: men trapped in burning compartments, desperate attempts to launch damaged aircraft, and the frantic struggle to abandon sinking ships. Many accounts highlight the difficulty of maintaining order amidst the chaos, with the overwhelming nature of the attacks leading to confusion and a breakdown of command structures.

The stories from surviving Japanese sailors and airmen are frequently punctuated by the experience of witnessing the death of their shipmates, the agonizing wait for rescue (often non-existent) as their vessels were sinking, and the struggle to survive in the ocean after abandoning their sinking vessels. Descriptions of burning ships, sinking men, and the screams of the dying paint a horrific picture of the immediate aftermath. The scarcity of reliable lifeboats and the overwhelming number of survivors attempting to escape the destruction created conditions ripe for even greater loss of life amongst the Japanese Navy and air force personnel.

The accounts also reveal the impact of the initial shock of defeat on morale. The belief in the impregnability of Truk Lagoon had been shattered, leaving a profound sense of vulnerability and fear among those who survived. Many accounts speak of a desperate hope for rescue, coupled with a chilling sense of resignation to their fate as their chances of escape seemed to dwindle with every passing moment of the relentless attack.

The lack of a significant coordinated defensive response, as noted earlier, is also evident in many of these Japanese accounts. While there were certainly acts of bravery and resistance on the individual level, the overall effectiveness of the Japanese response was severely hampered by the devastating initial blows inflicted during the beginning of the operation. Many sources speak of a complete lack of communication amongst different units or the near complete absence of capable command and control once the attacks began in earnest.

The human toll extends beyond those who died during the fighting. The survivors, many of whom endured weeks or even months in life rafts or on makeshift debris, faced incredible hardships. Starvation, thirst, exposure to the elements, and the constant threat of sharks and other hazards took their toll. The physical and psychological trauma experienced by these survivors often manifested later in life in the form of PTSD, physical ailments caused by malnourishment and exposure, and other conditions related to the extreme conditions of the aftermath of the operation. These men, who survived the initial attacks, then faced another protracted struggle for survival amidst horrific conditions.

Post-war interviews with Japanese survivors, conducted by historians and investigators, reveal further details about the lingering effects of Operation Hailstone. These interviews reveal stories of widespread grief and loss, not only for those killed, but also for the missing, whose fate often remained unknown for years, leaving a gaping hole in the lives of their families and loved ones. The long-term physical and psychological damage inflicted upon the surviving Japanese personnel is a testament to the extreme violence and brutality inflicted by Operation Hailstone.

By examining these diverse narratives, piecing together the incomplete and sometimes contradictory evidence, a fuller understanding of Operation Hailstone emerges. It's a story not only of military strategy and technological superiority, but also one of profound human resilience, courage, and overwhelming loss. The sheer scale of destruction and the suffering endured by both
American and Japanese participants serve as a stark reminder of the devastating human cost of war, a testament to the unrelenting brutality of the Pacific conflict, and a haunting echo of the battles fought in the waters of Truk Lagoon. The ghostly remains of sunken ships are a fitting monument to those who fell, but the personal accounts of survivors offer a deeper, more profoundly moving understanding of the human cost of Operation Hailstone.

The Psychological Impact of the Battle

The psychological toll of Operation Hailstone extended far beyond the immediate carnage. While the physical devastation of Truk Lagoon was undeniable – the sunken hulks of ships, the shattered remains of aircraft, and the scarred landscape – the invisible wounds inflicted on the minds of the participants proved equally enduring, if not more so. For the American forces, the experience, though ultimately victorious, was one of intense pressure and constant, albeit controlled, chaos. The sheer scale of the operation, with its relentless bombing runs and strafing attacks, fostered an environment of heightened anxiety and fear. Even amidst the successes, the sights and sounds of war – the explosions, fires, and screams – created a visceral experience that imprinted itself on the psyches of the participants.

Post-mission debriefings, while focusing on tactical successes and failures, often contain subtle hints of the psychological strain experienced by the aircrews and naval personnel. Many pilots reported feelings of sensory overload, a blurring of sights and sounds that left them disoriented and emotionally exhausted. The constant threat of anti-aircraft fire, the near misses, and the witnessing of the destruction wrought upon the Japanese fleet contributed to a pervasive sense of unease and anxiety. While the official narratives often emphasized the swift and decisive victory, the personal accounts revealed a deeper, more complex reality –one of intense pressure, fear, and a profound awareness of their own mortality.

The surprising lack of determined Japanese resistance, while tactically advantageous, also had a subtle yet significant impact on the American psyche. The expectation of a fierce counterattack, fueled by pre-battle intelligence and the perceived strength of Truk Lagoon's defenses, had been a significant source of pre-operation tension. The relative ease of the victory, therefore, may have created a sense of unease or even guilt in some participants. This unexpected ease of victory, while not diminishing their accomplishments, could have inadvertently contributed to a sense of detachment or a lack of appreciation for the true gravity of the human cost, both on the Japanese side and amongst their own ranks.

The accounts of American casualties, though comparatively fewer than those suffered by the Japanese, also serve as a reminder of the inherent risks of naval aviation and warfare. The loss of even a single life, the injury of a comrade, serves as a sobering counterpoint to the celebratory nature of the victory. These losses, however minor in comparison to the overall scale of the operation, would have contributed to a collective sense of grief and loss amongst those who survived, reminding them of the inherent fragility of life and the ever-present danger of war.

For the Japanese, the experience of Operation Hailstone was one of unmitigated horror. The attack's suddenness and overwhelming force left many feeling helpless and terrified. The Japanese accounts, often fragmented and incomplete, paint a picture of utter chaos and destruction. Survivors described scenes of unimaginable brutality: men trapped in burning compartments, ships exploding around them, and the desperate, often futile, attempts to escape the sinking vessels. The overwhelming scale of the attack, coupled with the rapid and widespread devastation, shattered the sense of security and invincibility that had been previously associated with Truk Lagoon.

The psychological impact on Japanese survivors was profound and long-lasting. The sheer scale of death and destruction witnessed during the attack, combined with the subsequent struggles for survival in the ocean, left deep emotional scars. Many survivors suffered from severe trauma, a condition that often went undiagnosed and untreated at the time. The prolonged exposure to the elements, starvation, thirst, and the constant threat of sharks and other dangers further exacerbated their psychological distress. Their suffering extended beyond the immediate aftermath of the battle, impacting their lives for years to come.

The experience of witnessing the deaths of shipmates, friends, and colleagues added another layer of profound psychological trauma. The loss of comrades-in-arms would have significantly impacted morale and the sense of camaraderie amongst the remaining

survivors. Moreover, the uncertain fate of many missing sailors and airmen added to the sense of grief and unresolved loss among the survivors, with many families left to wonder about the final
moments of their loved ones.

Post-war accounts and interviews with Japanese survivors reveal the lasting impact of Operation Hailstone on their lives. Many reported experiencing symptoms consistent with PTSD, including flashbacks, nightmares, anxiety, depression, and difficulty
concentrating. These psychological issues were often compounded by the physical injuries sustained during the battle or during their subsequent struggle for survival. The long-term health implications of these experiences extended far beyond the immediate aftermath, demonstrating the enduring legacy of the battle on the mental and physical well-being of those who survived.

The lack of a significant, coordinated Japanese defensive effort is also directly related to the psychological impact of the operation.

The initial surprise and overwhelming nature of the American attack resulted in a breakdown of command and control structures. The psychological shock and utter disorientation stemming from the unexpected attack created chaos, hampered communication, and severely diminished the effectiveness of any organized resistance.

Many accounts from survivors highlight the pervasive feeling of helplessness and despair that characterized the early hours of the attack, a state that inhibited coordinated defensive actions, further fueling the feeling of overwhelming defeat.

In conclusion, Operation Hailstone's legacy extends beyond its strategic importance and decisive victory. The psychological impact of this pivotal battle, profoundly felt by both American and
Japanese forces, serves as a stark reminder of the invisible wounds of war. The emotional scars, the long-term psychological trauma, and the persistent grief and loss endured by the survivors illustrate the immeasurable human cost of conflict. The battle's chilling resonance continues to echo through the personal accounts of those who witnessed its destruction, a lasting testament to the enduring psychological toll of Operation Hailstone and the human cost of war. The ghostly, submerged remains of Truk Lagoon serve as a haunting memorial not only to the physical destruction of war but

also to the indelible marks left on the human spirit.

Remembering the Fallen and Honoring Their Sacrifice

The waters of Truk Lagoon, once a bustling hub of Japanese naval power, now serve as a somber, silent testament to the human cost of Operation Hailstone. The ghostly silhouettes of sunken warships, the scattered debris of aircraft, and the coral-encrusted remnants of a once-proud base all whisper tales of sacrifice and loss.

Remembering the fallen, both American and Japanese, is crucial to understanding the true weight of this pivotal battle in the Pacific Theater. It is a reminder that beyond the strategic gains and tactical victories, the heart of the conflict lay in the courage, resilience, and ultimately, the lives of the individuals who fought and died.

The official casualty figures, while stark, offer only a glimpse into the human toll. For the Japanese, the numbers were staggering. The loss of twelve warships, including cruisers and destroyers, and hundreds of aircraft represented not merely military hardware but the lives of thousands of sailors and airmen. Many perished in the initial attacks, trapped within the burning hulls of their ships, their cries swallowed by the roar of explosions and the crashing waves.

Others survived the initial blasts only to perish in the days and weeks that followed, succumbing to wounds, starvation, dehydration, or exposure to the relentless tropical sun while adrift in life rafts or clinging to debris. The stories of those lost remain largely fragmented, gleaned from scattered survivor accounts and official Japanese records that often downplayed the full extent of the losses. Yet, each lost life represents a unique story—a son lost to a grieving mother, a husband torn from his wife, a father absent from his children's lives.

The stories of individual Japanese sailors often remain untold.

While detailed accounts of specific heroic acts from the Japanese side are rare due to the overwhelming nature of the attack and the subsequent loss of records, several accounts hint at the bravery and resilience shown amidst the utter chaos. There are accounts of individuals working tirelessly to save shipmates despite the perilous conditions, crewmembers offering aid to the injured and fighting to keep their spirits up, and officers maintaining discipline in spite of the mounting losses. These glimpses of courage and sacrifice, even in the face of overwhelming odds, stand in stark contrast to the utter devastation they faced. These acts, though rarely documented, remind us that the individuals involved, even on the losing side, were not mere statistics; they were men who experienced fear, demonstrated courage, and paid the ultimate price.

The American loss of life, though far smaller in comparison, still represented a significant human cost. Pilots returning from the relentless bombing runs faced the emotional burden of witnessing the destruction they wrought, and the knowledge that even with tactical precision, they claimed lives. The accounts of aircrew and carrier personnel recount the mental and physical stress of constant flight operations, the near misses with enemy fire, and the trauma of seeing comrades go down in flames. The losses during Operation Hailstone, though relatively small compared to other major battles, etched themselves onto the American consciousness, serving as a reminder that even amidst victory, the cost of war was always human. These losses, however small in scale when compared to Japanese losses, were nonetheless profoundly felt. Each loss represented a family's sorrow, a community's grief, and a nation's shared burden of war.

Specific examples, though difficult to fully document due to the nature of the conflict and the passage of time, highlight the individual sacrifices made on both sides. For instance, accounts of American pilots recount the bravery displayed when rescuing downed airmen under fire, risking their own lives to save comrades who had fallen into the lagoon. These acts illustrate the camaraderie and selflessness present within the ranks of the U.S.
Navy and Air Force. Conversely, while detailed heroism is less accessible on the Japanese side due to the widespread destruction and lack of centralized accounts, survivor testimonies hint at similar acts of courage, self-sacrifice and attempts at maintaining morale amidst the horror.

The aftermath of Operation Hailstone further amplified the human cost. For the survivors, the emotional and psychological scars proved as enduring as the physical wounds. American airmen and sailors grappled with the psychological weight of their experiences, the constant memory of the sights and sounds of battle, and the lingering trauma of witnessing widespread destruction. While many received attention upon their return, the long-term psychological impact of PTSD was often not fully understood at the time. For Japanese survivors, the struggle was even greater. Many faced not only physical injuries but also profound psychological trauma, leaving them with enduring mental health challenges.

The sunken ships of Truk Lagoon are more than mere wreckage; they are watery graves, each containing the stories of those who perished within their steel confines. The lagoon itself became a silent memorial, a haunting testament to the brutal reality of war. These vessels, now entombed in the coral, hold the silent secrets of countless individuals—their lives, their hopes, and their final moments of struggle. The underwater landscape provides a somber reminder of the sacrifices made and the losses endured. The eerie stillness of the submerged ships contrasts sharply with the violent and chaotic events that brought them to their watery graves.

The enduring legacy of Operation Hailstone lies not only in its strategic significance but also in the immeasurable human cost it exacted. The memory of the fallen, both American and Japanese, serves as a solemn reminder of the brutal realities of war and the profound importance of remembering those who served, sacrificed, and ultimately gave their lives. Honoring their sacrifice transcends the boundaries of nationality; it speaks to the universal human experience of loss, courage, and the enduring impact of conflict.

Truk Lagoon, a chilling underwater graveyard, remains a potent symbol of this enduring human cost, urging us to learn from the past and strive for a future free from the horrors of war. It is a place of reflection, where the weight of history rests heavy on the silent, sunken ships. Their silence speaks volumes, a stark testament to the immeasurable human cost of Operation Hailstone and a reminder of the enduring price of conflict. The ghosts of Truk Lagoon, silent witnesses to this pivotal battle, serve as a constant reminder of the fallen and the profound impact of their sacrifices. Their memory serves as a powerful imperative to remember, to learn, and to strive for a future where such devastation is never repeated.

The Current State of Truk Lagoon

Truk Lagoon today presents a stark contrast to its wartime past. The once-bustling naval base, a vital cog in the Japanese war machine, now lies submerged, a hauntingly beautiful yet somber underwater museum. The lagoon's transformation into a world-renowned dive site is a complex story, intertwining the passage of time, the
resilience of nature, and the enduring fascination with maritime history. The wrecks themselves, once symbols of Japanese military might, are now vibrant artificial reefs, teeming with marine life.

The sheer scale of the wreckage is breathtaking. Dozens of Japanese warships, ranging from destroyers and cruisers to submarines and cargo vessels, rest on the lagoon floor, their rusted hulls gradually being reclaimed by the ocean. Many remain remarkably intact, offering divers a chilling glimpse into their wartime lives. The USS Heian Maru, a large transport ship, lies relatively upright, its decks still bearing visible remnants of its cargo and internal structure. Divers can penetrate the ship's interior, exploring its rusted engine rooms, crew quarters, and even the remnants of its bridge, offering a visceral experience of navigating the ghostly corridors of a sunken warship. The eerie silence broken only by the sound of their own breathing and the gentle current accentuates the feeling of being transported back in time. Exploring these submerged vessels offers a sobering perspective on the cost of war, the lives lost, and the violent end met by these once powerful machines.

The Katori Maru, a training vessel, is another popular dive site. The ship lies mostly intact on the seabed, its gun emplacements still visible amidst the growth of coral and other marine organisms. The interior spaces of the Katori Maru present a different sort of
experience. While the outer structure offers opportunities for exploration and appreciation of the vessel's structure, the interior spaces often present a more intimate connection with the history of the ship. The remnants of daily life onboard can still be found, and many divers find it incredibly compelling to explore these preserved spaces, gaining a clearer understanding of the lives lived on board these vessels during wartime.

Beyond the larger vessels, the lagoon floor is scattered with the remnants of numerous smaller craft, aircraft, and assorted debris – a testament to the ferocity of Operation Hailstone. Scattered across the seabed lie the remnants of Japanese fighter planes, their wings torn and twisted, now encrusted with vibrant coral, a poignant symbol of the battle's destructive power, now absorbed by the sea's restorative capabilities. These aircraft, once symbols of Japanese aerial might, now provide homes for a variety of marine life,
highlighting the enduring resilience of nature, even in the face of war's devastation. The coral growth on these sunken planes has created colorful, vibrant reefs around them, transforming what were once instruments of death into vibrant and thriving ecosystems.

The ecological impact of these wrecks is a complex and fascinating aspect of Truk Lagoon's present state. Over the decades, the sunken ships have become artificial reefs, providing a habitat for a
remarkable diversity of marine life. Coral has colonized the hulls and decks, creating vibrant ecosystems teeming with fish,
invertebrates, and other organisms. Schools of brightly colored reef fish dart through the shipwrecks, and larger creatures like sharks and rays are often sighted in the surrounding waters. This
transformation demonstrates nature's ability to reclaim even the most heavily damaged environments, creating a testament to nature's tenacity and the restorative power of the ocean.

The wrecks themselves provide a unique habitat for numerous species of fish. The complex structures of the sunken vessels, with their numerous nooks and crannies, offer shelter and breeding grounds for a wide variety of fish. This, in turn, attracts other organisms, like sharks and rays that prey on the fish living within the wrecks. The interaction between these various marine creatures creates a vibrant and complex ecosystem within the lagoon. The artificial reefs formed by the wrecks support a much wider range of marine life than what the lagoon floor offered before the ships sank.

However, the ecological impact of the wrecks is not without its potential downsides. The rusting metal of the ships releases pollutants into the water, and some concern exists about the potential long-term effects of these pollutants on the marine environment. Furthermore, the popularity of the lagoon as a dive site raises concerns about the potential for damage to the fragile coral reefs and the wrecks themselves. Sustainable tourism practices are crucial to ensure the long-term preservation of this unique ecosystem. It remains a challenge to balance the preservation of this extraordinary underwater heritage site with its growing popularity as a dive destination.

Photographs of Truk Lagoon today often depict a surreal juxtaposition of destruction and beauty. The vibrant coral encrusting the decaying metal hulls of warships creates a visual paradox—a vibrant tapestry of life woven upon the bones of war. Images of divers exploring the ship interiors, silhouetted against the penetrating sunlight, create a stark and memorable contrast between the modern world and the ghosts of the past. These images capture the essence of Truk Lagoon—a place where the past and present are interwoven, where history and nature meet in a visually stunning, yet emotionally complex, setting.

The photographic record provides an essential tool for understanding the current state of Truk Lagoon. Images not only capture the visual beauty of the coral-encrusted wrecks but also document the deterioration of the ships over time, providing valuable data for researchers and historians. Photographs taken over several decades show the gradual changes in the marine environment, from the initial colonization of the wrecks by coral and other organisms to the present-day thriving ecosystem. High-resolution photography and even underwater videography are used to showcase the wrecks' conditions in detail, providing a unique opportunity to study these historical artifacts and the environmental processes shaping their transformation into artificial reefs. Such detailed documentation is essential to provide a comprehensive record of this extraordinary underwater landscape for future generations.

Truk Lagoon today serves as a chilling reminder of the destructive power of war, yet also a testament to the resilience of nature and the enduring fascination with maritime history. It's a place where history and nature intertwine, where the ghosts of the past mingle with the vibrant life of the present. The lagoon's transformation into a diver's graveyard is a powerful, almost paradoxical, combination

that captivates the imaginations of those who explore it. It is a powerful reminder of the enduring legacy of Operation Hailstone, one that should be both explored and preserved for future
generations. The preservation of this historical site and its unique ecosystem is a shared responsibility, demanding a delicate balance between access and protection. The ongoing monitoring and management of Truk Lagoon are crucial to ensuring that this underwater heritage site continues to inspire awe and
understanding while being protected for future generations to appreciate and learn from. The delicate ecosystem requires ongoing attention and care, and the potential for damage through
unsustainable tourism practices remains a significant concern.

The Wreckage and Its Preservation

The sheer number and variety of wrecks within Truk Lagoon present a unique challenge in preservation. While the coral growth has, in many ways, helped to stabilize the structures, the ongoing decay of the metal hulls poses a significant threat. Rusting steel releases pollutants into the water, potentially harming the vibrant ecosystem that has flourished around the wrecks. The Japanese freighter, the San Francisco Maru, for example, lies largely intact but shows significant signs of deterioration. Its cargo holds, once filled with war materials, are now slowly collapsing under the weight of the ocean and the encroaching coral. Divers can still discern the outlines of tanks, trucks, and other military equipment, but the metal is increasingly fragile, highlighting the need for careful management of access to these fragile historical artifacts.

The issue of pollution is a serious concern. Many of the wrecks contain remnants of fuel oil and other hazardous materials that continue to leach into the lagoon. While the immediate impact might be limited, long-term studies are needed to assess the
cumulative effects on marine life and the overall health of the lagoon's ecosystem. This necessitates ongoing monitoring of water quality and the development of strategies to mitigate the effects of these pollutants. One approach involves carefully planned and controlled interventions, perhaps involving the extraction of
remaining hazardous materials from accessible areas of the wrecks, although such operations are complex, expensive, and carry their own environmental risks.

Beyond pollution, the sheer number of visitors poses another challenge. Truk Lagoon's popularity as a dive site has grown
exponentially, placing increased pressure on the fragile ecosystem. The constant movement of divers, anchors dragging on the seabed, and accidental contact with the wrecks can all contribute to
damage. Sustainable tourism practices are therefore crucial, demanding careful regulation of dive operations, the establishment of protected zones, and the education of divers about responsible behavior. Stricter guidelines regarding anchoring, careful dive briefings emphasizing wreck fragility, and the limiting of divers at

specific sites during peak hours are vital steps in managing the influx of visitors without compromising the integrity of the underwater heritage.

Preservation efforts are multifaceted and involve a collaboration between various stakeholders. The Federated States of Micronesia, as the sovereign nation responsible for the lagoon, plays a crucial role in establishing and enforcing regulations. International organizations, such as UNESCO, are also involved, providing expertise and technical support for conservation efforts. Numerous research institutions and universities have conducted studies on the lagoon's ecosystem and the condition of the wrecks, providing valuable data that informs conservation strategies. These collaborations are essential in ensuring that preservation efforts are informed by the best available scientific knowledge and incorporate sustainable practices.

One prominent initiative is the meticulous documentation of the wrecks. High-resolution photography, video surveys, and 3D modeling are used to create detailed records of their current state. This documentation serves multiple purposes. First, it provides a baseline for monitoring the rate of deterioration and allows researchers to track changes in the wrecks' condition over time.

Second, it allows for the creation of virtual models, making it possible to study the wrecks without causing further physical disturbance. Finally, it provides valuable resources for educational purposes, creating virtual tours and educational materials that allow people worldwide to experience the historical significance of Truk Lagoon without physically visiting the site. These digital archives ensure that the history and significance of the wrecks are preserved and accessible, even if the physical wrecks themselves eventually disappear.

The ethical considerations surrounding the preservation of Truk Lagoon are complex. The wrecks are not simply historical artifacts; they are also war graves, containing the remains of countless Japanese sailors and soldiers. Respect for the deceased necessitates a sensitive approach to preservation, recognizing the human cost of war and the significance of the site as a final resting place. This requires balancing the need for exploration and research with the importance of treating the site with utmost respect and avoiding the disturbance of human remains. Regulations regarding penetration of certain wrecks, especially those known or suspected to contain human remains, are crucial.

Funding for preservation efforts is another significant hurdle. The task of protecting and preserving such a vast and complex site demands substantial financial resources. International grants, partnerships with private sector conservation organizations, and funding from tourist revenue can all contribute to securing the necessary funds. The economic benefits of responsible tourism, including the development of sustainable tour operator practices that contribute to conservation funds, should not be overlooked. Sustainable revenue streams are essential to long-term preservation, creating a virtuous cycle where the preservation efforts enhance the attraction of the site, attracting further sustainable revenue for continued conservation.

The long-term future of Truk Lagoon's preservation requires a multifaceted approach. Continuous monitoring of the wrecks' condition and the lagoon's ecosystem is crucial, along with ongoing research to identify and address potential threats. Educational initiatives to promote responsible tourism and public awareness of the site's historical and ecological significance are equally vital. The Federated States of Micronesia, working in collaboration with international partners, must maintain its commitment to establishing and enforcing stringent regulations to protect the site from further damage, ensuring the responsible management of tourism, and implementing effective pollution mitigation strategies.

The challenge of balancing the needs of tourism with the requirements of preservation demands a delicate balance. Truk Lagoon's economic viability is undeniably linked to its popularity as a dive site, but this must never overshadow the imperative of safeguarding the wrecks and the delicate ecosystem they support. The sustainable management of tourism, through strictly enforced regulations and the promotion of responsible diving practices, is paramount. This includes working with dive operators to ensure responsible behavior, enforcing limits on visitor numbers, and actively promoting educational materials that highlight the fragility of the environment and the importance of respectful exploration.

The preservation of Truk Lagoon is not simply a matter of preserving historical artifacts; it is about protecting a unique ecosystem and honoring the memory of those who lost their lives there. It is a testament to the enduring power of nature's restorative capabilities and a sobering reminder of the devastating consequences of war. The ongoing efforts to conserve this underwater heritage site are a shared responsibility, requiring a delicate balance between access, research, and the preservation of this extraordinary and poignant underwater landscape for future generations. The enduring legacy of Operation Hailstone continues to echo through the silent depths of Truk Lagoon, demanding that the world acknowledge its significance, both as a historical site and as a delicate and irreplaceable ecosystem. The task of preservation, therefore, is not just a practical necessity but a moral imperative.

The Ethical Considerations of Wreck Diving

The ethical dimensions of wreck diving in Truk Lagoon are multifaceted and deeply intertwined with the historical significance of the site. These wrecks are not merely inert objects; they are the tangible remnants of a devastating battle, silent witnesses to immense loss of life and a pivotal moment in World War II. Many vessels still contain the remains of Japanese sailors and soldiers, transforming these underwater graveyards into poignant memorials demanding profound respect. The challenge lies in balancing the legitimate interests of divers, researchers, and the tourism industry with the moral imperative of treating these sites with the utmost reverence.

Commercial dive operations, while contributing significantly to the local economy, must operate under a strict ethical framework. The pursuit of profit should never overshadow the sanctity of the war graves. Many dive operators already conduct themselves responsibly, providing detailed briefings that emphasize the importance of respecting the wrecks and refraining from disturbing any human remains. However, a uniform standard of ethical conduct across all operators is crucial. This requires robust regulations enforced by the Federated States of Micronesia, potentially including penalties for irresponsible behavior and clear guidelines on permissible dive practices near known or suspected burial sites. Independent audits and monitoring of dive operations could further ensure compliance with established ethical standards.

The potential for accidental damage, even by well-intentioned divers, is significant. The fragile condition of many wrecks, coupled with the inherent risks of underwater exploration, necessitates stringent guidelines. These should include mandatory briefings covering the delicate nature of the wrecks, the importance of maintaining buoyancy control to prevent accidental contact, and clear instructions regarding the prohibition of touching or removing artifacts. Dive operators should provide thorough training on safe diving procedures, emphasizing the importance of respecting the environment and the sensitive nature of the dive sites. Moreover, limits on the number of divers permitted at each site during peak periods could help minimize the risk of accidental damage and contribute to a more sustainable tourism model.

Beyond the immediate physical impacts of diving, the ethical implications extend to the longer-term preservation of the wrecks and the lagoon's ecosystem. The extraction of artifacts, even seemingly insignificant items, disrupts the historical context and contributes to the progressive degradation of the wrecks. The removal of artifacts not only diminishes the historical integrity of the sites but also raises concerns about the potential for black market trade in wartime relics, a practice that undermines the respectful treatment of these sensitive locations. Strict regulations, enforced through rigorous monitoring and penalties for violations, are essential to prevent such activities. Educating divers and the wider public about the ethical implications of artifact removal is equally crucial.

The issue of photography and videography also necessitates careful consideration. While documenting the wrecks through high-resolution images and video is invaluable for historical preservation and research, the manner in which this is done requires sensitivity. The use of powerful lighting or intrusive techniques could damage the delicate coral formations and other marine life that have become intertwined with the wrecks. Guidelines regarding lighting techniques, camera angles, and appropriate distance from the wrecks are needed to ensure that documentation efforts do not compromise the integrity of the environment. Furthermore, the dissemination of such visual material must be managed responsibly to avoid sensationalizing the sites and potentially encouraging disrespectful behavior by others.

Balancing the needs of research with the ethical considerations of respectful remembrance is another key challenge. Archaeological investigations, while essential for a deeper understanding of the wrecks' historical significance and the lives of those lost, should be undertaken with utmost caution and sensitivity. Any excavations must be conducted under rigorous ethical guidelines, prioritizing the preservation of human remains and the overall historical context. Collaboration between researchers, local authorities, and international organizations is essential to ensure that research projects adhere to the highest ethical standards and respect the dignity of the deceased. Strict protocols for the handling and cataloging of any discovered artifacts, along with clear guidelines on public dissemination of research findings, are vital to maintaining ethical practices.

The ongoing dialogue about ethical considerations surrounding Truk Lagoon's wrecks necessitates the involvement of multiple stakeholders. This includes the Federated States of Micronesia, as the sovereign nation responsible for the lagoon, as well as international organizations such as UNESCO, which possess expertise in the preservation of underwater cultural heritage. Furthermore, collaborations with research institutions, historians, archaeologists, dive operators, and tourism agencies are all crucial in establishing a unified approach to responsible wreck diving. This collaborative effort must strive to create a framework that protects the historical integrity of the sites, respects the dignity of the deceased, and ensures the long-term sustainability of the lagoon's ecosystem and its economic viability.

The development of comprehensive educational materials targeting divers, tour operators, and the general public is paramount. These materials should explain the historical context of Truk Lagoon, the human cost of the Battle of Truk, and the ethical implications of diving on these sensitive sites. They should also clearly articulate guidelines for responsible diving practices, emphasizing respect for human remains, the avoidance of damage to the wrecks and the ecosystem, and the prohibition of artifact removal. The widespread dissemination of these educational materials, through dive operator briefings, online platforms, and tourism information centers, is crucial to fostering a culture of responsible exploration and promoting awareness among visitors about the ethical dimensions of diving in Truk Lagoon.

Finally, the long-term preservation of Truk Lagoon's underwater heritage demands a sustained commitment to responsible management. This requires ongoing monitoring of the wrecks' condition and the lagoon's ecosystem, along with the continuous adaptation of regulations to reflect the latest scientific understanding and ethical considerations. The economic benefits

derived from sustainable tourism should be actively reinvested into preservation efforts, creating a virtuous cycle that ensures the long-term protection of this significant historical and ecological site. The ethical conduct of all stakeholders – from divers and tour operators to researchers and government agencies – is fundamental to
ensuring that Truk Lagoon's rich history and fragile ecosystem are preserved for future generations, a lasting tribute to the sacrifices made and a testament to the importance of respectful remembrance. The silent depths of Truk Lagoon continue to hold profound stories; our responsibility is to ensure these stories are told and
remembered with the utmost respect and sensitivity.

Truk Lagoon as a Historical Site

Truk Lagoon, now officially Chuuk Lagoon within the Federated States of Micronesia, transcends its status as a diver's graveyard; it stands as a potent symbol of a pivotal moment in the Pacific Theater of World War II. The sheer scale of the sunken vessels, aircraft, and other war remnants offers an unparalleled opportunity for historical research and education, a tangible connection to the past rarely seen elsewhere. The lagoon's significance lies not merely in the impressive spectacle of the wrecks but in the stories they silently tell—stories of courage, sacrifice, and the devastating consequences of war.

The wrecks themselves are invaluable primary sources for historians. Detailed examination of the sunken ships, meticulously documented through photographic surveys, sonar mapping, and even limited archaeological dives (conducted with utmost sensitivity), can reveal crucial details about ship design, armament, and the technologies employed during the war. The condition of the wrecks, the arrangement of their contents, and the presence of any remaining artifacts can shed light on the circumstances of their sinking, providing insights into the intensity of the attacks and the Japanese response. This information complements and enriches the existing historical record, challenging assumptions and offering new perspectives on the Battle of Truk. For instance, analysis of the damage sustained by particular vessels might reveal the effectiveness of different types of weaponry or the tactics employed by American forces. The discovery of personal effects belonging to the Japanese sailors and soldiers, treated with the utmost respect and only accessed under strictly controlled circumstances, can humanize the conflict, offering glimpses into the lives and experiences of those who served and perished. The meticulous cataloging and analysis of these artifacts can contribute greatly to our understanding of the human dimension of war.

The educational potential of Truk Lagoon is equally significant. The lagoon's underwater museum serves as a powerful and visceral teaching tool, allowing students and the public to connect with the realities of war in a way that traditional classrooms cannot replicate. Virtual tours, high-resolution photographic documentation, and interactive exhibits can bring the history of Truk Lagoon to a broader audience, fostering a deeper understanding of the Pacific War and its consequences. The lagoon's historical significance can be interwoven into educational programs focusing on naval strategy, maritime archaeology, and the human impact of conflict. This educational approach transcends simple factual recitation; it aims to promote critical thinking and empathy, encouraging individuals to consider the complexities of historical events and their human cost. Furthermore, by carefully preserving the site, future generations can learn firsthand from the tangible remains of this significant battle, ensuring the legacy of Operation Hailstone endures.

The economic benefits of Truk Lagoon's status as a dive destination are undeniable. The influx of divers generates significant revenue for the local economy, supporting businesses, creating jobs, and stimulating investment in infrastructure and tourism-related services. However, this economic engine must be managed sustainably and ethically to avoid jeopardizing the long-term preservation of the site. Responsible tourism practices, strict regulations governing diving activities, and a commitment to protecting the delicate marine ecosystem are essential to ensure that economic benefits do not come at the cost of environmental damage or disrespect for the fallen. This requires a delicate balance between economic development and environmental protection, a challenge that requires ongoing dialogue and collaboration between stakeholders, including local communities, the government of Micronesia, tourism operators, and environmental organizations.

Careful planning, implementation, and monitoring are crucial to ensuring this fragile ecosystem continues to thrive, supporting both tourism and the biodiversity of the lagoon.

The challenge lies in striking a balance between the economic potential of Truk Lagoon's wrecks as a dive site and the ethical responsibility of preserving its historical and environmental integrity. The lagoon's economic value is significantly linked to its historical significance. The allure of exploring these underwater relics draws divers from around the world, contributing substantially to the local economy. However, uncontrolled or

unethical diving practices could damage the wrecks and the fragile coral ecosystems surrounding them, diminishing both their
historical value and their appeal to future visitors. Consequently, effective management requires strict regulations, including
limitations on the number of divers allowed at specific sites, mandatory safety briefings, and clear guidelines on acceptable diving practices. Enforcement of these regulations is crucial, and penalties for violations should be significant enough to deter irresponsible behavior. The financial rewards from tourism need to be partly reinvested into conservation and preservation projects, establishing a cyclical system ensuring long-term benefits.

The management of Truk Lagoon as a historical site demands a multi-faceted approach. The Federated States of Micronesia, as the sovereign nation, plays a pivotal role in establishing and enforcing regulations governing access and use. International organizations, such as UNESCO, can offer valuable expertise in the management of underwater cultural heritage sites, assisting in the development of effective preservation strategies. This may include guidelines for sustainable tourism, archaeological research protocols, and methods for mitigating environmental damage. Collaboration between local communities, researchers, tourism operators, and government agencies is vital to developing a unified approach that respects the historical significance of the lagoon, safeguards its environmental integrity, and provides sustainable economic opportunities for the local population. Open and continuous dialogue involving all
stakeholders is essential to ensuring the long-term preservation of this unique and valuable site, balancing the needs of historical research, education, and tourism with the moral imperative of honoring the memory of those who lost their lives in the battle.

Moreover, the ethical framework governing Truk Lagoon must extend beyond physical preservation to encompass the intangible aspects of its history. The wrecks are not simply objects; they represent the lives and sacrifices of the individuals who served on those ships. This necessitates a sensitive approach to public
education and interpretation, avoiding the sensationalization or trivialization of the historical events associated with the lagoon. Educational programs and museum exhibits should emphasize the human cost of war, conveying the stories of both the American and

Japanese combatants who participated in the battle. This requires a delicate balancing act, aiming to inform and educate while simultaneously respecting the dignity of the deceased and avoiding any potentially offensive representations. Such an approach emphasizes the historical context, the personal narratives of the individuals involved, and the lasting impact of the battle, fostering respect and understanding among visitors.

The ongoing preservation and responsible management of Truk Lagoon as a historical site are vital, not just for the present generation but for those to come. It demands a concerted and sustained effort by all stakeholders, requiring robust regulations, responsible tourism practices, and a collaborative approach to ensuring that the lagoon's rich history, its fragile ecosystem, and its profound significance are protected for generations to come. The underwater remnants of Operation Hailstone serve as a poignant reminder of the devastating cost of war, and our responsibility is to ensure that this legacy is honored, remembered, and protected for future generations. The silence of the depths holds a powerful message; it is our duty to listen carefully and to ensure that Truk Lagoon's story is told with respect, integrity, and a deep understanding of its immense historical importance. The lagoon's future depends on a collective commitment to ethical stewardship, balancing historical preservation, sustainable tourism, and the enduring remembrance of those lost in the heart of the Pacific.

The Future of Truk Lagoon and Its Preservation Efforts

The preservation of Truk Lagoon presents a complex challenge, demanding a delicate balance between the economic opportunities offered by wreck diving tourism and the ethical imperative to protect this significant historical and ecological site. The sheer scale of the sunken vessels, coupled with the fragile coral reefs and diverse marine life, necessitates a multifaceted approach that
considers environmental sustainability, historical accuracy, and the cultural sensitivities of the local community. Short-term gains must never outweigh the long-term integrity of the lagoon.

Sustainable tourism is paramount. Currently, the lagoon generates substantial revenue for the Federated States of Micronesia (FSM) through dive tourism. However, uncontrolled growth threatens the very assets that drive this revenue. Over-visitation to sensitive wreck sites can lead to damage from careless divers, anchors, and even the exhaust plumes of dive boats. The fragile coral ecosystems, home to a vibrant array of marine life, are susceptible to damage from physical contact, sedimentation, and pollution. The FSM government, in collaboration with international organizations and local stakeholders, needs to implement and rigorously enforce regulations that limit the number of divers per site, designate protected zones, and mandate environmentally friendly dive practices. This includes restricting the use of anchors, promoting buoyancy control techniques, and prohibiting the removal of artifacts.

A crucial aspect of sustainable tourism lies in educating divers and tourists about the significance of Truk Lagoon. Before entering the water, all divers should receive comprehensive briefings on
responsible diving practices, the historical context of the wrecks, and the importance of preserving the lagoon's delicate ecosystem.

Interactive museums and visitor centers on the islands could provide engaging presentations, utilizing multimedia displays and historical artifacts recovered from the wrecks (with appropriate ethical considerations and respect for the remains of those who perished). These educational initiatives aim to foster a sense of responsibility and stewardship among visitors, ensuring their actions contribute to the preservation of the site rather than its deterioration.

The ongoing conservation efforts require substantial investment in long-term strategies. These strategies should focus not only on mitigating the immediate impacts of tourism but also on addressing longer-term threats, such as climate change, coral bleaching, and the accumulation of marine debris. Regular monitoring programs are essential to assess the health of the coral reefs, the condition of the wrecks, and the effectiveness of implemented conservation measures. This data will inform adaptive management strategies, allowing for adjustments in response to changing conditions. The FSM government, in partnership with international organizations and research institutions, can collaborate on scientific studies focused on coral reef restoration, wreck stabilization techniques, and methods to mitigate the effects of climate change on the lagoon.

International collaboration plays a vital role in Truk Lagoon's long-term preservation. UNESCO, in conjunction with other relevant organizations, can provide technical assistance, funding, and
expertise in the management of underwater cultural heritage sites. This could include the development of comprehensive management plans, the creation of training programs for local stakeholders, and the implementation of monitoring and evaluation systems.

International partnerships can facilitate the transfer of knowledge and resources, ensuring that the preservation efforts are informed by best practices and cutting-edge research. Funding mechanisms need to be explored to ensure the sustainability of these initiatives, encompassing both government support and private philanthropic contributions.

The local community's involvement is critical to the success of any long-term preservation strategy. Truk Lagoon's history is
intrinsically linked to the lives and experiences of the people of Chuuk. Their knowledge, perspectives, and participation are essential in crafting and implementing sustainable management plans. The FSM government needs to actively engage with local communities, incorporating their traditional ecological knowledge and cultural values into the preservation process. This engagement

should extend beyond simple consultation, ensuring that the local community has a genuine role in decision-making and benefits directly from the revenue generated by tourism. This might involve job creation in tourism and conservation related fields, economic support for local businesses, and investments in infrastructure that enhance the local community's quality of life.

Furthermore, ethical considerations must guide all aspects of preservation and tourism. The wrecks within Truk Lagoon are not simply dive sites; they are memorials to those who perished during the Battle of Truk. Any activities within the lagoon must be conducted with the utmost respect for the fallen, avoiding sensationalism or disrespectful behavior. Strict regulations prohibiting the disturbance of human remains, the removal of personal artifacts, and the inappropriate use of the wrecks for recreational purposes need to be implemented and enforced. Public education programs and signage should sensitively convey the historical significance of the site, emphasizing the human cost of war and the need for respectful remembrance.

The long-term preservation of Truk Lagoon requires a multi-pronged strategy combining scientific research, sustainable tourism management, community involvement, and international cooperation. The challenge is to strike a balance between the economic opportunities and the ethical imperative to preserve this unique underwater landscape. By fostering a culture of responsible tourism, investing in effective conservation measures, and actively involving the local community, the FSM can ensure that Truk Lagoon remains a testament to the past, a vibrant ecosystem, and a sustainable resource for generations to come. The future of Truk Lagoon depends on the collective commitment to a vision that balances historical preservation, environmental sustainability, and the well-being of the local community. This is not merely about preserving underwater wrecks; it is about preserving history, respecting memory, and safeguarding a vital part of the Pacific Ocean's biodiversity. The legacy of Operation Hailstone must be one of both remembrance and responsible stewardship. The silence of the depths should continue to speak, but its message should be one of respect, preservation, and a harmonious relationship between humanity and the ocean's fragile beauty. The challenge is immense, but the rewards – a preserved legacy for future generations and a thriving ecosystem – are immeasurable.

American CarrierBased Aircraft

The decisive victory at the Battle of Truk Lagoon in February 1944 wasn't solely attributable to superior tactical planning or the sheer number of attacking vessels. A significant contributing factor to the American triumph lay in the technological superiority of their carrier-based aircraft. While the Japanese possessed capable aircraft and skilled pilots, the technological gap between the two nations' air power proved insurmountable, particularly in the context of the Pacific theater's vast distances and challenging operational
environments. This technological edge manifested in several key areas: range, speed, payload, and overall aircraft design.

The American carrier air groups boasted a significant advantage in range. Crucially, this extended operational reach allowed American aircraft to strike deep into the heart of the Japanese defenses at Truk, while remaining within range of their carriers for a safe return. Japanese aircraft, by contrast, often faced limitations in their operational radius. The Grumman F6F Hellcat, for instance, possessed a significantly longer range than its Japanese
counterparts, like the Mitsubishi A6M Zero. This meant that Hellcats could engage in longer patrols, escort bombers over greater distances, and provide more robust air cover for the American fleet.

The extended range of the Hellcat and other American fighters, coupled with the greater range of their dive bombers and torpedo planes, significantly expanded the operational envelope of the American carrier task forces, enabling them to strike targets well beyond the Japanese reach. The limitations in Japanese aircraft range contributed to their inability to effectively counter the American air attacks, leaving many Japanese planes grounded or forced to operate at a disadvantage.

Furthermore, the speed of American aircraft proved a crucial factor. Planes like the F6F Hellcat and the Vought F4U Corsair exhibited superior speed and maneuverability compared to many of their Japanese adversaries, particularly at higher altitudes. The Hellcat, in particular, proved to be a formidable opponent in dogfights, outclassing the Zero in terms of speed and firepower. The Zero, while renowned for its maneuverability at lower altitudes, struggled

to match the Hellcat's speed and firepower, particularly in head-on engagements. This superiority in speed allowed American pilots to choose their engagements, dictate the terms of aerial combat, and maximize their chances of success. The speed advantage also allowed American aircraft to quickly respond to changing tactical situations and effectively engage multiple targets. This speed advantage was crucial in Operation Hailstone, allowing the
Americans to overwhelm the Japanese defenses and inflict heavy losses on their air power.

Beyond speed, the American aircraft possessed a significant advantage in terms of armament. The Hellcat, for example, boasted superior firepower compared to the Zero, with its six .50 caliber machine guns delivering a significantly heavier and more accurate barrage. Similarly, American dive bombers and torpedo planes carried larger payloads of bombs and torpedoes, enabling them to inflict more devastating damage on Japanese ships and
installations. The difference in armament translated directly into a higher kill ratio for the American pilots, significantly impacting the effectiveness of Japanese air defenses. The increased firepower allowed American aircraft to rapidly destroy Japanese aircraft and to inflict critical damage to ships and ground installations. The overwhelming firepower of the American air strikes at Truk was a key element in the battle's decisive outcome.

The design philosophy underlying the American aircraft also contributed to their superiority. American aircraft were designed with a greater emphasis on durability and survivability. While Japanese aircraft often prioritized maneuverability and speed at the expense of structural strength, the American designs incorporated features like self-sealing fuel tanks and more robust airframes, allowing them to withstand more damage and remain operational even after sustaining significant hits. Japanese aircraft were often lighter and more agile, but they were less resistant to damage, leaving them vulnerable to the superior firepower of the American aircraft. This difference in design philosophy resulted in a
significant disparity in the survival rates of American and Japanese pilots and aircraft. The ability of American aircraft to absorb
damage and return to base gave them a significant advantage in prolonged engagements. The sturdy design of American aircraft was

clearly visible in Operation Hailstone where they successfully endured the intense anti-aircraft fire and sustained combat to carry out their mission.

The differences extended beyond fighters and interceptors.

American dive bombers, such as the Douglas SBD Dauntless and the Curtiss SB2C Helldiver, were crucial in inflicting damage on Japanese ships and installations. These aircraft benefited from improved dive-bombing techniques and the reliability of their bombsights, enabling them to deliver more accurate and effective strikes. These improvements, coupled with the superior firepower of American aircraft, greatly amplified their destructive capability.

Japanese bombers and dive bombers, while possessing some strengths, lacked the range, speed, and payload to deliver the same level of damage to the extent of their American counterparts.

The technological edge of American carrier-based aircraft in Operation Hailstone was not merely a matter of individual aircraft performance. It was a product of a more integrated and effective system. The American aircraft carriers themselves were larger, more robust, and better equipped than the Japanese carriers. Their sophisticated radar systems allowed for better detection and tracking of enemy aircraft, giving American pilots a tactical advantage. The well-developed training programs for American pilots contributed to their higher level of proficiency and effectiveness in combat. The combination of advanced aircraft, superior training, and effective operational procedures proved instrumental in the crushing defeat inflicted upon the Japanese at Truk Lagoon. The coordinated deployment of diverse aircraft types—fighters for air superiority, dive bombers for precision strikes, torpedo planes for crippling capital ships, and scout planes for reconnaissance—exhibited a level of tactical sophistication that the Japanese struggled to match.

The contrast between the American and Japanese aircraft further highlights the technological disparities. The American aircraft benefited from advanced engineering, superior materials, and more effective manufacturing processes. The Japanese, facing resource constraints and the challenges of wartime production, were not able to keep pace with the rapid advancements in American aircraft technology. This gap was particularly evident in the later stages of the war, as American aircraft continued to improve and outpace their Japanese counterparts.

In conclusion, the technological superiority of American carrier-based aircraft played a decisive role in the outcome of Operation Hailstone. The combination of longer range, greater speed, superior firepower, robust designs, and effective operational procedures created a formidable force that overwhelmed Japanese defenses and inflicted heavy losses. This technological advantage, combined with skilled pilots and effective leadership, contributed significantly to the Allied victory in the Pacific and marked a turning point in the war. The dominance of American air power was not just about numbers, but about the significant technological leap forward that decisively tilted the balance of the Pacific War in favor of the Allies. The legacy of Operation Hailstone underscores the profound impact of technological innovation on modern warfare. The battle served as a stark reminder of the importance of technological development and its effect on shaping the outcome of conflict. The advanced capabilities of the American carrier-based aircraft proved to be a critical factor in the successful execution of Operation Hailstone, significantly influencing the strategic course of the war in the
Pacific.

Radar Technology and its Impact

The technological superiority of the United States Navy in the Pacific theater during World War II extended far beyond the capabilities of their aircraft. A crucial, often overlooked, element in their success at Truk Lagoon, and indeed throughout the Pacific campaign, was the significant advantage held in radar technology.

While the roar of engines and the flash of gunfire dominated the battlefields, the silent, unseen work of radar played a pivotal role in shaping the engagement, enabling the Americans to anticipate, react to, and ultimately overwhelm the Japanese forces.

The Japanese Navy, while possessing some radar systems, lagged significantly behind their American counterparts in terms of range, accuracy, and overall effectiveness. Their radar technology, while functional, suffered from limitations in range and sensitivity, often failing to detect American aircraft and ships until they were already within striking distance. This meant that the Japanese were often reacting to attacks rather than proactively defending against them, significantly hindering their ability to effectively counter the American offensive. Furthermore, the Japanese lacked the integrated radar networks that the Americans possessed, hindering their ability to share information and coordinate their defenses. This fragmented approach to radar deployment left significant gaps in their defensive capabilities, which the American forces skillfully exploited.

In stark contrast, the US Navy deployed a sophisticated and integrated radar system. The American system, constantly refined and improved throughout the war, offered several crucial advantages. First, its longer range allowed American forces to detect Japanese aircraft and ships at a much greater distance than the Japanese could detect American forces. This gave American commanders valuable time to prepare for incoming attacks, allowing them to scramble fighters, position their ships defensively, and coordinate their responses effectively. The early warning provided by radar allowed for a more deliberate and coordinated response, optimizing the effectiveness of American forces. This early warning capability was critical in mitigating the surprise element often employed by the Japanese.

Second, the improved accuracy of American radar enabled more precise targeting of enemy aircraft and ships. American radar systems could more reliably determine the location, altitude, and speed of enemy assets, allowing American pilots and gunners to engage their targets with greater precision. This enhanced accuracy translated directly into a higher rate of hits and a greater degree of damage inflicted on enemy forces. The ability to accurately
pinpoint targets reduced the need for large-scale, indiscriminate attacks and allowed for a more focused and surgical approach to targeting enemy assets.

Third, the integration of radar data across multiple platforms was a key differentiator. The American system allowed information from different radar stations, aircraft, and ships to be shared almost instantaneously, creating a comprehensive and dynamic picture of the battlefield. This level of situational awareness enabled
commanders to make informed decisions, adjust their tactics in real time, and coordinate the actions of different units effectively. The integrated nature of the radar system facilitated seamless
coordination among various elements of the naval force. Japanese forces, lacking this network, operated in relative isolation, making coordination a challenging and often ineffective process.

The impact of this radar disparity was particularly evident during Operation Hailstone. American radar detected the approaching Japanese aircraft and ships well in advance, giving them ample time to prepare their defenses and launch counter-attacks. This allowed American pilots to intercept Japanese aircraft before they reached their targets, minimizing the threat to American ships. The advanced radar warning system allowed for a more efficient
deployment of resources and minimized the losses suffered by the American forces. Conversely, the limitations of Japanese radar systems hampered their ability to effectively anticipate American attacks, leading to significant losses of aircraft and ships. The surprise element, often a key component of Japanese strategy, was significantly neutralized by the superior radar technology of the US Navy.

The technological gap in radar extended beyond mere detection and tracking. The Americans also utilized radar-guided fire control systems, allowing for more accurate targeting of anti-aircraft guns and significantly improving the effectiveness of their defenses against air attacks. This enhanced defensive capability further diminished Japanese offensive capabilities and increased American survival rates during the air combat. The ability to accurately target and eliminate incoming enemy planes played a significant role in the success of Operation Hailstone.

The radar advantage was also instrumental in the coordination and execution of the American air strikes. Radar allowed American aircraft to locate and attack Japanese ships and installations with far greater precision than was possible with visual sighting alone. This increased the effectiveness of the American bombing raids and ensured that their attack caused maximum damage and disruption to the Japanese fleet at Truk Lagoon. The coordinated strikes facilitated by the use of radar technology greatly overwhelmed the Japanese defenses and caused significant losses.

Furthermore, the radar technology facilitated the effective use of American air power. The longer range and improved accuracy of the radar allowed the American aircraft to carry out their operations effectively, even against a numerically superior adversary. The advanced radar systems improved the operational efficiency and reduced the risks associated with air operations. American pilots were able to accurately identify and target enemy assets, greatly maximizing their effectiveness.

The impact of radar technology during Operation Hailstone goes beyond the immediate tactical success. The ability of the US Navy to detect and track enemy movements played a crucial role in shaping the strategic outcome of the battle and the broader Pacific War. The intelligence gathered through advanced radar systems provided crucial insights into enemy strengths and vulnerabilities, enabling US strategists to design more effective war plans and strategies. The accumulated intelligence improved the overall conduct of war, resulting in higher operational efficiency and strategic effectiveness.

In conclusion, the technological advantage in radar technology possessed by the US Navy played a pivotal role in securing the decisive victory at the Battle of Truk Lagoon. It was not simply a matter of superior numbers or better pilot training; the ability to see the enemy before they could see the Americans, to accurately track their movements, and to share that information effectively across the fleet profoundly shaped the course of the battle. The radar technology provided an unparalleled level of situational awareness, enabling the Americans to coordinate their efforts with precision and effectiveness, ultimately overwhelming the Japanese defenses and inflicting crippling damage on their forces. The legacy of Operation Hailstone underscores not only the importance of air power and naval might, but also the crucial contribution of often-unsung technologies like radar in winning the war in the Pacific.

The seemingly silent work of radar played a crucial role in the narrative of victory, a testament to technological innovation's significant impact on the outcome of modern warfare.

AntiAircraft Defenses and Their Effectiveness

The technological disparity between the US and Japanese navies during Operation Hailstone extended beyond radar; it also manifested significantly in the realm of anti-aircraft defenses. While both sides employed anti-aircraft guns, the effectiveness of these defenses varied drastically due to several factors, including weapon technology, deployment strategies, and the overall integration with other defensive systems. The American advantage in this area, while not as pronounced as their radar superiority, still played a crucial role in shaping the outcome of the battle.

The Japanese anti-aircraft defenses at Truk Lagoon were largely composed of a heterogeneous mix of weaponry, reflecting their resource constraints and the decentralized nature of their defense strategy. This included a variety of guns, ranging from relatively light, quick-firing cannons to heavier, more powerful artillery pieces. The light guns, often found on smaller ships and defensive installations, provided a relatively dense curtain of fire, but lacked the range and accuracy to consistently threaten American high-altitude bombers. Their effectiveness was further hampered by a shortage of effective proximity fuses, which would have greatly increased the lethality of their shells. The heavier guns, while possessing greater range and destructive power, suffered from slower rates of fire and less precise targeting systems. These heavier guns were mostly located in fixed positions on the islands, making them vulnerable to targeted attacks from American aircraft. The lack of effective coordinated fire control across different gun emplacements hindered their overall effectiveness, and American pilots frequently reported a lack of significant resistance compared to other battles. The interoperability between the various systems was largely absent, creating an overall defensive system lacking in coordination and efficiency.

Furthermore, the Japanese employed a less integrated approach to their air defenses, relying more on individual units acting independently rather than working together under a unified command structure. This lack of integration often resulted in ineffective distribution of fire, with multiple batteries targeting the same aircraft or leaving gaps in their defenses where American aircraft could exploit. The lack of a centralized command and control system prevented effective communication and coordination between different anti-aircraft units. The relatively primitive fire-control systems further reduced the accuracy of their anti-aircraft fire, resulting in low hit rates and a correspondingly limited ability to inflict significant damage on attacking American aircraft. The Japanese also lacked the sophisticated radar-directed fire control systems that greatly improved the accuracy of the American defenses.

American anti-aircraft defenses, in contrast, benefited from a more sophisticated and integrated approach. While they also utilized a range of weapons, including light and heavy guns, the American systems were better integrated with their radar networks, allowing for more accurate targeting and coordination. The integration of radar-directed fire control systems provided a significant advantage, dramatically improving the accuracy of their fire and allowing them to engage incoming aircraft with far greater effectiveness. The fire control systems were continually refined throughout the war, benefiting from advancements in radar technology and the lessons learned from earlier engagements. The accuracy of the American anti-aircraft fire was greatly enhanced, resulting in a much higher rate of hits and a significantly increased chance of inflicting damage on enemy aircraft.

The American strategy emphasized a layered defense, using a combination of light and heavy guns strategically positioned to defend against attacks from different altitudes and directions. This layered approach maximized the chances of intercepting incoming aircraft and ensured that even if some aircraft penetrated the outer defenses, they still faced a significant threat from the heavier guns closer to the ships and bases. The American Navy also utilized close-in weapons systems, such as Bofors 40mm and Oerlikon 20mm cannons, which proved exceptionally effective against low-flying aircraft. These rapid-firing guns were highly effective in defending against dive bombers and strafing runs, and played a critical role in protecting the American fleet from the more lethal close-range attacks. The widespread adoption of proximity fuses further increased the effectiveness of the American anti-aircraft shells. These fuses exploded near an aircraft rather than requiring a direct hit, greatly increasing the likelihood of inflicting damage.

The American emphasis on training also played a significant role in the effectiveness of their anti-aircraft defenses. American gun crews received extensive training in the use of their weapons and fire-control systems, significantly improving their proficiency and allowing them to engage targets with a much higher degree of accuracy. The training programs not only focused on technical skills but also emphasized teamwork and coordination among the
different crews. This level of training was lacking on the Japanese side, and the lower skill level of many of their gunners further contributed to their overall ineffective anti-aircraft defenses.

The effectiveness of the anti-aircraft defenses on both sides is reflected in the loss rates during Operation Hailstone. While the exact numbers are difficult to definitively determine, it's clear that the American fleet suffered significantly fewer losses from anti-aircraft fire compared to the Japanese forces. The Americans, despite facing a considerable volume of fire, were able to minimize their losses through a combination of superior technology, improved tactics, and enhanced training of their gun crews.

Analysis of post-battle damage reports further suggests that a significant portion of Japanese anti-aircraft fire was inaccurate, failing to inflict meaningful damage on American aircraft.

Conversely, the accuracy of American anti-aircraft fire, facilitated by technological advancements and sophisticated fire control, resulted in heavy losses for the Japanese aircraft.

Beyond the technological aspects, the differences in logistical support played a critical role. The Americans enjoyed a much more robust logistical network in the Pacific, allowing for the timely replenishment of ammunition, spare parts, and other essential supplies. This ensured that American anti-aircraft defenses
remained operational throughout the battle, unlike some Japanese emplacements, which ran low on ammunition and experienced mechanical failures due to the lack of adequate support. This logistical disadvantage further amplified the Japanese struggle to mount an effective defense.

In conclusion, the disparity in anti-aircraft defenses between the US and Japanese navies during Operation Hailstone contributed significantly to the overwhelming American victory. While the Americans possessed a decisive advantage in radar technology, their superiority in anti-aircraft weaponry, their integrated defense systems, better training, and superior logistical support played a critical, though often overlooked, role in neutralizing the Japanese air power and securing a decisive victory at Truk Lagoon. The battle highlighted the importance of not only individual weapon systems but also the broader strategic and logistical elements in determining the effectiveness of a nation's defenses in modern naval warfare. The legacy of Operation Hailstone serves as a stark reminder of the interconnectedness of technological advancement, training, strategy, and logistics in shaping the outcome of naval battles, and ultimately, the course of a war.

Submarine Warfare and Its Role

The aerial and surface dominance achieved by the US Navy during Operation Hailstone wasn't solely a product of carrier-based air power and superior surface warships. A crucial, yet often less-discussed, element of the operation was the contribution of the US submarine force. While the devastating air attacks captured the headlines, the relentless, unseen pressure exerted by American submarines significantly weakened the Japanese defenses and crippled their ability to resupply and reinforce Truk Lagoon, long before the main assault even began. The deployment of submarines in the lead-up to and during Operation Hailstone exemplifies the growing importance of undersea warfare in the Pacific theater.

The strategic importance of Truk Lagoon, as a major Japanese base, made it a prime target for submarine operations. Its vulnerability stemmed from its geographical location: a relatively enclosed
lagoon, making it difficult for Japanese surface vessels to maneuver effectively and to provide adequate anti-submarine protection across the entire area. This provided American submarines with considerable opportunities for ambush and attack. The US Navy had by 1944 developed highly effective submarine tactics, honed
through years of experience in the Pacific. They were able to
operate with a level of stealth and lethality that greatly surpassed their Japanese counterparts.

Unlike the relatively static nature of land-based air and naval defenses, submarine operations provided a degree of flexibility and unpredictability that significantly impacted the Japanese war effort.

Submarines could operate independently, launching attacks at opportune moments and locations, thus circumventing static defensive perimeters. This element of surprise, coupled with the destructive power of torpedoes, proved exceptionally effective in disrupting Japanese supply lines and morale.

The US Navy deployed several submarines to the Truk Lagoon area in the period preceding Operation Hailstone. These submarines, operating independently or in small groups, conducted extensive reconnaissance missions, gathering crucial intelligence about the strength, deployment, and activities of the Japanese fleet. This intelligence played a vital role in shaping the overall strategy of Operation Hailstone, providing essential data on Japanese ship movements, air defenses, and overall readiness. The information gathered was then carefully analyzed and integrated into the overall operational plan, resulting in more effective attacks and minimizing American losses.

Reports from these reconnaissance missions were critical in pinpointing the high concentration of Japanese ships within Truk Lagoon. These reports detailed the types of vessels, their locations, and any indication of their defensive capabilities. This precise intelligence reduced the uncertainties involved in the main assault, allowing the US Navy to concentrate their forces on the most vulnerable targets. This accurate intel significantly increased the efficiency of the air strikes, maximizing the damage inflicted on Japanese ships and infrastructure.

Beyond reconnaissance, the submarines launched a series of attacks against Japanese shipping in the waters surrounding Truk Lagoon.

This sustained pressure on Japanese supply lines had a profound impact on their ability to resupply the base. The submarines targeted tankers, cargo ships, and other support vessels, disrupting the flow of fuel, ammunition, food, and other vital materials. The Japanese navy struggled to adequately protect their supply lines, often lacking the resources and effective anti-submarine capabilities to respond effectively to this persistent submarine threat. These attacks effectively strangled the logistical support systems needed to sustain the Japanese presence in Truk Lagoon.

The impact of the submarine attacks was not solely limited to the disruption of material supplies. The psychological effect on Japanese personnel was also significant. The constant threat of unseen submarines created a climate of fear and uncertainty.

Japanese sailors and airmen, already strained by the relentless American attacks, now had to deal with the anxiety of potential submarine ambushes, even while in port. This heightened psychological stress further reduced their operational effectiveness and contributed to the perception of vulnerability and overwhelming odds, further impacting morale.

Specific instances of successful submarine attacks during the period leading up to and during Operation Hailstone are well documented. Several submarines scored direct hits on Japanese ships, sinking or damaging a variety of vessels. These attacks not only reduced the Japanese naval strength directly but also contributed significantly to the overall sense of vulnerability and defeat. The cumulative effect of these attacks, however devastating individually, created a debilitating effect that significantly aided the overall success of the Operation Hailstone.

The detailed logs and operational records of the participating submarines shed light on the challenges and successes faced during these operations. These records provide valuable insights into the tactical decisions made by submarine commanders, the challenges posed by the difficult conditions of the lagoon, and the effectiveness of various torpedo types and firing strategies. Analysis of these primary sources reveals the significant contribution of submarine operations to the overall success of Operation Hailstone. These submarines were not simply supporting players; they were a critical part of a multi-pronged strategic approach designed to cripple the Japanese stronghold at Truk.

The success of the US submarine campaign against Truk Lagoon also highlighted the technological advancements made in submarine warfare by this point of the war. Improved sonar systems, more effective torpedoes, and enhanced navigational technology significantly increased the lethality and operational capabilities of American submarines. This technological superiority played a crucial role in the submarines' success in penetrating Japanese defenses, launching successful attacks, and escaping unscathed. The improvements in submarine technology also facilitated the ability to conduct more prolonged and complex missions, further enhancing their strategic impact.

In conclusion, while the aerial bombardment and surface fleet actions during Operation Hailstone captured the immediate dramatic impact of the battle, the contribution of submarine warfare was equally pivotal in shaping the outcome. The sustained campaign of reconnaissance, disruption of supply lines, and direct attacks on Japanese shipping played a significant role in weakening Truk's defenses and demoralizing its garrison. The submarines' silent, unseen effectiveness under the waves foreshadowed the increasing importance of anti-submarine warfare that would characterize future naval conflicts. The legacy of Operation Hailstone should not solely be remembered as a testament to carrier-based air power, but also as a demonstration of the vital role of submarines in achieving a decisive victory in the Pacific theater of World War II. The largely unseen work of the submarine crews was critical to setting the stage for the overwhelming success of Operation Hailstone.

Naval Gunnery and its Effectiveness

The overwhelming success of Operation Hailstone wasn't solely attributable to the devastating air power unleashed from the carrier decks or the strategic brilliance of the overall plan. A critical, often overlooked, element contributing to the decisive Allied victory was the superior firepower and accuracy of American naval gunnery.

While the submarines silently worked to disrupt Japanese supply lines and sow chaos, the surface actions demonstrated a clear technological edge in naval armament that significantly amplified the impact of the air attacks. The sheer destructive power unleashed by the American warships highlighted the considerable gap in naval technology between the two warring nations.

The Japanese fleet stationed at Truk Lagoon, though numerically significant before the operation, was ill-equipped to withstand the concentrated firepower of the US Navy's battleships, cruisers, and destroyers. The disparity was not merely a matter of quantity; it was a stark contrast in the quality and effectiveness of the weaponry itself. American naval guns possessed superior range, accuracy, and firepower compared to their Japanese counterparts.

This advantage stemmed from several factors, including advancements in gun design, powder technology, fire-control systems, and radar integration.

American battleships, like the USS Iowa and the South Dakota, boasted 16-inch guns capable of delivering devastating blows at significantly greater ranges than Japanese warships. These guns were not just larger; they were more precisely engineered, leading to improved accuracy and consistency in their projectile trajectories. The Japanese Navy, while possessing formidable battleships of their own, lacked the same level of technological sophistication in their main armament. Their guns, though powerful, often suffered from lower accuracy and shorter effective ranges, leaving them vulnerable to American fire before they could effectively retaliate.

The advancements in powder technology played a crucial role in enhancing the range and power of American naval guns. The improved propellants generated higher muzzle velocities, translating to greater range and more destructive impact upon impact. This meant that American ships could engage Japanese targets from a safe distance, minimizing the risk of return fire while maximizing the effectiveness of their bombardment. The Japanese navy's reliance on older propellant technology left their guns at a distinct disadvantage.

Beyond the guns themselves, American fire-control systems offered a critical advantage. These systems utilized advanced radar technology, allowing for precise target acquisition and tracking, even in challenging weather conditions. The integration of radar with sophisticated fire-control computers enabled American gunners to adjust their aim rapidly and accurately, achieving a level of precision that overwhelmed the Japanese defenses. Japanese fire-control systems, while improving, were not as advanced, resulting in a lower rate of successful hits and a diminished ability to effectively counter the American onslaught.

The difference in the effectiveness of fire control is starkly evident in comparing the battle reports and damage assessments. The accounts from American ships consistently detail high hit percentages against Japanese targets, often inflicting catastrophic damage with a relatively low expenditure of ammunition. In contrast, Japanese reports indicate significantly lower hit rates, with many shots falling short or wide of their intended targets. This discrepancy reflects the superior technology and training of American gunnery crews, coupled with the more effective fire-control systems. The accuracy of American gunnery was instrumental in neutralizing Japanese threats, limiting their ability to effectively respond.

The consequences of the superior American gunnery were evident in the sheer destruction inflicted upon the Japanese fleet and infrastructure within Truk Lagoon. The bombardment caused extensive damage to Japanese warships, many of which were sunk or severely crippled, rendering them effectively unusable. The American guns also heavily damaged or destroyed vital infrastructure in the lagoon, including fuel storage facilities, airfields, and repair yards. This damage severely hampered the

Japanese ability to resupply, repair, and maintain their forces, contributing significantly to the overall success of Operation Hailstone. The combination of aerial bombardment and surface gunnery effectively shattered the once formidable Japanese base, turning it into a strategic liability.

The American advantage extended beyond the capabilities of the guns themselves. The training and expertise of American gunnery crews played a crucial role in maximizing the effectiveness of their weapons. Years of rigorous training and experience in combat situations honed the skills of American gunners, enabling them to operate their weapons with remarkable speed and accuracy. The American Navy emphasized consistent practice, aiming drills, and the integration of the latest technological advancements into their training programs. The high proficiency of the crews significantly contributed to the successful execution of the bombardment.

In contrast, the Japanese Navy faced challenges in training and equipment. While dedicated and brave, Japanese gunners often lacked the same level of technological support and extensive
training opportunities available to their American counterparts. The disparity in the availability of advanced training simulators and target practice opportunities meant that Japanese gunnery crews were at a disadvantage. This was further compounded by issues with the quality and reliability of their equipment, contributing to inconsistencies in firing accuracy.

The technological disparity in naval gunnery extended to the types of ammunition used. American ships employed improved armor-piercing shells designed to penetrate the armor of Japanese
warships, causing significant internal damage even when they didn't achieve a direct hit. These shells utilized advanced metallurgy and explosive filler, maximizing their effectiveness against heavily armored targets. The Japanese ammunition, while adequate, lacked the same penetrative power and explosive yield, limiting their effectiveness against the heavily armored American warships.

Furthermore, American ships employed proximity fuses, which detonated shells near their target rather than upon direct impact, increasing their effectiveness even against moving ships and dispersed targets. This significantly boosted the killing power of anti-aircraft fire and made it far more difficult for Japanese ships to escape the onslaught of American artillery. These advanced fuses were not widely available in the Japanese Navy, again contributing to their overall inferiority in the gunnery aspect of the battle.

The bombardment of Truk Lagoon during Operation Hailstone thus provides a compelling case study in the impact of technological superiority in naval warfare. The advanced gunnery capabilities of the US Navy, coupled with superior training and tactics, proved to be a decisive factor in the battle's outcome. The extent of the damage inflicted on the Japanese fleet and infrastructure underscores the significant technological gulf that existed between the two navies by 1944. The effectiveness of American naval gunnery during Operation Hailstone not only crippled the Japanese stronghold at Truk but also served as a powerful demonstration of the crucial role of technological innovation in shaping the course of the war.

Beyond the immediate impact on the battle, the technological advantages demonstrated at Truk had lasting implications for the war in the Pacific. The success of American naval gunnery spurred further investment in research and development of naval weaponry, contributing to the even greater dominance of the US Navy in subsequent battles. The lessons learned at Truk underscored the crucial importance of technological superiority in achieving victory in naval warfare, influencing naval doctrines and strategies for years to come. The battle served as a stark reminder that technological advancements could be a decisive factor in shaping the outcome of naval battles, influencing the trajectory of the entire war. The legacy of Operation Hailstone, therefore, extends far beyond the immediate consequences of the battle itself; it serves as a pivotal chapter in the history of naval warfare, highlighting the pivotal role of technological advancement in achieving decisive victories.

Impact on the Pacific War

The crippling blow dealt to the Japanese Navy at Truk Lagoon during Operation Hailstone reverberated far beyond the immediate aftermath of the February 1944 assault. The destruction of significant naval assets, the crippling of vital infrastructure, and the demoralizing effect on Japanese forces had profound and lasting consequences on the course of the Pacific War, significantly accelerating the Allied advance towards ultimate victory. The strategic implications of the operation went far beyond the immediate losses inflicted upon the Japanese, impacting the overall war effort in several key ways.

Firstly, Operation Hailstone dealt a severe blow to the Japanese Navy's ability to project power in the central Pacific. Truk Lagoon had served as a crucial logistical hub, a vital resupply point, and a major repair facility for Japanese forces operating throughout Micronesia. Its neutralization effectively severed critical Japanese supply lines, leaving their forces in the region increasingly isolated and vulnerable. The loss of ships and aircraft, coupled with the destruction of repair facilities, severely hampered the Japanese capacity to respond effectively to subsequent Allied offensives. The lagoon, once a bastion of Japanese power, became a graveyard of their naval might, a potent symbol of their dwindling capabilities.

The impact on Japanese morale was equally significant. The sheer scale of the destruction inflicted at Truk, the precision and overwhelming power of the American attack, left the Japanese military leadership shocked and demoralized. This was not a minor skirmish; it was a resounding defeat that exposed the vulnerability of even their most heavily fortified bases. The psychological impact of Operation Hailstone extended beyond the immediate participants, undermining the confidence of Japanese forces throughout the Pacific and contributing to a sense of growing desperation. News of the massive losses undoubtedly spread through the ranks, eroding the already faltering belief in Japanese invincibility.

Operation Hailstone's success played a pivotal role in shaping

subsequent Allied strategies in the Pacific. The significant reduction in Japanese naval strength in the central Pacific opened up new avenues for Allied advance. The operation paved the way for the later campaigns in the Mariana Islands and the Philippines,
removing a significant obstacle to the Allied island-hopping
strategy. By neutralizing Truk, the Allies effectively eliminated a major threat to their supply lines and secured a strategic foothold in the region. This allowed the Allies to concentrate their forces on other key objectives, accelerating their progress towards Japan.

Beyond the immediate strategic impact, Operation Hailstone had a far-reaching effect on the allocation of Japanese resources. The massive losses sustained at Truk forced the Japanese to divert precious resources towards repairing the damage and replenishing their depleted forces. These resources, which could have been used elsewhere to bolster their defense against the Allied advance, were instead diverted to mitigating the losses from this single operation.

This diversion of resources created a cascading effect, further weakening the Japanese ability to effectively resist the relentless Allied advance across the Pacific. The necessity to repair the damage and re-establish the functionality of Truk as a base further strained Japan's already depleted resources and manpower.

The intelligence gathered during and after Operation Hailstone proved invaluable to the Allies. The meticulous reconnaissance efforts prior to the attack, combined with the analysis of the
damage inflicted and the captured Japanese documents, provided invaluable insights into Japanese naval capabilities, strategies, and vulnerabilities. This intelligence helped refine Allied tactics and strategies, allowing them to better anticipate and counter Japanese maneuvers. The detailed information gleaned from the sunken ships and the analysis of captured equipment provided a wealth of
knowledge about Japanese naval technology and procedures, significantly assisting in developing countermeasures for future engagements.

Operation Hailstone's impact extended beyond the purely military domain. The economic burden of replacing the lost ships, aircraft, and infrastructure further strained the Japanese economy, already struggling under the weight of the war effort. The immense cost of rebuilding Truk, both in material resources and manpower, drew resources away from other crucial areas, hindering Japan's capacity for sustained resistance. The significant investment required to repair the damage was a severe drain on an already stressed economy, worsening their situation. This economic strain further diminished their capacity for sustained military operations.

The success of Operation Hailstone also served as a powerful morale booster for the Allied forces. The decisive victory demonstrated the growing superiority of the American Navy in terms of both technological prowess and tactical skill. This reinforced Allied confidence and bolstered their determination to continue the offensive against Japan. The news of the overwhelming success at Truk undoubtedly spread throughout the Allied ranks, reinforcing the belief in their ultimate victory. This renewed sense of confidence had a palpable effect on troop morale and fueled further commitment to the war effort.

Furthermore, the legacy of Operation Hailstone extended beyond the immediate battlefield, influencing the strategic thinking and planning of both sides of the conflict. The operation highlighted the importance of air power in modern naval warfare, demonstrating the devastating potential of carrier-based aircraft in neutralizing enemy naval forces and infrastructure. The devastating effectiveness of the combined air and naval assault provided clear evidence of the growing importance of such combined force tactics. This realization shaped subsequent Allied strategies and led to increased investment in carrier-based aircraft and air support for naval operations. Japanese planners were forced to reassess their defensive strategies in light of the overwhelming defeat at Truk, leading to significant adjustments in their operational plans.

The aftermath of Operation Hailstone left Truk Lagoon a haunting testament to the ferocity of naval warfare. The sunken ships, still littered across the lagoon floor, became a chilling reminder of the battle's devastation. The lagoon, once a bustling Japanese stronghold, was transformed into an underwater graveyard, a poignant symbol of the war's destructive power and the shifting balance of naval power in the Pacific. This transformation made the area a perilous but intriguing destination for military archaeologists and wreck divers alike.

In conclusion, Operation Hailstone's impact on the Pacific War transcends the immediate losses inflicted on the Japanese. The operation significantly weakened Japanese naval capabilities in the central Pacific, facilitating the Allied advance and ultimately
contributing to their eventual victory. The battle's far-reaching consequences included the crippling of Japanese supply lines, a significant blow to Japanese morale, the diversion of crucial
resources, invaluable intelligence gathering, and an enhanced perception of American naval superiority. Operation Hailstone stands as a pivotal moment in the Pacific theater, a testament to the power of well-planned combined operations and a turning point that dramatically shifted the momentum of the war in favor of the Allied forces. Its legacy continues to resonate even today, offering a valuable case study in the complexities of naval warfare and the profound impact of decisive battles on the course of a global
conflict.

Shifting the Balance of Power

The strategic implications of Operation Hailstone extended far beyond the immediate destruction witnessed in Truk Lagoon. The loss of twelve ships, including several cruisers and destroyers, represented a significant depletion of Japan's already strained naval resources. These were not mere replacements; they represented irreplaceable losses of trained personnel, specialized equipment, and combat experience—elements crucial to effective naval operations. The sinking of these vessels, coupled with the destruction of hundreds of aircraft and the damage inflicted on vital infrastructure, profoundly impacted Japan's ability to project power across the vast expanse of the Pacific. The Japanese Navy, once the undisputed master of the Pacific, was demonstrably weakened, its offensive capabilities significantly curtailed.

The disruption of Japanese supply lines proved equally devastating. Truk Lagoon served as a crucial logistical hub, a central point for the resupply and repair of Japanese forces operating throughout Micronesia and the western Pacific. Its neutralization effectively severed these crucial lifelines, leaving isolated garrisons vulnerable and starved of reinforcements, ammunition, and fuel. The sheer distance between Truk and the home islands made resupply a logistical nightmare, a task further complicated by the increasing effectiveness of Allied submarine warfare. The consequences were far-reaching: Japanese units in the outer reaches of the empire found themselves increasingly isolated, their ability to mount effective resistance diminishing with each passing month. This logistical vulnerability, exacerbated by the damage inflicted upon Truk, played a significant role in the Allied successes in subsequent campaigns.

The battle also profoundly impacted Japanese strategic planning. Before Operation Hailstone, the Japanese envisioned a prolonged defense of the Pacific, relying on a combination of fortified bases and a powerful navy to repel Allied advances. The scale of the defeat at Truk, however, forced a reassessment of this strategy. The crippling blow exposed the vulnerability of even their most heavily fortified bases to well-executed combined operations involving carrier-based air power and coordinated naval attacks. This realization led to a shift in Japanese defensive strategy, a move away from ambitious offensive operations and towards a more defensive posture focused on the protection of the home islands.

Resources were diverted from offensive campaigns to bolster defenses closer to Japan, a strategic shift that reflects the profound impact of Operation Hailstone.

The loss of experienced personnel further compounded the damage inflicted at Truk. The destruction of ships resulted in the loss of thousands of trained sailors, pilots, and support personnel. These were not easily replaceable losses; years of training and experience were lost in a single battle, undermining the effectiveness of the remaining Japanese naval forces. The impact went beyond simply the numerical loss of manpower; it represented a loss of institutional knowledge, skills honed through years of operation, and the intricate web of relationships and expertise that characterized highly effective naval units. This loss of human capital, coupled with the material losses, further weakened the Japanese war effort.

Operation Hailstone's effect extended beyond the purely military realm. The economic cost of replacing the lost ships, aircraft, and infrastructure was staggering. Japan, already facing economic hardships under the strain of the war, was forced to divert precious resources away from other crucial areas to address the damage inflicted at Truk. This diversion of resources —from industrial production to civilian goods—exacerbated the existing economic strain, further limiting Japan's capacity to sustain the war effort.

The sheer scale of the losses meant that rebuilding Truk would require not only extensive material but also significant manpower, pulling resources from other critical sectors of the war effort.

Beyond the material and economic cost, Operation Hailstone inflicted a significant psychological blow on the Japanese military and civilian population alike. The scale of destruction at Truk, once perceived as an impregnable stronghold, revealed the vulnerability of Japanese power. News of the devastating defeat spread rapidly, undermining the image of Japanese invincibility that had been carefully cultivated by the propaganda machine. This eroded morale among the armed forces, impacting troop readiness and willingness to fight. In the civilian population, the defeat at Truk further intensified anxieties about the ultimate outcome of the war.

The intelligence gleaned from Operation Hailstone provided the Allies with invaluable insights into Japanese naval capabilities and strategies. Analysis of the wreckage, captured documents, and interrogation of surviving personnel gave the Allied forces a clearer understanding of Japanese naval tactics, technological limitations, and defensive strategies. This detailed information allowed the Allies to refine their own war plans, anticipate Japanese
countermeasures, and exploit their vulnerabilities more effectively in subsequent operations. The detailed study of the sunken ships provided valuable information on Japanese shipbuilding techniques, damage control measures, and fire control systems, all of which proved invaluable in planning future engagements.

Moreover, the success of Operation Hailstone acted as a considerable morale booster for the Allied forces. The decisive victory confirmed the growing superiority of the US Navy in terms of both technology and tactical skill. It reinforced the Allies'
confidence in their ability to continue their offensive in the Pacific and pushed them further toward their ultimate goal of a total victory. This renewed confidence was demonstrably crucial in pushing through subsequent campaigns, boosting troop morale, and solidifying the resolve of the Allied commanders.

The strategic shift resulting from Operation Hailstone had significant ramifications for the overall conduct of the war. The operation effectively neutralized a major Japanese base, disrupted their supply lines, and weakened their naval power in the Central Pacific. This facilitated subsequent Allied advances, paving the way for the Mariana Islands Campaign and the liberation of the
Philippines. The shift of Japanese strategic focus towards the defense of the home islands, a direct consequence of the losses at Truk, allowed the Allies to concentrate their resources and
manpower on other strategic objectives, accelerating the pace of the war in the Pacific.

In essence, Operation Hailstone stands as a pivotal turning point in

the Pacific theater of World War II. The operation's profound and far-reaching consequences—military, economic, and psychological—marked a significant shift in the balance of power. The damage to the Japanese Navy, the disruption of their supply lines, the
significant drain on their resources, and the profound impact on morale all contributed to the accelerating Allied advance and ultimately to Japan's defeat. The legacy of Operation Hailstone continues to resonate within the annals of naval warfare, serving as a stark reminder of the devastating potential of well-executed combined operations and the enduring impact of decisive battles on the course of history. Truk Lagoon remains, even today, a powerful and haunting reminder of this significant moment in naval warfare and the ultimate Allied victory in the Pacific.

The Psychological Impact on Japan

The psychological impact of Operation Hailstone reverberated far beyond the physical destruction wrought upon Truk Lagoon. The meticulously planned and flawlessly executed American assault shattered a carefully cultivated image of Japanese invincibility, a cornerstone of the nation's wartime propaganda. For years, the Imperial Japanese Navy had been portrayed as an invincible force, a symbol of national pride and military prowess. Truk Lagoon, a strategically vital base, had been presented as an impregnable fortress, virtually immune to attack. The reality of Operation Hailstone starkly contradicted this narrative.

The sheer scale of the destruction was almost incomprehensible. The loss of twelve major warships, hundreds of aircraft, and the devastation of vital infrastructure shocked the Japanese military and civilian population alike. News of the defeat, initially suppressed or heavily censored, inevitably leaked through various channels, spreading rapidly through whispers and rumors, ultimately reaching even the most isolated communities. The official reports, attempting to minimize the extent of the losses, only added to the growing sense of unease and mistrust. Soldiers and sailors stationed far from Truk, initially insulated from the immediate impact, sensed the chilling implication of the battle's outcome - if Truk could fall, what base was truly safe?

The psychological toll extended far beyond the immediate loss of life and material. The destruction of Truk Lagoon represented more than just the loss of a strategic base; it symbolized the erosion of Japanese confidence and military capability. The meticulously constructed defenses, intended to withstand any Allied attack, had proven utterly ineffective against the combined air and naval assault. This revelation profoundly impacted the morale of the Japanese military. The formerly unshakeable belief in their superior fighting prowess and the invincibility of their defenses began to crumble, replaced by a growing sense of doubt and apprehension.

The impact on the morale of the Japanese Navy was particularly devastating. The veterans of countless battles, the elite forces responsible for Japan's initial string of successes, found themselves facing a new reality. The men who had once exuded unwavering confidence now grappled with questions of their own invincibility. The loss of experienced sailors, pilots, and support personnel was a blow that went far beyond the mere numerical reduction in manpower. The loss of institutional knowledge, combat experience, and the shared camaraderie of long-serving crews profoundly impacted the Navy's effectiveness. The deaths of comrades, often under circumstances where resistance had proven futile, introduced an element of demoralization that extended into subsequent engagements.

The psychological impact extended beyond the armed forces, affecting the civilian population as well. The Japanese government, relying on a steady stream of propaganda and carefully curated news reports, had striven to maintain a sense of national unity and resilience. The scale of the defeat at Truk, however, made it increasingly difficult to maintain this carefully crafted narrative. The reality of the losses, both in terms of manpower and material, could not be entirely concealed. The ensuing uncertainty, coupled with the government's attempts to downplay the defeat, only heightened the existing anxieties among the civilian population.

The once pervasive confidence in a victorious outcome began to wane, replaced by a rising tide of doubt and fear.

The destruction of Truk also impacted Japanese strategic thinking. Prior to Operation Hailstone, the Japanese military had envisioned a prolonged war of attrition, relying on a combination of fortified bases and their powerful, albeit dwindling, naval force to repel the Allied advance. The swift and decisive defeat at Truk fundamentally altered this strategic outlook. The realization that even their most heavily defended bases were vulnerable to well-coordinated Allied attacks forced a reassessment of their defensive strategy. The previously ambitious plans for offensive operations were shelved in favor of a more defensive posture, focused on the protection of the home islands. This strategic shift, largely driven by the psychological impact of Operation Hailstone, reflected a fundamental shift in the Japanese military's perceptions of its own capabilities and the Allied threat.

The propaganda efforts of the Imperial Japanese government, once remarkably effective, struggled to maintain their credibility in the wake of Operation Hailstone. The disparity between the government's portrayal of invincibility and the stark reality of the defeat left many deeply disillusioned. This loss of trust in the government's pronouncements further destabilized the morale of both the military and civilian populations. The government's attempts to control the flow of information about the battle further exacerbated the psychological impact, fostering distrust and speculation. The lack of transparency only served to heighten the sense of fear and uncertainty, undermining the morale of those who were already grappling with the implications of the defeat.

The psychological consequences of Operation Hailstone were far-reaching and long-lasting. The defeat at Truk was not merely a military setback; it was a profound psychological blow that eroded Japanese morale, undermined military confidence, and contributed significantly to the accelerating decline of the Japanese war effort.

The shock of the defeat shattered the image of invincibility carefully cultivated by the government, revealing the vulnerability of the Japanese war machine and contributing to the growing disillusionment within the nation. The lingering psychological impact of the battle served as a harbinger of the ultimate outcome of the war, foreshadowing Japan's eventual surrender. The haunting silence left in the wake of the battle's fury served as a sobering testament to the magnitude of the Allied victory and the psychological price paid by the Japanese. The shadows of Truk Lagoon's sunken fleet became a potent symbol of defeat, a chilling reminder of the war's immense cost, both material and psychological, for the nation of Japan. The once impregnable stronghold transformed into an underwater graveyard, not merely of ships and aircraft, but also of dreams and hopes, a stark reminder of the profound psychological impact of Operation Hailstone. Even today, the battle's legacy continues to serve as a case study in the crucial intersection of military strategy and psychological warfare, a stark reminder of the far-reaching consequences of a single decisive battle on the fate of a nation. The psychological scars inflicted by Operation Hailstone would remain a part of Japan's collective memory for generations to come.

Operation Hailstone as a Turning Point

Operation Hailstone's impact transcended the immediate destruction at Truk Lagoon; it served as a pivotal turning point in the Pacific Theater, significantly altering the strategic landscape and influencing the course of subsequent battles. The scale of the Japanese losses – twelve major warships sunk or heavily damaged, hundreds of aircraft destroyed, and irreplaceable infrastructure crippled – sent shockwaves through the Imperial Japanese Navy and the Japanese high command. This wasn't merely a tactical defeat; it was a strategic blow that exposed the vulnerability of Japan's seemingly impregnable defenses and shattered the carefully cultivated myth of Japanese invincibility.

Before Operation Hailstone, the Japanese had enjoyed a period of relative success in the Pacific. Their initial victories had established a sense of confidence, bordering on arrogance, within their military ranks. Truk Lagoon, positioned at the heart of their defensive network, was considered the linchpin of their Pacific operations. The sheer size and extent of its defenses, coupled with the perceived strength of the Japanese forces stationed there, had convinced many that it was virtually unassailable. Operation Hailstone shattered this illusion. The speed and decisiveness of the American attack, the overwhelming superiority of Allied air power, and the surprisingly weak Japanese response exposed the flaws in Japanese strategy and significantly undermined their morale.

The loss of experienced personnel proved particularly devastating. The destruction of so many ships and aircraft meant not just a loss of material, but also the loss of highly trained crews, skilled pilots, and seasoned commanders. This human cost far outweighed the purely material losses. The death of experienced personnel severely hampered the Japanese ability to replace lost assets, and more critically, disrupted the transmission of crucial combat knowledge and experience within the Imperial Japanese Navy. Replacing a damaged ship was a significant undertaking, but rebuilding the skills, experience, and leadership embedded within the crews was far more difficult and significantly prolonged the Japanese recovery period.

The aftermath of Operation Hailstone saw a tangible shift in the Allied strategy. Empowered by the resounding success, the Americans were emboldened to launch even more aggressive offensives across the Pacific. The destruction of Truk Lagoon effectively neutralized a major Japanese base of operations, opening up new avenues of advance towards the Japanese home islands. The psychological advantage gained by the Allies was almost as significant as the material gains. The decisive nature of the victory boosted Allied morale while simultaneously undermining Japanese confidence. This shift in momentum was evident in subsequent battles.

The battle at Iwo Jima, for example, showcased the stark contrast in morale and strategic thinking. While the Japanese fought fiercely and with considerable bravery, their overall strategy was marked by a sense of desperation, in contrast to the earlier battles, where they had employed more proactive and confident tactical decisions. This desperate defense is partially attributed to the devastating blow dealt at Truk, the loss of which significantly weakened their overall strategic position and morale. The fight for Iwo Jima was brutal, illustrating the lengths to which the Japanese would go to defend their homeland, but the shift from assertive offense to desperate defense highlighted the impact of Operation Hailstone. This change was noticeable in the way the Japanese deployed their forces, the intensity of their resistance, and even in their communications – a tangible reflection of the psychological impact of the previous defeat.

Furthermore, the intelligence gathered during and after Operation Hailstone provided invaluable insights into Japanese capabilities and weaknesses. The analysis of captured documents, intercepted communications, and the assessment of the damage inflicted allowed the Allies to refine their strategies, anticipate Japanese tactics, and exploit their vulnerabilities in subsequent engagements.

This intelligence, gathered from the wreckage and the surviving Japanese personnel, proved crucial in planning later campaigns and contributed significantly to the Allied victories in the months and years that followed. Operation Hailstone, therefore, served not only as a military victory but also as a crucial intelligence-gathering operation, shaping the course of the Pacific War in the period leading up to the final push towards Japan.

The strategic implications of Operation Hailstone extended beyond the immediate battlefield. The loss of Truk Lagoon disrupted Japanese supply lines, hampered their ability to reinforce other bases, and limited their capacity for offensive operations. This strategic disruption forced a reassessment of Japanese war aims and strategies, leading to a more defensive posture as their resources were stretched thin. The once-ambitious expansionist policies of the Imperial Japanese Navy were effectively thwarted by the loss of their crucial central base in the Pacific. This shift from offensive to defensive tactics is a significant marker of the turning point Operation Hailstone represented. The Japanese were forced to re-evaluate their war plans and focus on the defense of their home islands, a fundamental shift in their strategic thinking directly attributable to the crushing blow inflicted at Truk.

The legacy of Operation Hailstone is not solely confined to the military arena. The economic implications of the losses were substantial. The destruction of ships, aircraft, and infrastructure represented a significant drain on Japan's already strained resources. The replacement of lost materials, coupled with the ongoing cost of the war, placed an immense burden on the Japanese economy and further contributed to the nation's decline. The economic strain only exacerbated the psychological impact, creating a sense of scarcity and hardship among the civilian population. This financial aspect, frequently overlooked in military analyses, played a significant role in undermining Japan's overall war effort.

Operation Hailstone stands as a stark example of the devastating effects of a well-executed naval operation. The meticulously planned and flawlessly executed American assault showcased the effectiveness of superior air power and the importance of precise intelligence. The battle's success significantly altered the strategic balance in the Pacific, contributed significantly to the Allied advance towards Japan, and served as a crucial turning point in the war. The echoes of the explosions, the ghostly silhouettes of sunken ships, and the haunted silence of the lagoon continue to serve as a testament to the battle's impact, a lasting reminder of the power of decisive action and the psychological toll of military defeat. The impact of Operation Hailstone wasn't limited to the immediate losses; its reverberations continue to be felt even today in the strategic analysis of naval warfare and the understanding of the complex interplay between military success and psychological warfare.

Historical Significance and Remembrance

The enduring legacy of Operation Hailstone extends far beyond the immediate aftermath of the devastating air and naval attacks on Truk Lagoon. The battle's impact resonates through the annals of naval history, shaping strategic thinking, influencing future military doctrines, and serving as a poignant reminder of the human cost of war. Its historical significance lies not only in the scale of the destruction inflicted upon the Japanese forces but also in the strategic implications that decisively shifted the balance of power in the Pacific Theater.

The near-total annihilation of the Japanese naval and air assets stationed at Truk Lagoon fundamentally altered the strategic landscape of the Pacific War. Truk, previously considered an impregnable fortress, was transformed into a graveyard of sunken warships and shattered aircraft, a stark symbol of Japanese vulnerability. This strategic defeat forced the Imperial Japanese Navy to abandon its offensive posture and adopt a largely defensive strategy. The loss of Truk crippled Japanese supply lines, hindering their ability to reinforce other vital bases and launch further offensives. This strategic shift profoundly affected the course of subsequent battles, weakening Japanese resistance and contributing to the Allies' relentless advance towards the Japanese home islands.

Beyond the immediate military repercussions, Operation Hailstone had significant long-term implications for naval warfare doctrine. The operation demonstrated the overwhelming effectiveness of carrier-based air power in neutralizing heavily defended enemy bases. The precision of the American attacks, coupled with the element of surprise, underscored the importance of intelligence gathering and coordinated strikes. This success served as a blueprint for future naval campaigns, influencing the development of carrier task forces and the strategic emphasis placed on air superiority in subsequent conflicts. The lessons learned at Truk were meticulously analyzed and incorporated into training programs, contributing to the increasing dominance of naval aviation in the latter stages of the war.

The human cost of Operation Hailstone is a crucial element that should never be forgotten. The destruction of Japanese ships and aircraft resulted in the loss of thousands of lives, both military and civilian. Many perished during the initial attacks, while others succumbed to injuries or were lost at sea. The tragedy extended beyond those who died immediately; countless families were left bereaved, their lives irrevocably altered by the war's devastating consequences. The submerged wrecks in Truk Lagoon serve as silent memorials to these lost lives, a haunting testament to the immense human suffering inflicted during the conflict. These silent monuments, scattered across the lagoon floor, are not just historical artifacts; they are poignant reminders of the human toll of war.

The remembrance of Operation Hailstone is not merely an exercise in commemorating past events; it is a vital act of learning from history. The battle's success and the subsequent Allied victory underscore the importance of strategic planning, meticulous intelligence gathering, technological superiority, and decisive action. By understanding the context of Operation Hailstone, we gain valuable insights into the dynamics of naval warfare, the complex interplay of military strategy, technological advancement, and human factors. Moreover, the battle highlights the moral ambiguities of warfare and the devastating consequences of conflict on both combatants and civilians. This reflection should contribute to a deeper understanding of the need for peace and international cooperation.

The historical significance of Operation Hailstone is further amplified by its impact on the subsequent development of post-war military strategies. The battle's analysis served as a case study for future generations of naval officers and strategists. The operational successes and failures were rigorously evaluated, allowing military planners to refine their strategies, optimize resource allocation, and improve operational effectiveness. The lessons learned from Operation Hailstone were incorporated into military doctrines and training programs, significantly influencing the conduct of naval operations throughout the Cold War and beyond. The echoes of the battle's strategic implications reverberate through subsequent naval conflicts, shaping the way modern navies operate and the strategic approaches employed in naval engagements.

Furthermore, the underwater graveyard of Truk Lagoon has become a site of historical preservation and somber contemplation. The wrecks, now encrusted with coral and teeming with marine life, have transformed into a unique and poignant underwater museum.

While offering a spectacle for scuba divers, these sites serve as a solemn reminder of the battle's devastating impact. The submerged remains of Japanese warships and aircraft are not merely remnants of a forgotten conflict; they are historical artifacts that hold invaluable information about naval technology, military strategy, and the human cost of war. Their preservation is essential for fostering future understanding and respect for the historical context of this pivotal event. The preservation efforts extend beyond the physical preservation of the wrecks. The narratives, stories, and accounts of those who participated in Operation Hailstone—both Allied and Axis forces—are vital components of the historical record. These oral histories, alongside official documents and analyses, provide a rich tapestry of human experience during this intense period in the Pacific Theater, enriching our understanding and reinforcing the gravity of the conflict.

The enduring significance of Operation Hailstone extends to the broader context of World War II in the Pacific. The battle marked a turning point in the war against Japan, signaling the shift from a protracted defensive posture on the part of the Allied forces to a more aggressive and successful offensive campaign. The success at Truk provided a much-needed boost to Allied morale, solidifying their confidence and determination to prevail. The psychological impact of Operation Hailstone cannot be underestimated; it had a demoralizing effect on the Japanese military, contributing to a decrease in their fighting spirit and overall capacity for effective resistance in subsequent engagements. This psychological impact, combined with the heavy material losses, paved the way for eventual Allied victory in the Pacific.

In conclusion, Operation Hailstone stands as a pivotal event in World War II, leaving an indelible mark on the course of naval warfare and the strategic landscape of the Pacific Theater. Its historical significance extends beyond the immediate destruction and losses, shaping military doctrines, influencing future conflicts, and prompting introspection on the human costs of war. The remembrance of this battle is not simply a retrospective exercise; it is a vital act of learning from the past, fostering a deeper understanding of naval history, and encouraging a commitment to peace and international cooperation. The silent testament of Truk Lagoon, a graveyard of sunken warships and shattered aircraft, serves as a powerful and enduring reminder of the magnitude of the battle, the sacrifice of those who fought, and the profound lessons learned from this pivotal moment in history. The ongoing preservation efforts, the meticulous historical research, and the continued analysis of the battle's strategic implications all ensure that Operation Hailstone's legacy will remain a subject of study and remembrance for generations to come. Its lessons are timeless and serve as a crucial reminder of the importance of strategic planning, decisive action, and the enduring human cost of armed conflict.

Truks Vulnerability and Defensive Shortcomings

The seemingly overwhelming success of Operation Hailstone, the February 1944 assault on Truk Lagoon, belies a deeper story of Japanese strategic miscalculations and defensive inadequacies. While the scale of destruction – the sinking of twelve ships, the loss of over 275 aircraft, and the crippling of the base's infrastructure –was undeniably devastating, the surprisingly light Japanese
resistance raises crucial questions about their preparedness and the overall effectiveness of their defensive strategy. A detailed
examination reveals a confluence of factors contributing to Truk's vulnerability and the ultimate failure of its defenses.

One significant factor was the inherent geographical limitations of Truk Lagoon itself. While the lagoon's natural defenses – a complex network of reefs and islands – offered some protection, this was far from insurmountable. The extensive shallows surrounding the islands, while hindering larger naval vessels, posed little obstacle to the numerous smaller, fast-attack aircraft employed by the
Americans. The carriers, operating beyond the range of Japanese land-based aircraft, could unleash their full air power without significant threat. The belief that the lagoon's natural barriers were sufficient protection proved to be a fatal miscalculation. The
Japanese underestimated the reach and capabilities of American carrier-based aircraft, and their concentration of resources in the lagoon created a tempting, and ultimately vulnerable, target. The dispersed nature of the defenses, relying heavily on smaller, less powerful installations rather than a unified, well-protected fleet, further compounded the problem.

Intelligence failures also played a crucial role in the Japanese inability to adequately defend Truk Lagoon. Japanese intelligence underestimated the scale and intensity of the impending American assault. They failed to accurately assess the size and capabilities of the attacking force, leading to an inadequate allocation of resources and a lack of preparedness for the devastating air strikes. The surprise element of the attack caught the Japanese completely off guard, leaving them ill-equipped to mount an effective defense. The lack of robust early warning systems, coupled with a failure to effectively interpret available intelligence, exacerbated this situation, resulting in a disastrous lack of readiness. Analysis of post-battle reports reveals a significant disconnect between the intelligence gathered and the operational responses implemented, highlighting a critical breakdown in communication and strategic decision-making.

Furthermore, the state of Japanese naval aviation at Truk was significantly depleted. The constant pressure of the ongoing Pacific campaign had taken its toll. Many experienced pilots were lost in previous battles, while aircraft suffered from a chronic shortage of spare parts and fuel. The effective strength of the Japanese air force at Truk was considerably lower than official reports indicated. This inherent weakness, coupled with the surprise attack, left the Japanese air defenses vulnerable and unable to effectively counter the overwhelming American air power. The lack of adequate fighter aircraft coverage in particular, left the Japanese ground installations and fleet exposed to sustained and virtually unopposed bombardment. The detailed records of Japanese aircraft losses during Operation Hailstone provide chilling evidence of the decimation of their air power at Truk.

The organizational structure of the Japanese defenses further contributed to their failure. The command structure lacked the necessary coordination and responsiveness required to counter a large-scale attack. Communications were often fragmented, resulting in delays in reacting to the unfolding events. The decentralized nature of the command structure hampered the efficient deployment of resources and the swift implementation of defensive strategies. The lack of a unified, centralized command center further hindered effective response to the developing crisis.

The Japanese command struggled to react decisively, often responding with piecemeal and ineffective countermeasures that failed to deter the American assault. This lack of effective coordination was clearly evident in the analysis of the battle's aftermath.

The overall state of Japanese morale and preparedness at Truk was also a significant factor. The prolonged campaign had taken a considerable toll on the fighting spirit of the Japanese troops

stationed there. Many were fatigued and demoralized, lacking the same levels of fighting spirit exhibited in earlier battles. This factor, combined with the unexpected ferocity and scale of the American attack, resulted in a less-than-robust defense. The lack of sufficient anti-aircraft defenses and the overall sense of unpreparedness exacerbated this situation, leading to a widespread lack of
resistance in the face of the overwhelming American assault. This was particularly evident in the analysis of the numerous eyewitness accounts of the battle.

The limitations of Japanese radar technology also contributed significantly to Truk's vulnerability. Their radar systems were relatively primitive compared to those of the United States,
providing inadequate detection and warning capabilities. The short range and limited accuracy of these systems meant that the
American fleet could approach undetected until it was within striking distance. This gave the Americans a decisive advantage in the initial stages of the attack. The subsequent analysis of radar records confirms the significant shortcomings of Japanese radar technology in detecting and tracking the incoming American forces. This technological inferiority played a crucial part in the successful execution of Operation Hailstone.

Finally, the lack of effective air cover further aggravated the Japanese defenses. The relative scarcity of effective fighter planes, the shortage of fuel and munitions, and the lack of coordination among Japanese pilots prevented the establishment of an effective aerial defense barrier. The American planes had a clear advantage in both numbers and advanced technology. The Japanese planes were quickly overwhelmed, leaving the installations and ships below vulnerable to repeated attack waves. The detailed air combat reports provide compelling evidence of the overwhelming American air superiority during Operation Hailstone, revealing the dire state of Japanese air defenses.

In conclusion, the fall of Truk Lagoon was not simply a result of overwhelming American firepower, but a confluence of factors highlighting critical vulnerabilities in Japanese strategic decision-making and defensive capabilities. Geographical limitations,
intelligence failures, depleted naval aviation, flawed organizational

structure, low morale, inferior radar technology, and inadequate air cover all contributed to the surprisingly light resistance and the devastating outcome of Operation Hailstone. The battle's legacy serves as a powerful illustration of how a combination of strategic miscalculations and operational inadequacies can lead to a
catastrophic military defeat, even when facing a numerically superior opponent. The detailed study of these elements is crucial for a full understanding of the strategic significance and
implications of the battle, offering invaluable lessons about naval warfare and the importance of meticulous planning, robust
intelligence gathering, and a well-coordinated defense. The analysis of Operation Hailstone underscores the need to learn from past mistakes to prevent similar failures in future conflicts.

Intelligence Failures and Miscalculations

The catastrophic failure of Japanese defenses at Truk Lagoon during Operation Hailstone in February 1944 stemmed not solely from the overwhelming American firepower, but also from a profound and multifaceted intelligence failure. This failure extended beyond a simple lack of information; it encompassed a systemic underestimation of American capabilities, a flawed interpretation of available data, and a critical breakdown in communication and response mechanisms within the Japanese command structure. The consequences were devastating, contributing significantly to the scale of the Japanese defeat.

One of the most glaring aspects of this intelligence failure was the underestimation of the size and scope of the impending American attack. Japanese intelligence assessments consistently underestimated the scale of the American carrier task force involved. Reports circulating within the Japanese Navy leadership painted an incomplete and arguably misleading picture of the approaching threat. This underestimation stemmed partly from the limitations of Japanese reconnaissance capabilities. Their long-range reconnaissance aircraft were not consistently effective in penetrating American air and naval patrols, resulting in incomplete and often outdated information reaching Truk. The intelligence gathered was often fragmented, inconsistent, and lacked crucial detail about the specific composition of the attacking fleet – its number of carriers, the types of aircraft deployed, and the overall operational plan. This lack of precise and timely information severely hampered the development of an effective defensive strategy.

The limitations were not only quantitative; the qualitative aspect of intelligence gathering was equally deficient. Japanese analysts failed to adequately assess the technological advancements made by the United States Navy. They underestimated the range and striking power of American carrier-based aircraft, particularly their dive bombers and torpedo planes. The technological gap was particularly evident in radar technology. The Japanese radar systems, while present, were far less sophisticated than those deployed by the

Americans. This technological inferiority prevented timely and accurate detection of the approaching American fleet, giving the Americans a crucial element of surprise. The lack of sufficient early warning allowed the Americans to launch their attack unhindered, catching the Japanese completely off guard and significantly reducing their ability to effectively react.

Furthermore, the Japanese intelligence apparatus struggled with effective information processing and dissemination. The system suffered from a hierarchical structure that often hampered the flow of crucial information. Lower-level reports were not always effectively communicated upward to high-level decision-makers, and crucial assessments were often delayed or lost in the bureaucratic process. This lack of clear, timely, and comprehensive information prevented the Japanese command from reacting effectively to the unfolding situation. The fragmented nature of the intelligence reports, coupled with an apparent unwillingness to accept the gravity of the impending threat, contributed to a delayed and inadequate response. Decentralized intelligence gathering, further exacerbated by inter-service rivalries, led to a lack of cohesion in information analysis and dissemination. Instead of a unified picture of the developing threat, Japanese commanders were working with incomplete and conflicting data, resulting in a failure to develop a cohesive defensive strategy.

The lack of adequate counterintelligence also played a significant role. The Americans, meanwhile, had implemented a sophisticated intelligence operation, gathering information about Japanese activity and capabilities at Truk Lagoon, while successfully obscuring their own plans. The Japanese, in contrast, failed to detect or adequately respond to American intelligence-gathering activities, providing the Americans with a significant informational advantage. The successful execution of Operation Hailstone highlights the American mastery of deception and intelligence gathering, in stark contrast to the Japanese failures in these critical areas.

This intelligence failure extended beyond the technical and organizational aspects; it also involved a crucial element of strategic miscalculation. The Japanese leadership demonstrated a degree of

complacency and overconfidence in the defensive capabilities of Truk Lagoon. The lagoon's geographical features, while offering some natural protection, were clearly inadequate against a
determined and well-equipped American assault. The Japanese belief in the invulnerability of Truk, fueled partly by their prior successes in the Pacific and partly by their incomplete and flawed intelligence reports, contributed significantly to their
unpreparedness for the American attack.

Beyond the specifics of intelligence gathering and processing, the Japanese failure at Truk also reflected a broader strategic weakness: a lack of appreciation for the evolving capabilities of the American Navy. Their strategic assessments underestimated the capacity of the United States to sustain and deploy a carrier-based air force capable of striking deep into the Pacific. The successful launch and execution of Operation Hailstone demonstrated that the Americans had achieved a decisive technological and operational superiority, which the Japanese failed to adequately acknowledge or address.

The consequences of these intelligence failures were dire. The lack of early warning, coupled with the underestimation of the American attack force, resulted in the near-total destruction of Japanese air power based in Truk Lagoon. The Japanese planes, caught on the ground or unprepared for the scale and intensity of the attack, suffered heavy losses. This loss significantly reduced Japan's ability to provide effective air cover for the ground installations and ships within the lagoon, contributing to the catastrophic damage inflicted by American air strikes. The inadequate intelligence was not a simple contributing factor; it was a fundamental cause of the
overwhelming Japanese defeat. The legacy of this intelligence failure served as a stark reminder of the critical importance of comprehensive, accurate, and timely intelligence in modern naval warfare. It underscores the necessity of developing robust
intelligence gathering and analysis capabilities, as well as effective communication and decision-making processes within a military command structure. The failure at Truk served as a pivotal lesson in the devastating consequences of intelligence shortcomings in the crucible of war.

Command Structure and Coordination Issues

The devastating losses suffered by the Japanese at Truk Lagoon during Operation Hailstone were not solely attributable to the overwhelming American firepower or the crippling intelligence failures previously discussed. A critical contributing factor was the inherent weakness and inefficiencies within the Japanese command structure and the resulting lack of effective coordination amongst their forces. The complex web of command, plagued by internal rivalries and communication breakdowns, proved disastrous in the face of a coordinated and technologically superior enemy.

The Japanese naval command structure in the Pacific was characterized by a highly centralized system, with ultimate authority resting with the Combined Fleet headquarters in Tokyo. This centralized structure, while seemingly offering a clear chain of command, suffered from significant delays in communication and decision-making. Information from Truk Lagoon had to travel a considerable distance, often through multiple layers of command, before reaching the highest echelons of power. This process was further complicated by the reliance on outdated communication methods, which were susceptible to disruption and delays. Even with the relatively rapid means of communication available at the time, the sheer distance and the hierarchical nature of the system meant that crucial decisions were often delayed, hindering the capacity for a timely and effective response to the unfolding American attack.

The geographic dispersion of Japanese forces at Truk Lagoon further compounded these problems. The lagoon itself, while offering some protection, also posed challenges for effective communication and coordination. Japanese units were scattered across numerous islands and anchorage points within the lagoon, making unified command and control exceptionally difficult. This geographical dispersion, coupled with the aforementioned communication difficulties, meant that the various elements of the Japanese defense—air units, naval vessels, and ground installations—were unable to coordinate their actions effectively. They lacked a comprehensive, unified plan to counter the American assault, leading to fragmented and largely ineffective responses.

Furthermore, the command structure suffered from significant inter-service rivalries. The Japanese Navy, Army, and Air Force operated with limited coordination and a degree of inter-service mistrust. This lack of cooperation was evident during the battle. The Navy, primarily responsible for the defense of the lagoon, had limited control over the Army and Air Force units stationed there. This lack of centralized control hindered the coordinated deployment of resources and ultimately reduced the effectiveness of the overall defense. Information sharing between the services was often
inadequate, leading to a situation where each service operated largely in isolation, responding to the American attack
independently rather than as part of a cohesive strategy. The resulting lack of a unified front allowed the Americans to exploit the weaknesses, isolating and destroying Japanese forces piecemeal.

Compounding the inter-service rivalries were significant differences in operational doctrine and priorities. The Navy, focused on
maintaining naval superiority, often prioritized the defense of its own ships and assets. The Army, responsible for ground defenses, concentrated on protecting the crucial infrastructure and
installations within the lagoon. The Air Force, meanwhile, was tasked with providing air cover, but its limited capacity was further compromised by the absence of effective coordination with the other two services. This divergence in priorities and operational approaches resulted in a disjointed response to the American attack, effectively reducing the potency of the overall defense. The lack of a unified strategy, stemming from inter-service rivalry and
divergent priorities, allowed the Americans to exploit individual vulnerabilities within the Japanese defense.

The deficiencies in command and control extended beyond inter-service relationships; they also affected intra-service coordination. The Japanese Navy, despite its emphasis on centralized command, suffered from a rigid chain of command that stifled initiative and adaptability. Lower-level commanders were often hesitant to deviate from strict orders, even when circumstances called for independent action. This rigidity limited the ability of the Japanese forces to respond effectively to the changing tactical situation during the American attack. The American forces, in contrast, were granted more leeway to take independent action based on their assessment of the situation, a characteristic that was crucial to their success in exploiting the weaknesses in the Japanese defense.

Beyond the formal command structure, the decision-making processes within the Japanese Navy were also flawed. The emphasis on hierarchical authority and the lack of open communication frequently hindered rapid decision-making. Reports from lower-level units often took too long to reach the higher echelons of command, hindering the timely response to the changing situation. Furthermore, the Japanese commanders often displayed a degree of rigidity and reluctance to accept bad news, contributing to a
delayed and inadequate response. This reluctance to confront the reality of their situation stemmed partly from a culture that valued unquestioning obedience and discouraged dissent. The result was a system that prioritized maintaining outward appearances of order and control, even at the cost of effective responsiveness to the rapidly evolving battlefield conditions.

The lack of effective pre-battle planning and wargaming contributed to the overall failure of Japanese defenses. There is scant evidence to suggest that the Japanese high command undertook thorough wargaming exercises to anticipate potential scenarios and strategize for a coordinated response. Instead, it seems that the defense
strategy was largely reactive, developed in response to the ongoing American attacks. This lack of proactive planning, combined with the rigid and centralized command structure, meant that the
Japanese forces were ill-prepared for the scale and intensity of the American assault. The opportunity to pre-position forces strategically and to develop contingency plans was missed, leaving the Japanese defense vulnerable to the American offensive.

In summary, the failure of Japanese defenses at Truk Lagoon during Operation Hailstone was a result of a confluence of factors, with command structure and coordination issues playing a critical role. The centralized and hierarchical command structure, coupled with inter-service rivalries and communication breakdowns, resulted in a fragmented and ineffective response to the American attack. The rigid chain of command stifled initiative and adaptability, while a flawed decision-making process delayed and hampered efforts to counter the American offensive. The lack of pre-battle planning further compounded these deficiencies, leaving the Japanese forces ill-prepared for the intensity of the assault. The consequences were catastrophic, highlighting the vital importance of effective command, control, and coordination in modern naval warfare. The failure at Truk stands as a stark lesson in the devastating consequences of organizational weaknesses in the face of a determined and technologically superior enemy. The lack of flexibility and adaptability in the face of overwhelming force underscore a fundamental flaw in the Japanese strategic thinking, a flaw that ultimately contributed significantly to their defeat. The legacy of Operation Hailstone continues to serve as a cautionary tale for military strategists and planners alike, emphasizing the critical role of efficient command, communication, and coordinated action in ensuring success on the modern battlefield.

Resource Allocation and Logistical Problems

The crippling defeat suffered by the Japanese at Truk Lagoon during Operation Hailstone was not solely a consequence of tactical failures or command deficiencies. A crucial, often overlooked, factor contributing to their vulnerability was the inherent weakness in their logistical system and the resulting resource allocation problems. The vast distances involved in supplying and maintaining a major naval base like Truk Lagoon in the central Pacific presented enormous challenges, challenges that the Japanese Imperial Navy (IJN) was ill-equipped to overcome.

The IJN's logistical system, built around a rigid, centralized structure mirroring the command hierarchy, proved woefully inadequate for the demands of a prolonged war in the Pacific.
Unlike the Allied powers, who benefited from a vast industrial capacity and a sophisticated network of supply lines, the Japanese relied on a relatively limited industrial base and extended, vulnerable sea lanes. This disparity became acutely apparent in the months leading up to Operation Hailstone, as the IJN struggled to maintain the flow of supplies and reinforcements to Truk Lagoon.

The sheer distance between the Japanese home islands and Truk Lagoon constituted a primary logistical challenge. Supplies had to travel thousands of miles across the vast expanse of the Pacific Ocean, traversing areas increasingly vulnerable to Allied submarine attacks. The IJN's merchant fleet, already strained by the demands of supporting operations across the vast Pacific theater, struggled to keep pace with the escalating needs of Truk Lagoon. The frequency and efficiency of convoys were severely hampered by the ever-present threat of Allied submarine activity, which inflicted
substantial losses on Japanese shipping.

Furthermore, the IJN's reliance on a relatively small number of major supply bases meant that any disruption in the flow of supplies to these hubs had cascading effects across the entire theater. The vulnerability of these bases to Allied air and submarine attacks became increasingly evident as the war progressed. The successful targeting of key supply points, even if seemingly minor in scale, could have a devastating impact on the overall logistical capacity. The Japanese lacked the diversified, decentralized supply system employed by the Americans, making them inherently more vulnerable to disruption.

The limited capacity of Japanese shipyards also played a critical role in exacerbating their logistical problems. Unlike the Allied powers, with their vast industrial capacity, the Japanese struggled to replace lost vessels and to keep pace with the demands of a protracted war. The destruction of ships during naval battles and submarine attacks was not easily compensated, leading to a chronic shortage of transport vessels needed to sustain the logistical
demands of Truk Lagoon. The damage to Japanese shipyards caused by Allied air raids further constrained their ability to replace lost tonnage, exacerbating the logistical strain.

The IJN's prioritization of combat vessels over support vessels further hampered their logistical efforts. While significant resources were dedicated to building powerful warships, relatively little attention was paid to expanding the capacity of their merchant fleet or investing in improved logistical technologies. This imbalance meant that the IJN lacked the sufficient tonnage to support the sustained flow of supplies required by a major base like Truk
Lagoon, even under ideal circumstances. The limited availability of transport ships created a chronic bottleneck, preventing the timely delivery of essential supplies and equipment.

Beyond the sheer tonnage, the organization and management of the logistical process itself were plagued by inefficiencies. The centralized control system, mirroring the command structure, resulted in bottlenecks and delays in decision-making. Requests for supplies often took considerable time to reach the appropriate authorities, leading to significant delays in delivery. The lack of a flexible, responsive logistical system meant that the IJN was unable to adapt quickly to changing circumstances or to respond effectively to unforeseen events, such as major battles or severe weather.

The inadequate infrastructure at Truk Lagoon further hindered logistical operations. While the lagoon itself provided a sheltered anchorage for ships, the limited port facilities and storage capacity hampered the efficient handling of supplies. The capacity to offload cargo, store it securely, and distribute it to various units within the lagoon was far below the level required to sustain a large naval base in the face of a sustained campaign. This limited capacity exacerbated the impact of disruptions in the supply chain and limited the ability of the Japanese forces to replenish their stocks.

The storage and maintenance of supplies also presented a significant challenge. The tropical climate of Truk Lagoon caused rapid deterioration of some materials, resulting in loss of valuable equipment and supplies. The limited storage capacity further exacerbated this problem, leading to inadequate protection from the elements and exposure to damage. The lack of suitable warehousing facilities resulted in significant losses through spoilage and deterioration.

The scarcity of fuel represented a particularly acute logistical problem. The IJN relied heavily on oil imports, leaving them critically vulnerable to disruption of shipping lanes. The Allied submarine campaign severely compromised the Japanese ability to replenish their fuel stocks, severely limiting the operational capacity of their air and naval forces. The depletion of fuel supplies at Truk Lagoon played a significant role in the inability of Japanese aircraft and ships to mount an effective defense against Operation Hailstone.

The shortage of spare parts also had a profound impact on the operational readiness of Japanese forces at Truk Lagoon. The inability to quickly repair damaged aircraft and ships limited their combat effectiveness, contributing to their inability to resist the American assault. The limited capacity to replace or repair essential equipment had a direct impact on their ability to fight effectively.

In conclusion, the logistical problems facing the Japanese at Truk Lagoon represent a significant factor contributing to their defeat during Operation Hailstone. The long supply lines, limited shipping capacity, inadequate infrastructure, ineffective management, and climate-related issues all converged to cripple their ability to sustain a major naval base in the face of an aggressive enemy. The logistical deficiencies exposed the fragility of the Japanese war effort in the central Pacific, highlighting the critical need for a robust and flexible logistical system in modern warfare. The contrast between the Japanese struggles and the efficient logistical operations of the United States Navy underscores the significant advantage enjoyed by the Allies in this crucial area and played a pivotal role in the Allied victory in the Pacific. The failure to adequately address these logistical shortcomings proved to be a significant strategic weakness, contributing directly to Japan's eventual defeat in the Pacific War.

The Impact of Previous Battles and Losses

The vulnerability exposed at Truk Lagoon during Operation Hailstone wasn't solely a product of the logistical shortcomings already discussed. The cumulative effect of prior battles and losses, both material and psychological, played a crucial, and often overlooked, role in the Japanese inability to effectively defend the vital base. The string of defeats suffered across the Pacific throughout 1943 and early 1944 had significantly eroded the fighting spirit and combat readiness of the IJN forces stationed at Truk.

The Battle of the Coral Sea in May 1942, while a tactical draw, marked a turning point in the Pacific war. It halted the Japanese advance southward and demonstrated, for the first time, the effectiveness of carrier-based air power against the IJN's fleet. The psychological impact of this near-miss, the realization that their previously invincible navy could be challenged, was significant.

Subsequent battles, like Midway in June 1942, reinforced this unsettling truth, inflicting devastating losses on the IJN's irreplaceable veteran pilots and experienced aircrews. These losses weren't merely numerical; they represented a catastrophic blow to the IJN's institutional knowledge and expertise. The highly trained pilots, who had honed their skills in the early stages of the war, were difficult, if not impossible, to replace. The newer, less experienced pilots lacked the tactical acumen and honed reflexes of their predecessors, a deficiency that would become increasingly evident in later engagements.

The Guadalcanal campaign, lasting from August 1942 to February 1943, further drained Japanese resources and morale. The brutal, protracted struggle for the island, characterized by intense air and naval battles, resulted in significant losses of ships, aircraft, and personnel. This campaign stretched the IJN's logistical capacity to its breaking point, highlighting the limitations of their supply lines and the difficulties in reinforcing and resupplying far-flung bases. The relentless Allied air attacks on Japanese airfields and supply lines continuously weakened the Japanese hold on Guadalcanal, ultimately forcing a costly retreat. The experience left the IJN with a deep sense of exhaustion, both physically and psychologically. The constant pressure of the campaign, combined with the heavy losses suffered, severely impacted morale and eroded confidence in the IJN's ability to prevail.

The subsequent battles in the Solomon Islands, including the Naval Battle of Kula Gulf and the Battle of Vella Lavella, continued to inflict heavy losses on the IJN. Each defeat further chipped away at their combat strength, depleted their remaining resources, and deepened the growing sense of despair within their ranks. The relentless Allied offensive, combined with the cumulative impact of previous losses, made it increasingly difficult for the IJN to maintain a coherent and effective defense in the region. The constant pressure forced the Japanese to spread their limited resources ever thinner, further diminishing their ability to react effectively to any major threat.

The material consequences of these prior engagements were equally severe. The IJN suffered significant losses of warships, including battleships and cruisers, during these battles. The repair facilities in Japan and its occupied territories, already strained by the demands of the war, struggled to keep pace with the increasing losses. The limited capacity to repair and replace damaged vessels, combined with the increasing scarcity of raw materials, hampered the IJN's ability to maintain a strong naval presence in the Pacific. The heavy losses in aircraft and trained pilots also had a profound impact on the IJN's air power. The IJN found itself consistently outmatched in terms of both the number and quality of aircraft.

The depletion of experienced personnel extended beyond just pilots. The experienced sailors, gunners, and other skilled personnel lost in these prior battles were equally irreplaceable. The loss of these individuals represented not just a reduction in numbers but also a significant decline in expertise and battle experience. The IJN's ability to coordinate complex naval operations, to execute tactical maneuvers effectively, and to react to unforeseen situations was directly impacted by the absence of these veterans. The constant stream of losses forced the IJN to rely increasingly on less experienced personnel, who were often poorly trained and lacked the necessary skills to effectively operate complex naval equipment.

This deficiency significantly impacted the effectiveness of the Japanese forces in the Pacific.

Beyond the material and personnel losses, the psychological impact of these repeated defeats was profound. The IJN's once unwavering confidence and fighting spirit began to waver. The sense of invincibility that had characterized the early years of the war was replaced by a growing awareness of their vulnerability and diminishing capabilities. Morale suffered as the repeated setbacks eroded the belief in the possibility of eventual victory. The relentless Allied offensive, coupled with the cumulative effect of losses, demoralized the troops and diminished their willingness to engage in further conflict.

The cumulative effect of these losses and the resultant psychological impact contributed directly to the weak defense mounted against Operation Hailstone. The Japanese forces at Truk Lagoon were depleted, demoralized, and poorly equipped to face the overwhelming American assault. The lack of sufficient aircraft, the scarcity of fuel, and the shortage of experienced personnel severely limited their ability to respond effectively. The limited air cover and weak anti-aircraft defenses allowed the American planes to inflict devastating damage on the Japanese ships and installations at Truk. The IJN's ability to resist the attack was significantly hampered by these factors, contributing directly to their resounding defeat.

The strategic decisions made by the Japanese high command, hampered by the cumulative weight of past failures and a growing sense of desperation, exacerbated the situation. The decision to concentrate significant naval assets at Truk, rather than dispersing them, made the base an attractive target for the Americans. The failure to adequately reinforce the defenses of Truk, despite accumulating evidence of the growing American threat, highlighted the inadequacy of Japanese strategic planning and resource allocation. The underestimation of American capabilities and the overestimation of their own strength led to disastrous consequences.

The impact of previous battles and losses at Truk Lagoon cannot be overstated. The combination of material depletion, loss of experienced personnel, diminished morale, and flawed strategic decisions created a perfect storm that allowed the Americans to inflict a devastating blow on a critical Japanese base. The consequences of Operation Hailstone resonated far beyond the immediate destruction of ships and aircraft at Truk Lagoon. It marked a significant turning point in the Pacific War, drastically altering the balance of power and paving the way for the eventual Allied victory. The analysis of these prior defeats reveals a crucial lesson about the long-term implications of military losses and the importance of maintaining a strong, well-equipped, and well-trained fighting force, both materially and psychologically, in order to effectively wage war. The case of Truk Lagoon starkly highlights the cost of repeated defeats and the devastating consequences that can arise when a nation fails to learn from its past mistakes.

Carrier Warfare and its Development

The vulnerability of Truk Lagoon, as exposed by Operation Hailstone, was not solely a consequence of logistical deficiencies or the psychological impact of prior defeats. A significant factor was the evolving and increasingly effective American doctrine of carrier warfare, a doctrine that had undergone a rapid and transformative development in the preceding years. The success at Truk was not merely a matter of superior numbers, but a testament to the strategic thinking and tactical proficiency of the US Navy. This evolution involved a complex interplay of technological advancements, strategic planning, and tactical innovation, culminating in the devastatingly effective air assault launched against the Japanese base.

Before Pearl Harbor, the US Navy's carrier doctrine was still in its infancy, largely shaped by the limited experience of the interwar period. The emphasis was primarily on scouting and reconnaissance, with carrier air power viewed as a supplementary force to the battle line. This approach reflected a more traditional naval mindset, with battleships still seen as the backbone of naval power. The devastating attack on Pearl Harbor, however, irrevocably altered this perspective. The vulnerability of the Pacific Fleet's battleships, anchored in a seemingly secure harbor, underscored the need for a more decisive and offensive role for carrier-based aviation.

The Coral Sea and Midway battles proved to be crucial turning points. While the Battle of the Coral Sea was tactically inconclusive, it marked the first time that carriers engaged in a decisive battle without direct surface contact. The focus shifted decisively from surface actions to aerial combat, highlighting the overwhelming advantage of carrier-based air power in a war of attrition. Midway, a resounding American victory, cemented this paradigm shift. The destruction of four Japanese fleet carriers, representing a significant portion of the IJN's carrier strength, underscored the offensive potential of carrier-based air power and its capacity to decisively shape the course of a naval campaign.

Following Midway, American carrier doctrine began to evolve rapidly, moving from a defensive posture to a decidedly offensive one. The emphasis shifted from the protection of fleet carriers to their aggressive employment as the primary offensive weapon. This involved developing sophisticated techniques for launching coordinated air strikes from multiple carriers, utilizing different types of aircraft for various missions such as scouting, bombing, and fighter cover. The development and implementation of more advanced radar technology, coupled with improved communication systems, enhanced the coordination and effectiveness of these operations. This technological leap allowed for more precise targeting and improved the survival rate of American aircraft.

The strategic planning for operations like Operation Hailstone directly reflected this doctrinal shift. The target selection, the concentration of forces, and the execution of the operation were based on the central role of carrier-based air power. Truk Lagoon, a crucial Japanese base, was targeted because of its strategic importance and its vulnerability to air attacks. The decision to launch a massive air strike, rather than relying on a more traditional surface engagement, was a deliberate strategic choice informed by the experience and confidence gained in preceding battles.

The operational planning emphasized the coordination of multiple carrier task forces, each providing different types of aircraft and capabilities. The carriers' aircraft were not deployed indiscriminately. They were assigned specific tasks and targets, based on a detailed assessment of the enemy's defenses and capabilities. Dive bombers were tasked with attacking ships, torpedo planes with crippling capital ships, and fighter aircraft provided both escort and air superiority. This division of labor, coordinated across multiple carriers, allowed for a more efficient and effective attack than would have been possible with a less refined approach.

Operation Hailstone itself provides a compelling example of this developed doctrine in action. The meticulously planned assault, involving several carrier groups, demonstrated the effectiveness of coordinated, multi-carrier strikes. The massive scale of the attack, both in terms of the number of aircraft and the weight of ordnance dropped, overwhelmed the Japanese defenses, effectively neutralizing their ability to respond effectively. The attacks focused on not only ships and aircraft but also fuel storage, repair facilities, and other crucial infrastructure elements, further crippling Japanese forces at Truk.

The success of Operation Hailstone was not just a product of superior numbers. The American pilots, benefiting from superior training, advanced aircraft, and effective support systems, achieved a level of air superiority that allowed them to inflict devastating damage with minimal losses. This marked a significant change from the early battles of the war, where air-to-air combat often resulted in significant losses on both sides. The improved training and better coordination of American aircrews, combined with their technological advantage, resulted in a much higher success rate for missions.

Moreover, the operation showcased the effectiveness of the American intelligence gathering and analysis. The pre-operation intelligence gathering significantly contributed to the success of Operation Hailstone, with detailed maps of the lagoon and the positions of Japanese ships and facilities being crucial in the planning and execution of the operation. This emphasis on intelligence-driven operations marked a significant departure from earlier naval battles, where relying on chance and luck was more common.

The development of American carrier warfare doctrine extended beyond the tactical level. It also involved significant advancements in logistics and support. The maintenance and resupply of the carrier task forces during extended operations became crucial for sustaining offensive operations. The vast logistical challenges inherent in sustaining a large carrier fleet across the Pacific were addressed through the efficient use of logistics networks, including the deployment of fleet oilers, repair ships, and supply ships that provided essential support to the carrier task forces, enabling them to stay at sea for extended periods and launch sustained offensive operations.

The doctrinal changes also reflected improvements in communication and coordination. Improved radio technology and cipher systems allowed for faster and more secure communication between the carriers, the fleet, and shore-based commands. This improved coordination played a pivotal role in the success of Operation Hailstone, allowing for a rapid response to changing circumstances during the operation, and improving the synchronization of the massive air attacks.

Finally, the evolution of American carrier warfare doctrine reflects the broader strategic goals of the US Navy in the Pacific Theater. The objective of island-hopping, with its reliance on the seizing and securing of strategically important islands, required a naval strategy that could support amphibious landings. Carrier-based air power was crucial for neutralizing Japanese air and naval opposition during amphibious assaults and securing air superiority for ground operations. The success at Truk demonstrated the capability of carrier task forces to effectively neutralize enemy bases, preparing the way for the subsequent amphibious assaults that would lead to the eventual defeat of Japan.

In conclusion, the American victory at Truk Lagoon during Operation Hailstone was not merely a product of overwhelming firepower or technological superiority. It was a testament to the well-defined and expertly executed doctrines of carrier warfare that had been refined and honed throughout the early years of the Pacific War. The evolution of this doctrine, from a supporting role to a primary offensive capability, was a process of adaptation, learning, and innovation, resulting in a powerful and decisive weapon that played a pivotal role in shaping the outcome of World War II in the Pacific. The lessons learned at Truk, and the experiences that led to the development of this effective doctrine, continued to shape American naval strategy for decades to come.

Fleet Coordination and Combined Arms Operations

The success of Operation Hailstone wasn't solely attributable to the raw power unleashed upon Truk Lagoon; it was a testament to the refined coordination and integration of American naval forces across different arms. The operation showcased a mature doctrine of combined arms warfare, a far cry from the nascent approaches of the pre-war era. This sophisticated coordination involved not just the carriers, but also the crucial contributions of submarines, destroyers, cruisers, and supporting logistical elements. The seamless interplay of these different branches of the Navy is a crucial aspect of understanding the American victory.

Submarines played a vital, albeit largely unseen, role. Before the main air assault, submarines conducted reconnaissance, mapping the lagoon's defenses and pinpointing key targets. This underwater surveillance provided invaluable intelligence that informed the targeting decisions of the carrier-based aircraft. Subsequent to the airstrikes, submarines patrolled the area, disrupting any potential Japanese attempts at reinforcement or salvage. Their ability to operate independently and undetected meant they provided continuous pressure on the Japanese forces, preventing any meaningful counter-offensive. The integration of this intelligence gathered from submerged assets directly enhanced the efficacy of the air and surface strikes.

The destroyer and cruiser squadrons acted as a crucial protective shield for the carrier task forces. Their primary role was anti-aircraft defense, intercepting any Japanese aircraft attempting to retaliate against the carriers during and after the airstrikes. The coordination between the anti-aircraft fire of the destroyers and cruisers and the fighter aircraft was essential in maintaining air superiority. The destroyers' speed and maneuverability allowed them to screen the carriers from torpedo attacks, while the cruisers provided additional firepower and longer-range anti-aircraft capabilities. This layered defense, carefully orchestrated and precisely executed, effectively neutralized the threat posed by Japanese counterattacks. Analysis of post-battle reports shows a remarkable synchronization of actions between the surface fleet's anti-aircraft capabilities and the actions of the carrier-based fighter squadrons. The close coordination was crucial in mitigating damage to the American carriers.

Beyond the direct combat roles, the logistical support provided by the supporting fleet was equally critical to the operation's success.
The efficient resupply of fuel, ammunition, and spare parts to the carrier task forces was paramount in sustaining the lengthy
operation. Dedicated oilers, repair ships, and supply ships ensured the carriers could remain at sea, continuously launching waves of attacks. The sheer volume of ordnance expended at Truk
necessitated a robust logistical network, a testament to the
American Navy's ability to plan and execute complex operations far from their home bases. The timely delivery of critical supplies minimized downtime, allowing the carriers to maintain the pressure on the Japanese forces.

The success of Operation Hailstone further underscored the
importance of effective communication and command structures within the American Navy. The ability to coordinate the actions of multiple carrier task forces, submarines, cruisers, and destroyers across such a vast area required a sophisticated command and control system. Advances in radio technology and encryption played a vital role in ensuring that information flowed smoothly and securely. The centralized command structure enabled rapid decision-making, adjustments to the plan based on real-time intelligence, and efficient coordination of the various components of the operation. This technological and organizational superiority translated directly into tactical advantages. The effectiveness of the American command and control system contrasts sharply with the apparent lack of coordination within the Japanese forces, further illustrating the disparity between the two navies.

The integration of air and sea power was not merely additive; it was synergistic. The air attacks weakened Japanese defenses, paving the way for the submarines to operate more effectively. The surface fleet's anti-aircraft defense protected the carriers, allowing them to deliver sustained attacks. The logistical support ensured that the entire operation could be maintained for an extended period. This integrated approach, a hallmark of American naval doctrine by

1944, represented a major shift from the more compartmentalized approaches seen in earlier naval conflicts. The careful balance of resources and the understanding of the interconnectedness of each naval element contributed to the operation's overwhelming success.

Analysis of the operation shows a clear hierarchy of targeting priorities. The initial air strikes focused on neutralizing Japanese air power. Once air superiority was established, the focus shifted to high-value targets such as capital ships, aircraft, and fuel storage facilities. Subsequent attacks targeted other crucial infrastructure elements to cripple Truk's operational capacity. This systematic approach, executed with precision, maximized the impact of the air strikes. The strategic targeting methodology was based not only on the immediate destruction of enemy assets, but also on a long-term consideration of crippling their ability to recover and mount any effective counterattack.

This structured approach extended to the types of aircraft deployed. Dive bombers, with their accuracy and high explosive payloads, were deployed to inflict maximum damage on surface ships.
Torpedo planes targeted capital ships, aiming to inflict crippling damage that would hinder or even eliminate their operational capabilities. Fighter aircraft maintained air superiority and
provided close air support to the bombers, ensuring their survival and maximizing the effectiveness of the strikes. The careful
selection and coordinated deployment of these diverse aircraft contributed substantially to the overall effectiveness of the
operation. Post-battle analyses revealed the remarkable precision of the air strikes, a testament to the expertise of the pilots and the sophisticated targeting information they received.

Furthermore, the integration of intelligence gathering and analysis was pivotal to Operation Hailstone's success. Pre-strike intelligence identified key targets, their defenses, and the overall strength of the Japanese forces. This intelligence drastically improved the chances of success by allowing the American forces to focus their attacks on the most vulnerable points. The intelligence helped to predict Japanese responses, anticipate their defensive measures, and thus to plan the operation to mitigate those challenges. Post-strike
intelligence confirmed the extent of the damage inflicted, proving

the effectiveness of the tactical decisions made prior to the mission.

The seamless integration of all these components, from the submarine reconnaissance to the logistical support, from the sophisticated targeting procedures to the sophisticated intelligence gathering, and the effective utilization of different types of aircraft all contributed to the comprehensive defeat of the Japanese forces at Truk. Operation Hailstone was not merely a demonstration of American firepower, but a sophisticated display of coordinated naval warfare, demonstrating the full potential of integrating different naval assets into a unified and highly effective force. The operational lessons learned at Truk were instrumental in shaping American naval strategy for the remainder of the Pacific War. The doctrine of combined arms, honed and refined through this and other crucial battles, proved decisive in securing Allied victory. The success at Truk served as a blueprint for future operations, showcasing the destructive potential of a meticulously planned and expertly executed combined arms strategy. The systematic and comprehensive nature of the assault, aimed at crippling the Japanese fleet's operational capabilities, became a defining characteristic of future American naval operations in the Pacific.

The success at Truk served as a powerful demonstration that superior technology and firepower alone were insufficient; careful planning, intelligent coordination, and the effective integration of different naval forces were essential for achieving decisive victories in the complex battles of World War II.

Air Power and its Strategic Importance

The overwhelming success of Operation Hailstone, the February 1944 assault on Truk Lagoon, cannot be understood without acknowledging the pivotal role played by American air power.

While the coordinated efforts of submarines, cruisers, and destroyers were crucial, the devastating blows delivered by carrier-based aircraft were the decisive factor in crippling the Japanese stronghold. The sheer scale of the air attacks – involving hundreds of aircraft launching wave after wave of strikes – overwhelmed Japanese defenses, exposing the limitations of their air and anti-aircraft capabilities. The destruction of Japanese air power at Truk was not merely a tactical victory; it was a strategic triumph that significantly altered the balance of power in the Pacific.

The effectiveness of the American carrier-based air attacks stemmed from a combination of factors. First and foremost was the superior technology of American aircraft. The Grumman F6F Hellcat, the Grumman TBF Avenger, and the Douglas SBD Dauntless were superior in performance and armament to their Japanese counterparts. The Hellcat, in particular, established a clear air superiority over Truk, effectively neutralizing Japanese air defenses before the main attack even commenced. The superior range and payload capacity of the American aircraft allowed them to deliver devastating blows from a safe distance, minimizing the risk to the carriers themselves.

Furthermore, the American aircrews displayed exceptional skill and training. Years of rigorous training and combat experience had honed their abilities, leading to a high degree of precision and effectiveness in their attacks. Analysis of post-battle photographic reconnaissance reveals the accuracy of the bombing runs, with many hits concentrated on key targets such as ships, aircraft, and fuel storage facilities. The proficiency of the American pilots is evident in their ability to effectively overcome the challenges of targeting moving ships in a complex lagoon environment. This contrasted sharply with the less effective bombing runs observed by the Japanese.

The strategic planning behind the air attacks was equally crucial to their success. Intelligence gathered from various sources, including reconnaissance flights, submarine patrols, and code-breaking efforts, provided crucial insights into the layout of Truk Lagoon, the locations of key Japanese assets, and the strength of their defenses.

This pre-emptive intelligence allowed the American planners to develop a carefully orchestrated plan of attack, targeting high-value targets in a systematic fashion. The prioritized targeting methodology maximized damage and disruption while minimizing unnecessary risks. Instead of haphazard attacks, American forces employed a structured approach.

The initial waves of strikes focused on neutralizing Japanese air power, clearing the skies for subsequent attacks on surface targets.

This initial phase was vital in securing air superiority. Once the threat from Japanese aircraft was significantly reduced, subsequent waves of attacks targeted high-value assets. Capital ships, such as cruisers and destroyers, along with aircraft parked on the airfield and vital fuel storage facilities, were systematically destroyed. The air attacks were not only destructive, but also designed to cripple Japanese logistical capabilities. By destroying fuel supplies and repair facilities, the Americans aimed not just to inflict immediate damage, but to prevent the Japanese from repairing or replacing their losses.

The success of the air attacks was further amplified by the support provided by the supporting elements of the fleet. The anti-aircraft fire from the destroyers and cruisers provided a defensive umbrella over the carriers, protecting them from Japanese counterattacks. The close coordination between the surface fleet and the carrier-based fighter aircraft ensured the safety of the bombers while they carried out their attacks. Moreover, the logistical support provided by the supply ships and oilers ensured that the carriers could sustain the intense pace of operations for an extended period. The ability of the fleet to maintain a continuous flow of aircraft and ordnance was instrumental in the overall success of the operation.

The impact of Operation Hailstone on the Pacific War was profound. The destruction of Japanese naval power at Truk Lagoon dealt a crippling blow to Japan's ability to project power in the

Central Pacific. The loss of numerous ships and aircraft severely weakened their naval forces, impacting their ability to effectively respond to the Allied advance. The destruction of the base infrastructure, including airfields, fuel storage facilities, and repair yards, severely hampered their operational capacity for an extended period. This significantly hindered their logistical and operational capacity across the wider theater. Truk, once a formidable bastion, became a crippled and vulnerable base.

Moreover, the victory at Truk Lagoon served as a powerful demonstration of the growing power of American naval aviation. It confirmed the dominance of carrier-based aircraft, and their ability to deliver decisive blows against even well-defended targets. This significantly shaped the strategic thinking of both the US and Japanese commands. The operation highlighted the vulnerability of static base facilities to devastating air power and impacted subsequent naval planning.

The lessons learned from Operation Hailstone regarding the strategic importance of air power and the need for careful planning and coordination had a lasting impact on the conduct of naval warfare throughout the Pacific. The success of the operation solidified the American Navy's emphasis on carrier-based air power as a crucial component of its strategy. The close integration of air, surface, and submarine forces, coupled with the effective use of intelligence, proved to be an unbeatable combination. The operation stands as a testament to the power of sophisticated planning and superior execution, a potent example of American naval doctrine in its most effective form. The victory at Truk signaled a major shift in the balance of power in the Pacific, paving the way for the subsequent Allied offensives across the region. The effective deployment of air power was not just an operational success but a strategic watershed moment in the Second World War.

Intelligence Gathering and Targeting

The devastating success of Operation Hailstone hinged not only on the superior capabilities of American aircraft and the skill of its aircrews but also, crucially, on the meticulous intelligence gathering and precise targeting that preceded the assault. The operation wasn't a matter of simply sending waves of planes to bombard a vaguely defined enemy position; it was a surgically precise operation born from comprehensive and accurate intelligence. This intelligence effort involved a multifaceted approach, drawing on various sources and integrating them into a cohesive picture of Truk Lagoon's defenses and vulnerabilities.

One primary source of intelligence was aerial reconnaissance. Long-range patrol planes, operating from bases further afield, conducted repeated reconnaissance flights over Truk. These flights, often performed at high altitudes to avoid detection, painstakingly mapped the lagoon's geography, identifying key Japanese installations, including shipyards, fuel depots, and airfields. High-resolution photography, painstakingly developed and analyzed by photo-interpreters, provided detailed images of the Japanese fleet's composition and disposition. This included not only the identification of individual vessels but also their types and their condition, enabling the Americans to prioritize targets based on their strategic importance and vulnerability. For example, the identification of large fuel storage facilities – a vital resource in a remote island base – placed these installations at the forefront of targeting priorities. The aerial reconnaissance further revealed the layout and defenses of the airfields, enabling American planners to anticipate the likely response from Japanese fighter aircraft and to develop strategies to neutralize them.

Submarine patrols played a complementary role in intelligence gathering. American submarines, operating secretly in the waters around Truk, were tasked with observing Japanese shipping movements, reporting on the number and type of vessels entering and leaving the lagoon, and providing information about the defenses of the lagoon's entrance. Submarines, operating undetected, provided real-time updates on the activity within Truk

Lagoon, complementing the periodic information gleaned from aerial reconnaissance. Their covert surveillance provided vital situational awareness, which was crucial in forming a complete and updated picture of the defenses. These reports, meticulously recorded and transmitted through secure channels, provided invaluable insights into the dynamic nature of the Japanese defenses.

Crucially, the breaking of Japanese naval codes provided American intelligence with a significant advantage. Through the dedicated efforts of codebreakers at stations such as OP-20-G, the Americans were able to intercept and decipher Japanese communications, providing invaluable insights into their operational plans, fleet movements, and the overall state of their defenses. This intelligence offered a rare look inside the enemy's decision-making process, allowing American planners to anticipate Japanese responses to the upcoming attack and to adjust their own strategies accordingly. The insights gleaned from code-breaking were particularly effective in revealing the strength and disposition of Japanese air and anti-aircraft capabilities, which were central to the planning of the air assault. The decoded messages often revealed detailed information about the number of aircraft available, their types, and their locations, helping pinpoint the most effective points for attack.

Once the intelligence was gathered, the process of target selection and prioritization began. American planners meticulously analyzed the accumulated information, creating a comprehensive picture of the strategic importance of various targets within Truk Lagoon. This wasn't a random bombardment; the attacks were precisely targeted to maximize their impact and to cripple the Japanese base's capabilities. The high-value targets were identified based on their potential to inflict the maximum damage on the Japanese war effort.

The primary targets included the Japanese warships moored within the lagoon. The destruction of these vessels would not only inflict immediate losses but would also significantly reduce Japan's capacity to project naval power across the Pacific. The prioritization of capital ships such as cruisers and destroyers was a key aspect of the targeting strategy. These vessels represented the most immediate threat to American forces, and their removal significantly reduced the likelihood of a coordinated Japanese counterattack. Similarly, airfields were key targets to neutralize Japanese air power and prevent an effective response to the air raids. The elimination of Japanese aircraft and their ground support was seen as crucial to the success of the operation. This strategy successfully prevented a powerful counterattack that could have significantly hampered the American effort.

Along with naval vessels and airfields, the targeting plan included significant infrastructure, most notably fuel storage facilities. Truk Lagoon was a remote base, and the supply lines were extended and vulnerable. The destruction of these fuel facilities aimed to cripple the base's long-term operational capabilities, reducing its ability to sustain itself even if it could recover from the immediate damage. Repair facilities, shipyards, and other essential infrastructure also received high priority on the target list. The idea was to ensure that any immediate damage inflicted would be followed by a longer-term crippling of the Japanese war effort. The strategic aim was not just immediate destruction but long-term incapacitation.

The final targeting plans incorporated this detailed analysis, establishing a precise sequence of attacks. The initial waves of aircraft focused on neutralizing the Japanese air defenses. This was a crucial first step, creating the conditions for the subsequent waves of bombing and torpedo attacks to hit their targets with minimal opposition. Once air superiority was secured, the attacks shifted to the high-value targets identified through intelligence: warships, airfields, and fuel storage facilities. This phased approach ensured that the American forces were able to effectively achieve their goals while minimizing their own losses. The entire operation represented a remarkable confluence of sophisticated intelligence gathering, accurate targeting, and flawless execution.

The success of Operation Hailstone underscores the critical importance of intelligence gathering and precise targeting in modern naval warfare. The meticulous work of intelligence analysts, codebreakers, aerial reconnaissance pilots, and submarine crews directly contributed to the overwhelming success of the operation. It serves as a compelling case study illustrating how accurate intelligence can transform a military operation from a high-risk gamble to a strategically decisive victory. The American approach at Truk demonstrated the effectiveness of integrating different forms of intelligence to create a comprehensive and dynamic picture of the enemy. The lesson learned proved pivotal in shaping subsequent naval strategies, emphasizing the crucial role of detailed reconnaissance and meticulously planned targeting in achieving decisive victories in the Pacific Theater. The effectiveness of the intelligence and targeting efforts at Truk became a crucial component of America's successful strategy in the Pacific War, setting a high standard for future operations.

PostBattle Analysis and Lessons Learned

The immediate aftermath of Operation Hailstone saw a flurry of activity as the US Navy assessed the results of its daring assault on Truk Lagoon. Initial reports, compiled from pilot debriefings,
photographic reconnaissance, and submarine observations, painted a picture of overwhelming success. The destruction of Japanese naval assets was staggering: twelve ships sunk or severely damaged, including several cruisers and destroyers, represented a significant blow to the Japanese fleet's strength in the central Pacific. The loss of hundreds of aircraft, many destroyed on the ground, further crippled Japanese air power in the region. The destruction of vital infrastructure – fuel depots, repair facilities, and airfields –
effectively neutralized Truk Lagoon as a major operational base.

However, the post-battle analysis extended beyond the purely quantitative assessment of material damage. The Navy sought to understand the reasons behind the unexpectedly light Japanese resistance. While the element of surprise was certainly a factor, contributing to the initial disarray, the analysis revealed deeper issues within the Japanese naval strategy and operational
capabilities. The Japanese had clearly underestimated the scale and intensity of the American attack. Their intelligence gathering had fallen short, failing to anticipate the sophistication and precision of the American assault. The seemingly impenetrable defenses of Truk Lagoon, built up over years, proved surprisingly ineffective against the coordinated air and submarine attack.

A key area of post-battle analysis centered on the effectiveness of different types of munitions used in the operation. The analysis of bomb damage assessed the effectiveness of various types of bombs, including high-capacity general-purpose bombs and armor-piercing bombs, against different types of targets – warships, aircraft, and structures. This analysis was crucial in refining future bombing strategies and in informing the development of more effective munitions. The evaluation also extended to the use of torpedoes, studying their effectiveness against differently moored ships and their susceptibility to countermeasures. The data gathered from Operation Hailstone contributed to the development of better torpedoes and improved torpedo-launching techniques.

The role of carrier-based aviation in achieving the decisive victory at Truk was a subject of intense study. The analysis highlighted not only the effectiveness of the aircraft themselves – their speed, range, and payload – but also the importance of coordinated attack waves, effective air-to-air combat tactics, and the seamless integration of various aircraft types – dive bombers, torpedo bombers, and fighters – to achieve specific operational goals. This analysis informed the continued development of carrier-based aviation doctrine, emphasizing the importance of flexibility, adaptability, and close coordination between different elements of a carrier air wing. The success of Operation Hailstone cemented the role of the carrier as the primary offensive weapon in naval warfare.

The intelligence gathering efforts leading up to Operation Hailstone also came under scrutiny. While the operation was undeniably successful, the post-battle analysis aimed to identify areas for improvement in future operations. While the intelligence on the composition and disposition of the Japanese fleet and infrastructure was largely accurate, some inconsistencies and inaccuracies were noted, prompting a review of intelligence-gathering methods and procedures. This led to improvements in aerial and submarine reconnaissance techniques, greater emphasis on code-breaking efforts, and more effective integration of different intelligence sources. The analysis also underscored the importance of human intelligence (HUMINT) in supplementing and verifying data obtained from other sources.

The unexpectedly low level of Japanese resistance prompted a broader inquiry into the state of the Japanese Navy and its overall operational readiness. It became clear that the Japanese were struggling with shortages of fuel, trained personnel, and modern equipment. Their logistical problems were amplified by their reliance on extended supply lines that were vulnerable to American submarine attacks. Operation Hailstone demonstrated the profound impact of sustained submarine warfare on Japanese naval capabilities. The analysis highlighted the critical role of the US Navy's submarine campaign in strangling Japanese supply lines and weakening their operational capacity. This spurred further investment in submarine warfare and enhanced anti-submarine warfare training and technologies.

The post-battle analysis also extended to the organizational and command structures involved in Operation Hailstone. The successful coordination between different elements of the US Navy– carriers, submarines, and land-based aircraft – was a testament to improved inter-service cooperation and effective communication. The streamlined command structure enabled rapid decision-making and decisive action, crucial to the operational success. This aspect of the operation underscored the need for clear lines of authority, improved communication protocols, and the value of close cooperation between different branches of the armed forces.

The lessons learned from Operation Hailstone had a profound impact on the evolution of American naval doctrine. The emphasis shifted from attrition warfare to a more strategic approach focused on achieving decisive victories through superior intelligence, meticulous planning, and precision targeting. The operation demonstrated the effectiveness of overwhelming air power against even well-defended naval bases. The devastating success of carrier-based aircraft underscored their growing importance in naval strategy. The operation's success was also a pivotal point in recognizing the crippling effects of disrupting enemy supply lines and infrastructure through coordinated submarine and air operations.

The changes reflected in the revised naval doctrine included: an increased emphasis on intelligence gathering and analysis; more sophisticated target selection and prioritization strategies; enhanced training in air-to-air combat and anti-submarine warfare; advancements in the development and deployment of carrier-based aircraft; and a strengthened commitment to inter-service cooperation. The impact of these changes was clearly evident in subsequent naval campaigns in the Pacific. The refined doctrine and tactics helped shape the American victories at the Mariana Islands and Leyte Gulf, demonstrating the enduring legacy of the lessons learned from Operation Hailstone.

Finally, the post-battle analysis went beyond simply assessing operational aspects. It also considered the strategic implications of the operation's success. The crippling of Truk Lagoon as a major Japanese base significantly altered the balance of power in the Pacific Theater. It disrupted Japanese supply lines, weakened their operational capabilities, and paved the way for the Allied advance across the Pacific. The operation demonstrated the effectiveness of a combined arms approach, integrating air, sea, and submarine
operations to achieve decisive strategic objectives. This
comprehensive approach became a cornerstone of future American naval strategies, transforming the Pacific Theater, operation by operation, toward ultimate victory. The analysis confirmed that Operation Hailstone was not merely a tactical victory, but a
strategically decisive turning point in the war, a testament to the power of meticulous planning, precise execution, and the
adaptability of American naval doctrine.

Advances in Naval Aviation

The decisive victory at Truk Lagoon hinged not only on superior strategy and coordination but also on the technological advancements in American naval aviation. Operation Hailstone served as a stark demonstration of the growing disparity between US and Japanese air power, a gap that widened significantly throughout the course of the war. This technological advantage wasn't simply a matter of superior numbers; it stemmed from significant improvements in aircraft design, performance, and the capabilities of the supporting infrastructure.

One of the most crucial advancements was the overall improvement in aircraft design. American aircraft carriers, such as the *Intrepid* and *Yorktown* , launched a diverse array of aircraft, each optimized for specific roles. Dive bombers like the Douglas SBD Dauntless boasted impressive dive capabilities, allowing them to deliver devastating attacks on heavily armored targets. Their rugged construction and reliable performance were critical in achieving precise hits on Japanese warships. The Grumman TBF Avenger, a torpedo bomber, significantly improved upon its predecessors, offering greater range, payload, and survivability. Its ability to deliver torpedoes with accuracy proved crucial in crippling Japanese capital ships, a task that proved exceedingly difficult for earlier torpedo bombers.

In contrast, the Japanese relied heavily on aircraft such as the Nakajima B5N "Kate" and the Aichi D3A "Val," aircraft that, while effective in the early years of the war, were increasingly outmatched by their American counterparts. The "Kate" and "Val," though capable, lacked the range, speed, and defensive armament of their American rivals. Their technological inferiority became glaringly apparent during the Battle of Midway and continued to be a factor in subsequent engagements. Japanese pilots, renowned for their skill and bravery, were often forced to contend with an increasingly unfavorable technological landscape. This wasn't a matter of Japanese incompetence; it reflected the limitations imposed by resource constraints and a slower pace of technological innovation compared to the United States.

The advancements extended beyond individual aircraft design.

Improvements in aircraft engines provided American planes with superior speed, range, and climb rate. These enhanced capabilities translated directly into battlefield advantages. American pilots could reach their targets quicker, deliver their payloads with greater precision, and evade enemy fighters more effectively. This was particularly critical in the crowded skies above Truk Lagoon, where the ability to quickly engage and disengage was essential for survival. Japanese aircraft, hampered by less powerful engines, often found themselves at a disadvantage in terms of both speed and maneuverability, making them vulnerable to American fighters.

The technological gap was also evident in the realm of radar technology. American carrier groups were equipped with significantly more advanced radar systems than their Japanese counterparts. This provided crucial early warning of approaching enemy aircraft, allowing for more effective defensive measures and coordinated attacks. The ability to detect Japanese aircraft at a greater distance allowed American pilots to launch preemptive strikes and establish air superiority before the Japanese could mount an effective defense. The superior radar technology contributed significantly to minimizing American losses while maximizing the effectiveness of their attacks.

Furthermore, the American emphasis on developing reliable and high-capacity bombs also contributed to the success of Operation Hailstone. The availability of larger, more powerful bombs allowed American pilots to inflict more damage with fewer sorties. The consistent and reliable performance of these munitions, coupled with better bombing techniques, contributed to the high rate of successful hits on Japanese targets. In contrast, the Japanese faced limitations in both the quantity and quality of their bombs, reducing the effectiveness of their air attacks.

Another key factor was the improved reliability and maintainability of American aircraft. While Japanese aircraft were often praised for their design and aesthetic qualities, they suffered from a higher rate of mechanical failures compared to their American counterparts. This meant that fewer Japanese aircraft were available for combat operations at any given time. The American focus on standardization, mass production, and robust maintenance procedures translated into a more dependable aerial force, capable of sustaining sustained operations without significant losses due to mechanical issues.

Beyond aircraft themselves, the technological superiority extended to the support infrastructure. The advanced maintenance and repair capabilities of the US Navy ensured that aircraft were quickly repaired and returned to service, minimizing downtime. This superior logistical support system played a crucial role in sustaining the intensity of the air attacks during Operation Hailstone. In contrast, the Japanese struggled with logistical challenges and limited repair capabilities, contributing to their reduced operational capacity during and after the battle.

The improvements in pilot training also played a significant part. American pilots benefited from a more rigorous and sophisticated training regime that emphasized air-to-air combat, formation flying, and coordinated attacks. This superior training contributed to the higher kill ratio achieved by American pilots during Operation Hailstone. While individual Japanese pilots demonstrated remarkable skill and courage, the overall effectiveness of their air operations was hampered by their less extensive and structured training programs.

Finally, the success of Operation Hailstone highlighted the importance of effective communication and coordination. American carrier air wings benefited from advanced communication systems that enabled seamless coordination between different aircraft types, and between the air wings and the fleet itself. This precise coordination was essential to the success of the complex and multi-faceted air attacks launched during the operation. The Japanese, facing limitations in their communication systems, found it more challenging to coordinate their defenses effectively.

In conclusion, the American success at Truk Lagoon in February 1944 was not solely due to superior strategy and tactical brilliance. The technological advancements in naval aviation, encompassing aircraft design, engines, radar, bombs, logistics, and pilot training, played a crucial role in securing a decisive victory. Operation Hailstone serves as a powerful illustration of the critical impact of technological superiority in shaping the outcome of naval warfare during World War II. The differences between the American and Japanese aircraft and supporting systems highlight the increasing disparity in technological capabilities, a disparity that would only continue to widen as the war progressed, ultimately contributing significantly to the Allied victory in the Pacific. The lessons learned from this operation, particularly regarding the importance of technological innovation and investment, had a lasting impact on the development of naval aviation in the postwar era.

Improvements in Radar and Sonar

The technological chasm separating the Allied and Axis powers during World War II extended far beyond the realm of aviation. The advancements in radar and sonar technologies, while perhaps less visually dramatic than the clash of carrier-borne aircraft, were equally pivotal in shaping the outcomes of naval engagements, including the decisive victory at Truk Lagoon. These advancements profoundly impacted intelligence gathering, target acquisition, and the overall operational effectiveness of the American fleet.

Prior to the war, radar technology was in its relative infancy. Early radar systems were bulky, unreliable, and possessed limited range and accuracy. However, the urgency of the conflict spurred rapid innovation, with significant improvements achieved on both sides of the Atlantic. The Americans, fueled by massive wartime
investment and a collaborative effort between government,
industry, and academia, made particularly impressive strides. By 1944, American warships and aircraft were equipped with radar sets that offered significantly enhanced performance. The improved range allowed for the detection of enemy ships and aircraft at much greater distances, providing crucial early warning of impending attacks. This advance was transformative, providing invaluable time for defensive measures and the launching of preemptive strikes.

The advancements in radar were not solely a matter of increased range. Improvements in resolution and accuracy allowed for more precise identification of targets. Earlier radar systems often
struggled to distinguish between friendly and enemy vessels,
leading to friendly fire incidents and confusion. The more sophisticated radar sets employed by the Americans in 1944 offered enhanced discrimination capabilities, enabling clear identification of targets, even amidst a complex electromagnetic environment. This reduced the risk of friendly fire and allowed for more efficient allocation of resources. The ability to precisely track multiple targets simultaneously provided a significant tactical advantage.

Furthermore, the integration of radar with other naval systems, such as fire-control computers, greatly enhanced the accuracy of gunfire. Radar-directed guns could track targets at longer ranges and maintain their lock even in rough seas, conditions that severely hampered the effectiveness of traditional optical sighting systems.

This resulted in a significant increase in the accuracy and effectiveness of naval bombardment, crucial in neutralizing enemy shore batteries and infrastructure.

Sonar technology also underwent significant advancements during the war. Early sonar systems, known as ASDIC (Anti-Submarine Detection Investigation Committee), were primarily used for anti-submarine warfare. Their limitations included relatively short ranges and susceptibility to interference from environmental factors such as water temperature and salinity gradients. However, the constant pressure to counter the submarine threat led to rapid technological improvements, leading to more powerful, sensitive, and reliable sonar systems. These systems provided invaluable situational awareness, allowing ships to detect submerged submarines, even at considerable distances.

The evolution of sonar also extended to the development of more sophisticated signal processing techniques. Earlier systems often struggled to discriminate between the echoes of submarines and other underwater objects. The improvements in signal processing enabled more accurate target identification and classification. This was particularly important in discriminating between potential submarine targets and other underwater features, like reefs or the seabed. This enhanced ability to accurately detect and classify targets decreased false alarms and improved the overall
effectiveness of anti-submarine operations.

The integration of radar and sonar data with other intelligence sources played a crucial role in enhancing the overall situational awareness of the American fleet. The combined information from these systems allowed for a more comprehensive understanding of the enemy's dispositions, intentions, and capabilities. This was especially valuable in the planning and execution of complex naval operations like Operation Hailstone. The integration process often involved central command centers where analysts could combine data from multiple sources, offering commanders a dynamic view of the battlefield. This significantly improved the ability to make informed decisions, deploy assets effectively, and anticipate enemy movements.

The contrast between the American and Japanese technological capabilities in radar and sonar was stark. While the Japanese did develop and deploy their own radar and sonar systems, they lagged significantly behind the Americans in terms of range, accuracy, and reliability. The Japanese systems often suffered from technical problems, resulting in inferior performance compared to their American counterparts. These limitations hampered the Japanese ability to detect incoming attacks, accurately track targets, and effectively coordinate their defenses. This technological deficit contributed significantly to the Japanese losses during Operation Hailstone and other naval battles.

The disparity in radar and sonar technology is clearly illustrated by examining the intelligence picture leading up to the Truk Lagoon operation. American intelligence, bolstered by advanced radar and sonar, had a far clearer understanding of the Japanese naval deployments in the lagoon. They knew the location, numbers, and types of ships and aircraft based at Truk. This enabled the Americans to plan a highly effective attack, targeting specific vessels and maximizing their chances of success. In contrast, the Japanese possessed a far more limited understanding of the approaching American forces, hampering their ability to prepare an effective defense.

Furthermore, the effectiveness of American anti-submarine warfare efforts was greatly enhanced by the superior sonar technology. The ability to detect and track Japanese submarines before they could launch an attack played a crucial role in protecting the vulnerable American carrier task force. This protective capability allowed the American forces to concentrate on their offensive operations, without the need to divert substantial resources to anti-submarine defense. The lack of similar capabilities on the Japanese side meant that they were far more vulnerable to attack, with limited options to effectively counter the American naval operations.

In conclusion, the improvements in radar and sonar technologies were crucial factors contributing to the American victory at Truk

Lagoon. The enhanced capabilities in detection, targeting, and situational awareness provided a significant tactical advantage. The gap between American and Japanese capabilities in this area amplified the already significant differences in air power and overall naval strength, further illustrating the crucial role that technological advancement played in determining the outcome of World War II naval engagements. The lessons learned from the operation, including the critical need for investment in research and development in these key areas, shaped naval strategies and technology development in the post-war era and continue to influence naval doctrines today. The superior intelligence derived from these technological advantages was as critical as the superior firepower employed at Truk Lagoon. This underscores that winning a naval battle in the mid-20th century required not only superior firepower, but also superior understanding of the battlespace.

Advances in Naval Gunnery

The technological superiority enjoyed by the United States Navy during World War II extended beyond radar and sonar; advancements in naval gunnery played a similarly crucial role in achieving decisive victories like Operation Hailstone. The improvements in accuracy, range, and sheer firepower of American naval guns created a significant disparity compared to the weaponry fielded by the Imperial Japanese Navy, contributing substantially to the lopsided outcome at Truk Lagoon.

One significant advancement was the refinement of fire-control systems. Prior to the war, the accuracy of naval gunfire was heavily reliant on optical sighting systems, highly susceptible to the effects of weather, distance, and the motion of the ship. These limitations restricted the effective range of naval guns, and the accuracy was often unreliable, especially in challenging conditions. The introduction of advanced fire-control directors, incorporating radar and sophisticated computing mechanisms, revolutionized naval gunnery. These systems could accurately track targets at significantly increased ranges, compensating for the movement of both the firing ship and the target.

The development of advanced rangefinders, incorporating both optical and radar technology, played a vital role in this enhanced accuracy. These systems could determine the precise distance to the target, even in poor visibility conditions. This data was fed into the fire-control computers, which calculated the necessary adjustments for trajectory, considering factors like wind speed, air density, and the curvature of the Earth. This resulted in a dramatic increase in the probability of hitting the target, particularly at longer ranges where optical sighting systems were severely limited.

The integration of radar into fire-control systems was a major leap forward. Radar provided an accurate and consistent means of tracking the target's position, regardless of visibility or weather conditions. This was a considerable advantage over relying solely on optical rangefinders, which were rendered virtually useless at night or in fog, rain, or smoke. The seamless integration of radar data with the fire-control computers allowed for continuous tracking and adjustment of the gunnery solution, even as the target moved.

Another crucial improvement was the development of more powerful and efficient propellants. These new propellants allowed for a significant increase in the range and velocity of naval shells.

Higher muzzle velocities translated into flatter trajectories, improving accuracy at long ranges. The increased range extended the effective firepower of American warships, allowing them to engage enemy targets from much greater distances, rendering many Japanese shore installations and ships vulnerable before they were even within range of effective return fire.

Furthermore, American naval guns benefited from improvements in shell design. High-explosive shells were improved, increasing their destructive power and blast radius. The development of armor-piercing shells, designed to penetrate heavily armored targets, further enhanced the effectiveness of American naval gunfire against enemy warships. The combination of increased range, higher muzzle velocity, and more potent shell designs dramatically increased the lethality of American naval gunfire.

The contrast between American and Japanese naval gunnery capabilities was stark. While the Japanese Navy possessed capable guns, their fire-control systems and shell technology were generally inferior to their American counterparts. They lacked the sophisticated radar-directed fire-control systems that were integral to the accuracy of American guns. Their optical sighting systems, while effective at closer ranges under ideal conditions, were far less effective at longer ranges or in adverse weather conditions, resulting in lower accuracy and a shorter effective range.

The limitations of Japanese fire-control systems severely hampered their ability to effectively counter the American naval bombardment during Operation Hailstone. The Japanese ships and shore installations were frequently caught in the open, exposed to accurate and devastating American gunfire. Their attempts to respond were often ineffective, with their shells falling short or missing their targets. This imbalance of naval gunnery technology played a significant part in the decisive American victory.

Moreover, the Japanese lacked the advanced shell designs and powerful propellants that significantly enhanced the range and effectiveness of American naval guns. Their shells often lacked the destructive power to effectively engage heavily armored targets, and their shorter range restricted their ability to effectively counter American fire. The differences in shell design also affected the efficiency of their attacks, with the American shells often achieving greater penetration and fragmentation than their Japanese counterparts.

The disparity in gunnery technology extended beyond the hardware. The American Navy also benefited from superior training and tactics. American gun crews received extensive training using advanced simulators and live-fire exercises, ensuring a high degree of proficiency in the use of their complex fire-control systems. The integration of radar and other technological advancements into naval doctrine resulted in significantly improved coordination and overall efficiency.

In contrast, the training and experience of Japanese gun crews were generally less thorough and sophisticated. The Japanese were often forced to fight defensively due to their lack of technological parity, hindering their capacity for maneuver and effective counterfire.

Their reliance on optical sighting systems often meant that their ships had to close to within dangerous proximity to engage American vessels effectively, exposing themselves to devastating return fire.

The advancements in American naval gunnery technology were not solely responsible for the victory at Truk Lagoon, but they certainly played a crucial role. The combined effect of improved range, accuracy, and firepower, coupled with superior training and tactical doctrine, created a significant advantage for the American Navy. This superiority in gunnery, alongside the advantages in radar and sonar, dramatically altered the balance of power in the Pacific, contributing significantly to the Allied advance across the Pacific and the eventual defeat of the Imperial Japanese Navy. The lessons learned in the realm of naval gunnery technology, like those in other areas of naval warfare, were meticulously studied and analyzed following World War II, shaping the development of naval weaponry and doctrine in the post-war era and influencing the strategies employed by naval forces to this day. The emphasis on precision and range, the integration of technological advancements into training and tactics, and the constant pursuit of more efficient and destructive weaponry, are enduring legacies of the Second World War's influence on naval warfare. The American victory at Truk Lagoon served as a powerful demonstration of this

technological dominance, a clear testament to the decisive role that advancements in naval gunnery played in shaping the course of the Pacific war. The ability to precisely deliver devastating firepower at extended ranges proved to be a critical factor in neutralizing the Japanese threat at Truk Lagoon, and indeed throughout the Pacific campaign.

Code Breaking and Intelligence Gathering

The technological triumph of Operation Hailstone wasn't solely a product of superior firepower and advanced radar; it was inextricably linked to the crucial role played by codebreaking and intelligence gathering. The ability to decipher Japanese naval codes and intercept their communications provided the US Navy with an unparalleled strategic advantage, profoundly influencing the planning and execution of the attack on Truk Lagoon. This intelligence wasn't simply a matter of knowing the enemy's movements; it provided a detailed understanding of their strengths, weaknesses, deployment patterns, and even their operational plans, transforming a potentially risky and complex operation into a strategically precise and overwhelmingly successful one.

The success of Operation Hailstone hinged on the meticulous work of codebreakers at stations like OP-20-G, the US Navy's cryptographic center. For years, they had been painstakingly working to decipher the Japanese naval code, known as JN-25b.

While complete decryption was elusive, significant progress was made, allowing American cryptographers to glean crucial pieces of information regarding Japanese fleet movements, deployments, and even the level of defenses at Truk Lagoon. This partial decryption, often providing fragments of information rather than complete messages, became a vital component in the intelligence picture.

Analysts pieced together these fragments, correlating them with other sources of intelligence like aerial reconnaissance and radio intercepts, to construct a clearer understanding of the Japanese disposition at Truk.

The information gleaned from codebreaking was not merely confirming existing assessments; it often revealed critical details that significantly impacted operational planning. For instance, the intercepted messages provided insights into the deployment patterns of Japanese naval aircraft and the overall strength of their air defenses at Truk. This information enabled Admiral Spruance to tailor his air and naval strikes, optimizing the allocation of resources and ensuring that the most vulnerable targets were prioritized. Without this knowledge, the operation would have been significantly more risky, with the potential for heavier casualties among American forces.

Aerial reconnaissance played a vital complementary role in confirming and refining the intelligence obtained through codebreaking. Reconnaissance flights over Truk Lagoon produced photographic evidence of the Japanese fleet, confirming the number and types of ships present, the arrangement of their moorings, and the level of defensive preparations. These photographs, when combined with the decrypted messages, painted a remarkably detailed picture of the Japanese defenses and vulnerabilities. The combined intelligence efforts thus allowed for a more refined targeting plan, minimizing the risk to American aircraft and maximizing the damage inflicted on the Japanese assets.

Beyond the visual evidence provided by aerial reconnaissance, intelligence gathering also involved the painstaking collection and analysis of other types of information. Radio intercepts, beyond the decoded messages, often provided crucial situational awareness. The frequency and content of Japanese radio chatter could indicate troop movements, the level of alertness, and even the morale of the enemy forces. These seemingly small details, when carefully analyzed, could paint a valuable picture of the overall operational situation. The combination of human intelligence, signal intelligence (SIGINT), and image intelligence (IMINT) provided a synergistic effect, building a much more comprehensive understanding of the enemy than any single intelligence source could provide.

The intelligence gathered had a profound impact on the choice of targets and the timing of the attack. The knowledge gained from codebreaking and reconnaissance revealed which Japanese ships were most vulnerable, and which areas had the weakest defenses. This allowed Admiral Spruance to concentrate his air strikes on the most high-value targets, maximizing the damage inflicted while minimizing the risk to his own forces. The intelligence also played a crucial role in selecting the optimal timing for the attack, ensuring that the Japanese forces were caught somewhat off guard, thereby increasing the effectiveness of the strike.

The success of Operation Hailstone, therefore, was not solely a result of superior naval power; it was also a testament to the power of effective intelligence gathering and codebreaking. The ability to decipher Japanese codes and collect comprehensive intelligence allowed the US Navy to plan and execute a highly effective attack, inflicting devastating losses on the Japanese fleet and significantly weakening their ability to operate in the Central Pacific. The
intelligence advantage, often overlooked in the narrative of brute force and naval power, was a critical element that enabled the decisive victory. The synergy between codebreaking, aerial
reconnaissance, and the analysis of radio intercepts provided a crucial informational advantage, transforming a potentially perilous undertaking into a resounding triumph. This demonstrates the importance of strategic intelligence and its crucial role in shaping the course of naval warfare in the Pacific theater during World War II.

The legacy of Operation Hailstone extends far beyond the
immediate destruction inflicted upon the Japanese forces at Truk Lagoon. The success of the operation highlighted the critical
importance of investments in codebreaking and intelligence
gathering. The insights gained from the operation underscored the decisive advantage conferred by having superior intelligence, shaping naval strategies and the allocation of resources in the subsequent years of the war. The success of Operation Hailstone also spurred further advancements in codebreaking technology and analysis techniques. The knowledge gained from deciphering Japanese codes was not only crucial for the immediate success of Operation Hailstone but also contributed to the Allied victory in other Pacific campaigns.

Moreover, the experience of Operation Hailstone influenced the development of combined intelligence operations, emphasizing the synergistic power of integrating different intelligence sources –human intelligence, signals intelligence, and imagery intelligence.
This coordinated approach became a defining characteristic of intelligence operations in the latter stages of World War II and continued to influence military planning long after the war ended.
The intelligence success of Operation Hailstone established a precedent for future operations, demonstrating the vital role that

superior intelligence gathering and analysis can play in achieving decisive military victories.

In conclusion, the impact of codebreaking and intelligence gathering on Operation Hailstone was profound and far-reaching. The ability to decipher Japanese communications and collect and analyze detailed intelligence provided the US Navy with an unparalleled strategic advantage, enabling them to plan and execute a highly effective and devastating attack on Truk Lagoon. The information obtained from intelligence sources was instrumental in selecting targets, timing the attack, and minimizing casualties among American forces. The success of Operation Hailstone highlighted the critical importance of investing in codebreaking and intelligence gathering, shaping naval strategies and resource allocation in the years to come. The operation's legacy continues to underscore the crucial role that strategic intelligence plays in achieving decisive military victories and shaping the course of warfare. The intelligence advantage gained through codebreaking and other intelligence gathering methods played a pivotal role in the American victory at Truk Lagoon, a victory that significantly altered the balance of power in the Pacific Theater and accelerated the Allied advance towards Japan. This underlines the often underestimated, yet crucial contribution of intelligence work to the overall success of military operations during World War II.

The Impact of Technological Superiority

The decisive American victory at Truk Lagoon during Operation Hailstone in February 1944 was not solely a product of superior manpower or strategic planning; it was fundamentally shaped by a significant technological disparity between the US Navy and its Japanese counterpart. This technological gap manifested in several key areas, contributing to the overwhelming success of the American operation and significantly weakening Japan's ability to project power in the Central Pacific.

One of the most significant technological advantages the Americans possessed was their superior naval aviation. The US Navy's carrier-based aircraft, such as those launched from the USS Intrepid and USS Yorktown, boasted greater range, speed, and payload capacity compared to their Japanese counterparts. The Grumman F6F Hellcat and the Vought F4U Corsair, for instance, significantly outperformed the Japanese A6M Zero in terms of speed, maneuverability at high altitudes, and firepower. The Hellcat, in particular, proved to be a superior dogfighter, inflicting heavy losses on the Japanese air defense during Operation Hailstone. This superiority in air power allowed the Americans to achieve air superiority relatively quickly, suppressing Japanese air defenses and paving the way for devastating attacks on the ships and installations within Truk Lagoon. The advanced radar systems equipping the American carriers also allowed for the early detection of Japanese aircraft, granting precious time for launching interceptors and preparing defensive measures. This capability was crucial in minimizing American losses during the air battles over Truk.

Beyond carrier aircraft, the Americans also possessed a technological edge in their dive bombers. The Douglas SBD Dauntless and the Curtiss SB2C Helldiver, employed extensively during Operation Hailstone, were capable of delivering heavier bomb loads with greater accuracy than their Japanese counterparts. This superior bombing capability, coupled with the effective use of airborne radar, allowed the American forces to inflict significant damage on Japanese ships and infrastructure with relatively few sorties. The precision bombing capabilities reduced the number of aircraft needed to achieve substantial results, minimizing potential losses and maximizing the effectiveness of the attacks. The Japanese, in contrast, lacked the equivalent precision bombing capability, often resulting in less accurate and less effective attacks.

Furthermore, the American technological advantage extended to their submarine fleet. The increased range, improved sonar technology, and enhanced torpedoes of the US Navy's submarines allowed them to operate effectively throughout the vast expanse of the Pacific Ocean. During Operation Hailstone, American submarines played a crucial role in disrupting Japanese supply lines, hindering reinforcements and resupply efforts to Truk Lagoon. Their ability to operate covertly and inflict damage without being detected significantly weakened the Japanese defenses and hampered their ability to react effectively to the American air and naval attacks. The Japanese, meanwhile, were struggling to keep pace with the advancements in submarine technology, making them more vulnerable to American attacks.

The technological superiority of the American Navy also extended to its surface combatants. The American battleships, cruisers, and destroyers were generally better armed, armored, and equipped than their Japanese counterparts. While the surface fleet did not engage in direct combat during Operation Hailstone, the potential for such engagement factored into the strategic calculations of both sides. The knowledge of the superior firepower and capabilities of the American surface fleet undoubtedly influenced Japanese defensive strategies, contributing to their relatively passive response during the air attacks. The Japanese fleet, already weakened by previous losses and constrained by a shortage of fuel and skilled personnel, was simply ill-equipped to meet the technological might of the approaching American fleet.

The technological advantages were not limited to hardware. The Americans also possessed superior training and maintenance procedures. American pilots, aircrews, and ship crews had undergone rigorous training programs that instilled a high level of proficiency and effectiveness. The superior maintenance infrastructure of the US Navy ensured that its aircraft and ships remained in optimal operational condition throughout the

campaign. These factors, while not strictly technological, played a critical role in maximizing the effectiveness of the superior
technology the Americans possessed. The Japanese, burdened by the strain of war and struggling with resource limitations, lacked the similar level of consistent training and efficient maintenance procedures.

In contrast to the technological sophistication of the American forces, the Japanese forces at Truk Lagoon suffered from a number of technological deficiencies. Their aircraft were, as previously mentioned, inferior to their American counterparts in various aspects. Their radar systems were less advanced and less effective, hindering their ability to detect incoming American aircraft. Their air defenses were consequently less effective and more easily overwhelmed. This lack of adequate technological means significantly hampered their ability to defend themselves against the overwhelming American air power. The inadequate early warning systems, coupled with the inferior performance of their aircraft, left the Japanese fleet and air bases vulnerable to the devastating American attacks. The damage inflicted, therefore, was far more significant than would have been possible had the
technological balance been more equal.

Furthermore, the Japanese Navy's reliance on outdated tactics and doctrines contributed to their vulnerabilities. Their defensive
strategies were not well-suited to counter the superior technology of the American forces. The Japanese had not effectively adapted their tactics to account for the increased range and striking power of American carrier-based aircraft and their superior technological capabilities. This contributed to their inability to effectively counter the American attacks. Their inability to develop and deploy
effective countermeasures highlights a significant shortcoming in their technological and strategic approach. They struggled to adapt to the rapidly evolving nature of naval warfare in the Pacific,
particularly in terms of the increasing capabilities of carrier-based air power.

Operation Hailstone, therefore, serves as a stark illustration of the profound impact of technological superiority on the outcome of naval warfare in World War II. The Americans' technological

advantage, encompassing superior aircraft, submarines, radar, and training, decisively shaped the battle, leading to the overwhelming destruction of Japanese forces at Truk Lagoon. The technological disparity wasn't merely a contributing factor to the victory; it was, in essence, the determining factor, demonstrating the critical role that technological advancements played in shaping the course of the war in the Pacific. The legacy of this operation underscores the importance of continuous technological innovation and adaptation in military operations. The decisive American victory at Truk
highlighted the critical need for naval forces to stay abreast of technological developments and to adapt their doctrines and tactics accordingly. The battle serves as a stark reminder that technological superiority, when coupled with effective strategy and execution, can be a decisive factor in determining the outcome of a military conflict. The imbalance in technological capabilities between the US Navy and the Imperial Japanese Navy at Truk Lagoon irrevocably shifted the balance of power in the Pacific theater, accelerating the Allied advance towards Japan and ultimately contributing to the Allied victory in World War II. The technological lessons of
Operation Hailstone continue to resonate in modern naval warfare, emphasizing the enduring importance of investment in research, development, and the adaptation of new technologies to maintain a decisive edge on the battlefield.

American Offensive Strategy

The American offensive strategy during Operation Hailstone was a masterful blend of overwhelming firepower, meticulous planning, and innovative tactical execution. It capitalized on the technological superiority already established, transforming it into a decisive blow against the Japanese stronghold at Truk Lagoon. The operation wasn't a spontaneous reaction; it was the culmination of months of strategic planning and intelligence gathering. Intelligence reports consistently highlighted Truk Lagoon's significance as a vital
Japanese base, a critical hub for resupply and operations
throughout the central Pacific. Its strategic location, combined with the substantial naval and air assets stationed there, made it a prime target for neutralization. The planners understood the potential risks, recognizing that Truk was heavily defended and that a direct assault could result in significant losses. However, the potential rewards—crippling Japanese logistics, disrupting operations, and securing a crucial stepping stone for further Allied advances—outweighed the perceived risks.

The American strategy revolved around achieving air and sea superiority before launching a concentrated attack. This wasn't a simple matter of brute force; it involved a sophisticated
understanding of Japanese defensive capabilities and
vulnerabilities. Intelligence analysis meticulously mapped Japanese radar coverage, anti-aircraft defenses, and the deployment of their air assets. This detailed knowledge informed the timing and
sequence of the American attacks. The initial phase focused on establishing air superiority. Waves of carrier-based aircraft, drawn from multiple carriers, including the USS Intrepid and USS
Yorktown, were launched in a carefully coordinated assault. The goal was not just to destroy Japanese aircraft but to systematically dismantle their radar network and anti-aircraft defenses. The
superior range and payload of American aircraft, such as the
Grumman F6F Hellcat and the Vought F4U Corsair, played a vital role in this phase. These aircraft were able to engage enemy fighters at longer ranges, minimizing exposure to Japanese anti-aircraft fire.

The success of the initial air attacks relied heavily on the effectiveness of American radar technology. Early warning systems, more sophisticated than their Japanese counterparts, provided crucial advance notice of enemy aircraft movements. This allowed American fighters to intercept incoming Japanese planes before they could effectively challenge American air superiority. The coordination between airborne early warning aircraft and the carrier-based fighters was seamless, a testament to the rigorous training and effective communication systems within the US Navy. Once air superiority was established, the focus shifted towards the destruction of Japanese naval assets within the lagoon. Dive bombers, like the Douglas SBD Dauntless and the Curtiss SB2C Helldiver, were unleashed, targeting the ships berthed in the lagoon. The precision bombing capabilities of these aircraft, coupled with the improved accuracy afforded by airborne radar, maximized the effectiveness of each sortie.

The selection of targets was also strategic. The American planners didn't simply focus on destroying the largest or most visible ships; they prioritized targets that would have the most significant impact on Japanese operational capabilities. This included oil storage facilities, ammunition depots, and repair yards, effectively crippling the ability of the Japanese to maintain and repair their fleet. The destruction of these support infrastructure severely limited the Japanese ability to recover from the losses inflicted during the air attacks. The subsequent attacks on the ships themselves were almost secondary to this strategic crippling of the base's operational infrastructure. The effectiveness of the American attack is also reflected in the remarkably low losses suffered by the American forces. This was a direct result of the comprehensive planning, superior technology, and coordinated execution. The meticulous targeting, coupled with effective air cover, ensured that American losses were kept to a minimum, maximizing the impact of the operation while minimizing risks.

The submarine component of Operation Hailstone also played a significant role. American submarines, operating in the vicinity of Truk Lagoon, launched attacks on Japanese shipping entering and exiting the lagoon. These attacks effectively disrupted the already strained supply lines to the base, further limiting the Japanese ability to reinforce and resupply their forces. The increased range,

advanced sonar technology, and superior torpedoes of the US submarines contributed significantly to their success. The
submerged attacks were particularly effective because they targeted ships outside the protection of the lagoon's defenses, striking at the vulnerable flanks of the Japanese supply chain. This aspect of the operation highlights the multi-pronged approach employed by the Americans, leveraging all available assets to achieve maximum impact.

The American success at Truk Lagoon wasn't simply a matter of superior technology; it also demonstrated superior strategic
thinking and operational execution. The decision to target Truk Lagoon was not taken lightly. It involved detailed analysis of
Japanese strengths and weaknesses, meticulous planning, and the seamless coordination of different naval assets. The effective use of intelligence, the precise execution of the air and submarine attacks, and the judicious selection of targets showcased the high level of operational expertise within the US Navy. The operational aspects were not only about the physical destruction of enemy assets but also about disrupting the Japanese ability to maintain their
presence in this strategically important location. The operation's success was also a testament to the American ability to integrate different forms of warfare effectively, combining air, sea, and submarine operations into a cohesive and devastating strategy. This strategic integration and ability to adapt to the challenges of naval warfare highlighted the American navy's effectiveness in applying modern strategic concepts.

However, the American strategy wasn't without its potential weaknesses. The reliance on carrier-based air power, while ultimately successful, exposed the American fleet to potential risks.

A strong Japanese counter-attack could have inflicted substantial damage, highlighting the inherent vulnerability of carrier forces. The vast distance between the American carriers and their support bases also presented logistical challenges. Maintaining the supply of fuel, ammunition, and spare parts across such distances demanded careful planning and efficient supply lines. These logistical
challenges were addressed through effective pre-planning and established supply chains, but a disruption of these chains could have significantly impacted the operation's success. Moreover, while

the operation was a resounding success, it didn't entirely eliminate the Japanese presence at Truk Lagoon. Japanese forces remained in the area, albeit weakened, posing a continuing threat, although a significantly diminished one.

In conclusion, the American offensive strategy during Operation Hailstone was a complex and multifaceted operation that skillfully combined technological superiority with meticulous planning, precise execution, and effective coordination of different naval assets. The operation demonstrated the effectiveness of a well-integrated approach to naval warfare, highlighting the crucial interplay between technology, intelligence, and tactical execution.

While not without its potential vulnerabilities, the operation ultimately resulted in a decisive victory, crippling Japanese naval power in the Central Pacific, and securing a crucial foothold for the continued Allied advance across the Pacific Ocean. Operation Hailstone was a pivotal turning point in the war, not just for the destruction it wrought, but also for the tactical lessons learned and the strategic implications it held for the rest of the Pacific
campaign. The lessons learned from this operation continue to inform naval strategies and tactical doctrines to this day,
emphasizing the enduring importance of technological innovation, strategic planning, and coordinated execution. The legacy of Operation Hailstone stands as a powerful example of the devastating consequences of technological and strategic disparity in modern naval warfare.

Japanese Defensive Strategy

The stark contrast between the meticulously planned American offensive and the Japanese defensive posture at Truk Lagoon during Operation Hailstone reveals much about the strategic and technological disparities between the two navies. While the American strategy was characterized by a sophisticated blend of air, sea, and submarine power, integrated through superior intelligence and coordinated execution, the Japanese defense, in retrospect, appears reactive and ultimately inadequate. This inadequacy stemmed not solely from a lack of resources, though that played a significant role, but also from fundamental flaws in strategic thinking, operational doctrine, and technological limitations.

The Japanese defensive strategy at Truk, at its core, relied on a layered approach. The first layer comprised the extensive anti-aircraft defenses stationed around the lagoon. Numerous anti-aircraft batteries, ranging from light to heavy caliber guns, were positioned on the islands surrounding the lagoon, intended to repel air attacks. However, these defenses proved woefully insufficient against the overwhelming air power unleashed by the American carriers. The sheer volume of American aircraft, coupled with their superior range and accuracy, overwhelmed the Japanese gunners.

The Japanese lacked effective radar warning systems, severely hindering their ability to coordinate a timely and effective response.

Their radar technology, inferior to its American counterpart, provided insufficient early warning, leaving their anti-aircraft crews with little time to react to the incoming waves of American aircraft. The relatively short range of their own fighters also proved to be a significant disadvantage, limiting their ability to intercept the attacking American planes before they reached their targets.

The second layer of the Japanese defense involved their own air assets based at Truk. However, these forces were already significantly depleted prior to the commencement of Operation Hailstone, suffering from a chronic lack of spare parts, fuel, and trained pilots. Continuous attrition from previous Allied attacks had taken a toll on the Japanese air power, leaving them in a weaker position to effectively counter the massive American air assault. The deployment of Japanese aircraft was further hampered by inadequate communication and coordination amongst their units. This lack of effective communication, coupled with the limitations of their radar systems, resulted in a fragmented and ineffective response to the American air attacks. The airfields themselves were poorly situated and vulnerable, failing to account for the range and precision of American bombing.

The third layer of defense, the Japanese naval forces stationed in Truk Lagoon, were largely caught unprepared. Despite the strategic importance of the lagoon, a significant portion of the Japanese fleet was not fully prepared for an attack of this magnitude. Many ships were undergoing repairs or were inadequately fueled and provisioned. The concentrated nature of the Japanese fleet within the lagoon, while intended for mutual support, proved to be a fatal vulnerability. The close proximity of the ships made them easy targets for the precision bombing of the American dive bombers. Furthermore, the Japanese lacked a coherent plan for coordinating a defensive action from their naval vessels. The surprise element and the relentless nature of the American assault overwhelmed the Japanese naval defense.

Beyond the immediate tactical failures, the Japanese defensive strategy suffered from several significant strategic flaws. The decision to concentrate so many assets in a single, geographically limited area, such as Truk Lagoon, proved to be a critical error. This concentration made the entire base vulnerable to a decisive blow. A more dispersed deployment, with assets spread across multiple bases, could have significantly reduced the effectiveness of the American assault. However, such a strategy would have also presented logistical and communication challenges, indicating a significant limitation in Japanese logistical capabilities and strategic coordination.

The Japanese assessment of American capabilities also appears to have been flawed. They underestimated the range, accuracy, and sheer volume of American air power, as well as the effectiveness of American submarines. Intelligence gathering and analysis were clearly inadequate. The surprise and scale of the American attack suggest a significant failure to accurately predict the American offensive strategy. This failure highlighted a lack of effective intelligence gathering and analysis in the Japanese war machine. The overestimation of their own defensive capabilities and the underestimation of the American offensive capacity directly contributed to the failure of their defense.

Finally, the Japanese defensive strategy lacked the flexibility and adaptability necessary to counter the American attack. They failed to adapt to the changing situation and to effectively employ their limited resources to mitigate the damage. Once the initial wave of American attacks had secured air superiority and commenced the destruction of their air and naval assets, the Japanese were left with limited options for effective countermeasures. This rigidity and lack of effective improvisation proved to be fatal.

In conclusion, the Japanese defensive strategy at Truk Lagoon during Operation Hailstone was a combination of technological inferiority, flawed strategic assessment, poor tactical execution, and inadequate logistical support. Their layered defense, while
theoretically sound, was undone by the superior American technology, meticulous planning, and the effective integration of air, sea, and submarine operations. The failure of the Japanese defense at Truk Lagoon serves as a powerful case study in the importance of accurate intelligence gathering, effective logistical support, adaptability, and strategic flexibility in modern naval warfare. The legacy of this failure profoundly impacted the course of the Pacific War, underscoring the critical need for a
comprehensive and dynamic defensive strategy in the face of a technologically and strategically superior adversary. The aftermath of Operation Hailstone marked not just a significant loss for the Japanese navy but a critical turning point in the war, showcasing the consequences of a defensive strategy incapable of countering a determined and well-prepared opponent. The lessons from this failure reverberate through military history, highlighting the
importance of continuous adaptation and the critical role of intelligence in shaping defensive strategies. The seemingly impenetrable bastion of Truk Lagoon, once a symbol of Japanese strength, crumbled under the weight of its own strategic weaknesses and the unrelenting power of the American offensive. The failure was not simply a matter of numbers or individual bravery, but a

systemic breakdown of planning and execution, amplified by a widening technological gap that the Japanese could not overcome.

Contrasting Naval Doctrines

The contrasting naval doctrines of the United States and Japan during World War II fundamentally shaped the outcome of engagements like Operation Hailstone. These doctrines, born from differing geopolitical realities, technological capabilities, and philosophical approaches to warfare, manifested in starkly different strategic and tactical approaches. The American doctrine, forged in the crucible of a vast ocean and a need for global projection of power, prioritized fleet mobility, integrated arms capabilities, and decisive offensive action. The Japanese doctrine, rooted in a more limited geographic scope and a belief in the decisive power of a concentrated strike force, emphasized decisive battles fought with overwhelming force and a strong emphasis on surprise.

The American approach, broadly characterized as a doctrine of "fleet in being," recognized the crucial role of naval power in controlling sea lanes and projecting power across vast distances. The US Navy, possessing a vast industrial base capable of building and maintaining a large fleet, favored a strategy of attrition. This involved deploying powerful carrier task forces, capable of projecting overwhelming air power far from their bases, coupled with robust submarine capabilities, capable of attacking enemy shipping and bases independently. The American focus was on achieving and maintaining air and sea superiority, using that dominance to cripple the enemy's ability to wage war. This was not merely a matter of destroying ships and aircraft; it was about severing supply lines, isolating enemy forces, and systematically eroding their capacity to resist.

The development of radar and other advanced technologies played a crucial role in the American naval doctrine. Radar greatly enhanced the effectiveness of both offensive and defensive operations, allowing for earlier detection of enemy aircraft and ships and more accurate targeting. The integration of radar into fire-control systems significantly increased the accuracy and lethality of naval gunfire. The US Navy also heavily invested in developing effective communication systems which enabled seamless coordination between fleet units, even across vast distances. This sophisticated communication network ensured effective communication among ships, aircraft, and shore-based installations, a critical factor in executing complex, coordinated operations. The ability to rapidly share intelligence, coordinate attacks, and adjust strategies based on real-time information was a distinct advantage over the Japanese Navy.

The American doctrine also placed a strong emphasis on combined arms warfare, recognizing the synergistic effect of integrating air, surface, and submarine forces. This approach, evident in the meticulous planning and execution of Operation Hailstone, involved carefully coordinated attacks, designed to maximize the impact of each element. Carrier-based aircraft provided air cover and delivered devastating airstrikes, while surface ships provided fire support and anti-submarine protection. Submarines, often operating independently, targeted enemy shipping and disrupted supply lines, thereby weakening the enemy's capacity to resist. This integrated approach maximized the effectiveness of each arm of the navy while minimizing vulnerabilities.

In contrast to the American approach, the Japanese naval doctrine reflected a more limited vision of naval warfare, rooted in a sense of national isolation and a reliance on decisive victories. Japanese naval strategy centered on the concept of a "decisive battle," a single, overwhelming engagement that would cripple the enemy fleet and secure victory. This doctrine prioritized the development of highly skilled and disciplined crews, advanced ship designs, and the cultivation of a warrior ethos within the fleet. The Japanese emphasis on elite personnel and superior technology reflected a conviction that a smaller but more highly trained and equipped navy could defeat a larger, less capable adversary.

However, this focus on the decisive battle had inherent limitations. It neglected the importance of sustained attrition and the crucial role of logistical support. While the Japanese Navy initially achieved remarkable success through daring attacks and meticulous planning, their strategy lacked the flexibility and sustainability necessary to cope with the sustained pressure of a larger, industrially more powerful enemy. Furthermore, the Japanese emphasis on the decisive battle led to a concentration of forces in key locations, making them highly vulnerable to preemptive strikes, as evidenced by the devastating results of Operation Hailstone at Truk Lagoon. The concentration of naval assets at Truk Lagoon, while intended to create a formidable defensive bastion, actually made it an attractive target for a powerful air assault. The resulting losses severely damaged Japanese naval capacity in the Pacific.

The Japanese also underestimated the importance of intelligence and the effectiveness of combined arms. Their intelligence gathering and analysis were less sophisticated than their American counterparts, leading to a flawed assessment of American capabilities and intentions. The lack of effective intelligence gathering significantly contributed to the strategic miscalculations that ultimately proved costly. They also lacked the comprehensive integration of air, surface, and submarine arms that characterized the American approach. Although the Japanese Navy possessed talented pilots and submarine crews, their ability to coordinate these assets effectively against a larger and technologically superior force was limited. The effectiveness of their submarines was hindered by a lack of effective reconnaissance and coordination with other units.

The technological disparity between the two navies also played a crucial role in shaping the outcome of naval engagements. The American Navy benefited from significantly superior radar technology, allowing for earlier detection of enemy aircraft and ships, enhancing both offensive and defensive capabilities.
American aircraft also had greater range and payload capacity, giving them a significant advantage in air-to-air and air-to-surface combat. The Japanese, while having some advanced technology, particularly in torpedoes, lacked the industrial capacity to mass-produce these technologies or consistently match American advances in areas such as radar, carrier-based aircraft, and fleet-wide communication systems. This technological gap widened over time, further exacerbating the existing strategic and tactical disparities between the two navies.

In conclusion, the contrasting naval doctrines of the American and Japanese navies reflected their differing geopolitical circumstances, technological capabilities, and philosophical approaches to warfare.

The American doctrine, prioritizing fleet mobility, combined arms warfare, and sustained attrition, proved to be more adaptable and ultimately more effective in the long run. The Japanese doctrine, while initially successful in achieving some spectacular victories, ultimately proved to be too rigid, inflexible, and overly reliant on the improbable success of a single, decisive battle. The decisive defeat at Truk Lagoon, and other engagements, illustrated the weaknesses of the Japanese strategy and highlighted the advantages of the American approach. The lessons drawn from this stark
contrast remain relevant today, emphasizing the importance of adaptability, effective intelligence, and the integration of all
available military assets in achieving success in naval warfare. The technological race, too, proved decisive, underscoring the necessity for consistent technological advancement and integration for any nation aspiring to dominance in the naval arena. The legacy of Operation Hailstone and the broader comparison of American and Japanese naval doctrines serves as a powerful testament to the critical interplay of strategy, technology, and adaptation in
determining the outcome of naval conflict.

Resource Allocation and Prioritization

The stark contrast in naval doctrines between the United States and Japan extended beyond strategic and tactical approaches to encompass fundamental differences in resource allocation and prioritization. These differences, deeply rooted in their respective industrial capacities, geopolitical ambitions, and philosophical orientations towards warfare, profoundly influenced the course of the Pacific War and the outcome of engagements like Operation Hailstone. The American approach, characterized by a vast industrial base and a global vision, prioritized a sustained, multi-pronged offensive, while the Japanese, operating under constraints of limited resources and a more insular perspective, focused on concentrated strikes and a decisive, singular victory.

The United States, possessing an industrial capacity far exceeding that of Japan, adopted a strategy of mass production and attrition. The sheer scale of American shipbuilding, aircraft production, and munitions manufacturing dwarfed that of its opponent. This allowed the US Navy to sustain heavy losses, replenish its fleet rapidly, and continuously exert pressure across the vast expanse of the Pacific. Resource allocation reflected this strategy: massive investments were poured into the expansion of shipyards, aircraft factories, and training facilities. The development and deployment of new technologies, such as improved radar systems, advanced aircraft, and effective communication systems, were also given top priority. The continuous upgrading of existing equipment and the rapid integration of new technologies into fleet operations were hallmarks of the American approach. The sheer volume of resources, both human and material, allowed for a degree of risk-taking and experimentation that was simply unattainable for the Japanese. Losses, though significant in some individual battles, were quickly offset by the vast industrial reserve. This allowed the US Navy to maintain a continuous and overwhelming presence in the Pacific, slowly but surely wearing down the Japanese forces through a protracted campaign of attrition.

A crucial aspect of American resource allocation was the prioritization of logistical support. The vast logistical network –

encompassing shipyards, supply depots, and lines of communication spanning the Pacific – was given paramount importance. This ensured a continuous flow of supplies, fuel, ammunition, and replacement personnel to fleet units deployed throughout the Pacific theatre. This logistical prowess provided the backbone of the sustained offensive pressure that ultimately overwhelmed the Japanese. The emphasis on maintaining the long supply lines and establishing secure bases along the advance route played a critical role in the success of American campaigns. The ability to quickly repair damaged ships and replace lost aircraft and equipment was a significant advantage, one that underscored the importance of resource allocation in sustaining long-term operations. The detailed planning and meticulous execution that characterized operations like Operation Hailstone were only possible due to this logistical strength.

In stark contrast, Japan's resource allocation reflected its limited industrial capacity and its strategic emphasis on a swift, decisive victory. Resources were concentrated on the development of a highly skilled, elite fighting force and advanced, albeit often less numerous, weaponry. The Japanese naval doctrine placed considerable value on highly trained personnel and cutting-edge technology, particularly in areas like torpedoes and specialized aircraft. While some sectors enjoyed substantial investment – particularly in advanced naval vessels and elite pilot training – others were comparatively neglected. This resulted in an unbalanced approach where the production of certain key components lagged significantly behind American output, hindering overall effectiveness. The emphasis on quality over quantity, while reflecting a certain strategic logic, ultimately proved insufficient to counter the overwhelming industrial might of the United States.

This constrained resource environment meant that Japanese planners had to make difficult choices about resource prioritization. Decisions concerning the allocation of aircraft, fuel, and trained personnel often meant prioritizing one front over another, a challenge that was exacerbated by the vast distances involved in the Pacific theatre. The Japanese lacked the logistical depth to sustain prolonged campaigns, relying instead on capturing and utilizing resources from conquered territories. This dependence on captured resources proved to be a major weakness, as the expansion of the war and the loss of territory greatly curtailed their access to vital supplies. The failure to adequately anticipate and plan for sustaining a long-term conflict significantly hampered their ability to effectively counter the American advance.

Further compounding the problem was the Japanese approach to technological development. While skilled in the development of certain advanced weaponry, Japan lacked the industrial capacity to mass-produce these technologies effectively. This focus on smaller quantities of highly advanced weaponry meant that even successes in certain technologies couldn't offset the lack of numerical superiority in many key areas. The advanced Type 93 torpedo, for instance, was a technological marvel, yet its production rate couldn't keep pace with the sheer number of weapons deployed by the American Navy. This technological imbalance, further compounded by inferior radar and communication systems, placed the Japanese at a disadvantage even where their individual weapons boasted superior capabilities.

The concentration of resources at Truk Lagoon, while strategically intended to create an impregnable bastion, ultimately proved to be a fatal flaw in Japanese resource allocation. The large number of ships, aircraft, and support personnel concentrated in a single location presented an irresistible target for a determined American assault. The devastating air raids of Operation Hailstone demonstrated the vulnerability of concentrating resources in a single location, particularly without adequate defensive capabilities or the logistical capacity to quickly reposition or replenish lost assets. The heavy losses suffered at Truk Lagoon represented not just the destruction of matériel, but also a significant depletion of irreplaceable human resources and experienced personnel, a drain that Japan could ill afford.

The contrasting approaches to resource allocation highlight a fundamental difference in strategic outlook. The Americans, with their vast resources and industrial capacity, opted for a strategy of sustained attrition, spreading their resources across various fronts while maintaining a robust logistical backbone. The Japanese, constrained by limited resources, concentrated their efforts on achieving a decisive victory, a gamble that ultimately failed due to the inability to effectively offset the industrial and logistical advantages of the United States. The outcome of Operation Hailstone, and indeed the broader Pacific War, serves as a powerful illustration of how resource allocation and prioritization decisions, informed by strategic doctrines and underpinned by industrial capacity, can profoundly shape the course of naval warfare and the fate of nations. The American ability to sustainably support a prolonged war of attrition, characterized by continuous replacement of equipment and personnel, stands in stark contrast to the Japanese gamble on a single decisive victory, highlighting a key factor in determining the outcome of the Pacific campaign. The analysis of resource allocation underscores the crucial connection between a nation's industrial capacity, strategic doctrine, and ultimate success or failure in large-scale naval conflict.

The Impact of Leadership and Command Structure

The contrasting approaches to resource allocation discussed earlier directly influenced the leadership and command structures of both the American and Japanese navies, ultimately shaping the strategic decisions made during Operation Hailstone and the broader Pacific War. The decentralized command structure of the US Navy, a reflection of its vast resources and industrial capacity, allowed for greater flexibility and adaptability on the battlefield. In contrast, the Japanese Navy's more centralized and hierarchical command structure, a product of its limited resources and emphasis on highly trained elites, proved less responsive to the rapidly evolving
circumstances of the war.

Admiral Raymond Spruance, commander of the Fifth Fleet during Operation Hailstone, epitomized the American approach to leadership. His style was characterized by a calm, deliberate, and highly analytical approach to decision-making. Spruance
meticulously planned the operation, delegating authority to his subordinate commanders while maintaining overall control. This distributed leadership structure facilitated the effective coordination of the diverse forces involved in the operation, encompassing
carrier-based aircraft, submarines, and surface vessels. His reliance on meticulous planning and his trust in the capabilities of his
subordinate commanders were key to the operation's success. He provided the overarching strategic vision while empowering his subordinates to execute their specific tasks with a high degree of autonomy. This decentralized command fostered initiative and independent action at various levels, proving vital in adapting to unforeseen circumstances during the battle. The operation benefited from the combined expertise of numerous skilled commanders, each responsible for a specific aspect of the assault. This distributed expertise mirrored the American industrial model of distributed manufacturing and supply chains.

The effectiveness of American leadership wasn't solely reliant on the top-down approach but benefited immensely from the robust communication systems employed. Real-time communication enabled effective coordination between the various elements of the fleet and facilitated rapid responses to changing battlefield conditions. The improved radar and communication systems, previously highlighted as an area of significant American advantage, not only contributed to the success of the operation but also supported the decentralized command structure by ensuring timely information flow. This allowed commanders at various levels to make informed decisions based on the latest available intelligence. Decentralization meant that individual unit commanders could take swift and decisive actions based on situational awareness.

Conversely, the Japanese Navy's leadership and command structure reflected its more centralized and hierarchical approach. Admiral Soemu Toyoda, the Commander-in-Chief of the Combined Fleet, held immense authority, making many key decisions concerning the allocation of resources and the deployment of forces. This centralized control, while promoting a degree of operational coherence, hindered flexibility and responsiveness. The distance between the highest levels of command and the operational units deployed at Truk Lagoon meant that decisions were often delayed and inflexible. The lack of real-time communication and situational awareness exacerbated this problem. Commanders at Truk Lagoon, even with their individual experience and expertise, were constrained by the inflexible strategic directives from the Combined Fleet headquarters. This hierarchical command structure, intended to ensure unity of purpose and effective execution, resulted in a slow and often inadequate response to the American assault.

The Japanese emphasis on highly skilled and elite commanders, while producing highly effective officers in peacetime and small-scale engagements, proved a critical vulnerability in the context of the vast Pacific theatre and a protracted war. This reliance on elite officers meant that the loss of experienced commanders disproportionately impacted the effectiveness of the Japanese fleet.

The death or incapacitation of key officers resulted in a serious leadership vacuum that the hierarchical structure struggled to fill swiftly, in contrast to the US Navy's ability to maintain operational strength even with battlefield losses due to the extensive training and operational experience across various levels of command. The centralized structure lacked the built-in redundancy of the

American system; the loss of a crucial commander created a significant disruption within the chain of command.

The contrast in command philosophies extends beyond the top levels to encompass the interaction between senior commanders and their subordinates. The American system fostered a greater degree of initiative and independent action from subordinate commanders, encouraging them to adapt to unforeseen circumstances on the battlefield. The Japanese system, conversely, tended towards a more rigid adherence to pre-planned directives, leaving subordinate commanders with less freedom to respond effectively to rapidly changing situations. This rigid structure often resulted in a failure to exploit opportunities and in inadequate responses to unforeseen developments in the heat of battle. This disparity in the degree of autonomy granted to subordinate commanders contributed significantly to the differing outcomes in strategic decision-making.

Furthermore, the cultural differences between the two navies played a crucial role in shaping their respective command structures and leadership styles. The American emphasis on individual initiative and decentralized decision-making reflected its broader cultural values of individualism and pragmatism. The Japanese emphasis on collective responsibility and strict adherence to hierarchy mirrored its own societal structures and cultural norms. While this sense of collective spirit and loyalty enhanced unit cohesion in some aspects, it also inhibited flexibility and responsiveness in the face of dynamic battlefield situations. The rigidity of the Japanese command structure, often leading to delays in decision-making and missed opportunities, was deeply intertwined with the hierarchical nature of Japanese society. The strong emphasis on saving face and avoiding dissent also contributed to the inability of the Japanese Navy to adapt its strategies in response to the evolving realities of the war.

The differences in intelligence gathering and assessment further amplified the disparities in leadership and command. The US Navy, with its advanced radar and communication systems, possessed a more robust and timely intelligence network. This enabled more accurate assessments of the enemy's capabilities and intentions, informing strategic decisions at all levels of command. In contrast, the Japanese Navy struggled with obtaining timely and accurate intelligence, hindered by less effective technology and a more centralized intelligence system that was less responsive to the dynamic realities on the ground. This intelligence deficit hampered the Japanese Navy's ability to make informed strategic decisions, resulting in deployments and responses that were often ill-suited to the prevailing circumstances. The failure to accurately assess the extent of American air power and the vulnerability of Truk Lagoon to sustained air attacks was a direct result of this intelligence failure.

In conclusion, the contrasting approaches to leadership and command structure adopted by the American and Japanese navies were deeply intertwined with their broader strategic doctrines, resource allocation strategies, and even cultural values. The American decentralized structure, supported by robust communication and intelligence systems, proved remarkably adaptable and effective, facilitating a rapid and coordinated response to the challenges of the Pacific War. The Japanese centralized structure, though emphasizing efficiency and unity in a more cohesive unit, proved less flexible and responsive to the dynamic realities of the vast and rapidly evolving battlefield. The stark differences in leadership and command, combined with the disparate approaches to resource allocation and technological development, culminated in a decisively American victory at Operation Hailstone and the broader Pacific campaign, underscoring the profound impact of these factors on the outcome of naval warfare. The legacy of these differences continues to provide valuable insights into the complexities of strategic leadership and the multifaceted factors that determine success in large-scale naval conflicts.

The IslandHopping Campaign

Operation Hailstone, while a stunning tactical victory in itself, was far from an isolated event. Its significance lies deeply within the broader context of the Allied island-hopping campaign across the vast expanse of the Pacific Ocean. This campaign, a meticulously planned and executed strategy, aimed to progressively secure
strategically important islands, thereby inching closer to the
Japanese home islands. The logic underpinning this strategy was multifaceted. Firstly, each captured island served as an invaluable stepping stone, providing advanced bases for air and naval power, significantly reducing the distances to subsequent targets. This reduced the logistical burdens associated with long-range
operations, enabling a sustained and increasingly powerful offensive against the Japanese.

Secondly, the island-hopping campaign aimed to progressively isolate the Japanese forces. By capturing key islands, the Allies disrupted Japanese supply lines, communication networks, and reinforcements, gradually strangling their ability to sustain their far-flung empire. Truk Lagoon, the target of Operation Hailstone, served as a crucial hub within this vast network, a critical logistical and operational base for Japanese forces throughout Micronesia. Neutralizing Truk, therefore, had a cascading effect, significantly weakening Japanese capabilities across a broad swathe of the Pacific.

The choice of Truk as a target was not arbitrary. Intelligence reports consistently highlighted its importance as a major supply and repair base for the Japanese Navy and Army. The lagoon sheltered a substantial fleet of ships, aircraft, and submarines, providing a vital springboard for Japanese operations in the central and western Pacific. The vast network of airfields around the lagoon allowed for the rapid deployment and support of Japanese aircraft, posing a considerable threat to Allied operations elsewhere in the Pacific.

The neutralization of this base, therefore, presented a compelling strategic opportunity: by crippling Truk, the Allies could
significantly curtail Japanese offensive capabilities and disrupt their logistical capacity, paving the way for further advances.

The success of Operation Hailstone was a testament to the careful planning and execution of the operation. The meticulous coordination between the various branches of the U.S. Navy – the aircraft carriers, submarines, battleships, and cruisers – demonstrated the growing synergy between different elements of the Allied war machine. The devastating air strikes launched from carriers like the *Intrepid* and *Yorktown* , combined with the effective submarine attacks, dealt a crippling blow to the Japanese fleet and infrastructure within the lagoon. The air superiority established by the U.S. Navy effectively neutralized Japanese air defenses, allowing the carrier-borne aircraft to operate with relative impunity, resulting in the catastrophic destruction of Japanese air power and surface ships.

However, the island-hopping campaign was not without its challenges. The Japanese, despite suffering substantial losses, proved remarkably resilient. Even after the devastating blows at Truk, they continued to fight tenaciously on other islands. The sheer geographical expanse of the Pacific, the harsh conditions in many of the islands, and the determined resistance of the Japanese forces made the campaign a long and arduous process. The Allies paid a price for each island secured, and every victory involved significant human and material costs. Operation Hailstone, though a major success, only represented a single step in a long and grueling campaign that spanned years.

The operation's success also highlighted the crucial role of intelligence gathering and analysis. The U.S. Navy's superior intelligence capabilities provided accurate assessments of Japanese strength and deployment, enabling the Allies to plan and execute the operation with a high degree of precision. This contrasted sharply with the Japanese intelligence apparatus, which failed to accurately assess the scale and scope of the impending attack, leading to a significant strategic miscalculation. This disparity in intelligence capabilities played a pivotal role in determining the outcome of the operation.

The aftermath of Operation Hailstone cemented Truk's transformation. The lagoon, once a vital Japanese stronghold, became a grim reminder of the Allied dominance in the Pacific. The sunken ships and aircraft, now resting on the seabed, serve as a haunting testament to the destructive power of modern warfare and the decisive victory of Operation Hailstone. Truk's strategic importance had been effectively neutralized, opening up the way for Allied operations to move further westward.

The island-hopping campaign, however, involved far more than just military operations. It required vast logistical support, including the transport of troops, equipment, and supplies across thousands of miles of ocean. The success of the campaign hinged on the ability of the Allied navies to maintain the flow of supplies and reinforcements to the islands under their control. The logistical complexities of sustaining a sprawling campaign across such a vast area presented a formidable challenge, highlighting the importance of efficient and effective logistical systems. The maintenance of this vast logistical network was crucial not only for the success of operations like Hailstone, but for the sustained advance toward the Japanese home islands.

Further, the island-hopping campaign had profound political implications. Each successful capture of a strategically important island brought the Allies closer to Japan, strengthening their diplomatic position and exerting increasing pressure on the Japanese government. The strategic gains made at Truk, for example, significantly diminished Japan's ability to mount significant offensive operations, bolstering Allied diplomatic pressure for an end to the conflict.

The socio-economic consequences of the campaign were also far-reaching. The war created widespread displacement and devastation in the Pacific islands. The capture of islands disrupted indigenous populations, changing the political, social and economic structure of these communities. Many of these islands were left ravaged, requiring significant reconstruction efforts following the war. The long-term effects of the war on the people and environment of these islands remain a complex and often overlooked aspect of the Pacific War.

Moreover, Operation Hailstone, and the wider island-hopping

campaign, contributed significantly to the overall Allied war effort in the Pacific. By securing strategically important islands, the Allies gained a foothold closer to Japan, making future invasions more feasible and reducing the overall cost of achieving victory. The progressive isolation and weakening of the Japanese war machine through the island-hopping strategy contributed substantially to the Allied victory in the Pacific.

In conclusion, Operation Hailstone's profound impact extended far beyond the immediate destruction inflicted upon the Japanese fleet and infrastructure at Truk Lagoon. It served as a crucial turning point within the larger Allied strategy of island-hopping, effectively crippling a key Japanese base and significantly weakening their capability to wage war across a broad sector of the Pacific theatre. The operation's success underscored the importance of coordinated naval warfare, superior intelligence, meticulous planning and the immense logistical resources that fueled the Allied war machine. While Hailstone was a significant military victory in its own right, its true significance rests within the broader context of the Allied Pacific campaign, underscoring its integral role in the overall strategy that eventually led to victory over Japan. The legacy of Operation Hailstone is not merely the physical remains of a once-mighty naval base, but also its strategic contribution to the Allied advance, shifting the balance of power in the Pacific and ultimately drawing the world closer to the end of World War II. This
operation, in its context, represents not just a battle won, but a critical chapter in the larger narrative of a global war. The ripples from this operation continued to shape the strategic landscape of the Pacific for months, even years, to come. The intelligence
garnered, the confidence built, and the lessons learned from Hailstone undeniably contributed to the further successes in the ongoing island-hopping campaign.

The Battle of the Pacific

Operation Hailstone, while a decisive victory in its own right, must be understood within the dynamic and evolving context of the broader Battle of the Pacific. To isolate it as a singular event risks diminishing its profound impact on the overall Allied strategy and the shifting balance of power in the Pacific theater. The battle, fought in February 1944, was not an isolated incident but a crucial link in a chain of naval engagements that progressively weakened the Japanese Empire's ability to project power and defend its vast, sprawling empire.

The Battle of the Pacific was characterized by a series of strategic offensives and counter-offensives, each shaping the subsequent course of the war. Early engagements, like the Battle of Coral Sea and the Battle of Midway, marked turning points, shifting the initiative from the Japanese Imperial Navy to the increasingly powerful US Navy. These earlier battles, while crucial in halting the initial Japanese advance, were fought on a different scale and scope than Operation Hailstone. Coral Sea and Midway were largely carrier-versus-carrier battles, focused on decisive engagements between fleet units. While Hailstone involved carrier aircraft, its scope was broader, encompassing a systematic dismantling of a major Japanese base, a more comprehensive operation targeting land-based assets in addition to naval forces.

The scale of destruction at Truk Lagoon was unprecedented for a single operation in the Pacific. The sheer number of ships sunk—twelve, ranging from cruisers to smaller support vessels—and aircraft destroyed—275—represented a significant blow to Japanese naval capabilities. This loss was not simply a matter of replacing vessels and aircraft; it also undermined the carefully constructed logistical infrastructure that supported Japanese operations across Micronesia. The destruction of the fuel and supply depots at Truk, for example, had a cascading effect, hampering Japanese operations far beyond the immediate vicinity of the lagoon. The loss of experienced aircrews and maintenance personnel, in addition to the physical losses, compounded the impact, making it extremely difficult to quickly regain operational strength.

Comparing Hailstone to other major Pacific battles highlights its unique contribution to the Allied war effort. While battles like the Battle of Leyte Gulf involved colossal fleet engagements and massive casualties, Hailstone achieved a strategic objective with comparatively fewer losses on the Allied side. The relatively light resistance encountered by the American forces at Truk is a notable feature of the battle. This was a result of several factors, including superior Allied intelligence, the element of surprise, and the already weakened state of the Japanese defenses in the area due to prior Allied offensives. The Japanese had already suffered significant losses in other battles, and their ability to reinforce and resupply Truk was constrained. This allowed for a more decisive and one-sided victory compared to engagements where the Japanese had been better prepared and deployed. Unlike the desperate struggles for Guadalcanal and Iwo Jima, Hailstone's success was comparatively swift and less costly.

The intelligence component that fueled Operation Hailstone's success deserves particular attention. The Allies possessed highly accurate intelligence regarding the strength and disposition of Japanese forces at Truk. This allowed for the meticulous planning and coordination of air and submarine attacks, maximizing the impact while minimizing Allied losses. This intelligence superiority contrasted sharply with the Japanese, who were largely caught off guard, underestimating the scale and intensity of the impending attack. This intelligence advantage, honed through months of code-breaking, reconnaissance, and analysis, played a critical role in determining the outcome. The ability of the Americans to anticipate the Japanese responses and thus neutralize their potential counterattacks significantly contributed to the stunning success of Hailstone.

Operation Hailstone's success was not solely attributable to the power of the American Navy's air and naval assault; it was also a consequence of the overall Allied strategy in the Pacific. The island-hopping campaign, with its incremental gains, gradually isolated and weakened the Japanese. Truk, as a vital hub within this network, was a natural target for neutralization. Its capture wasn't merely a tactical victory; it was a strategically decisive move, dismantling a critical link in the chain of Japanese supply and communications, further isolating their forces in the western Pacific. The success of the operation paved the way for subsequent Allied advances, facilitating the capture of key islands further west and drawing the Allies closer to the Japanese home islands.

The aftermath of Hailstone showcased the shift in the balance of power. Truk Lagoon, once a formidable Japanese stronghold, was transformed into a graveyard of warships and aircraft, a silent testament to Allied dominance. This dramatic shift was not simply a military achievement but also a psychological victory, further demoralizing the Japanese and undermining their confidence in their ability to defend their empire. The psychological effect of such a decisive defeat should not be underestimated. The loss of Truk significantly impacted Japanese morale and further eroded their resolve to continue the war.

Furthermore, the logistical impact of Operation Hailstone was profound. The destruction of Japanese supply and repair facilities at Truk significantly disrupted their ability to sustain operations in the central and western Pacific. This had a ripple effect across various fronts, undermining Japanese capabilities in other regions. The operation's long-term effects extended beyond the immediate
destruction. The loss of a major logistical center contributed to the steadily worsening logistical situation for the Japanese forces, further restricting their operational capacity.

In conclusion, Operation Hailstone stands as a significant victory within the broader context of the Battle of the Pacific. Its success was a result of a convergence of factors: superior Allied intelligence, meticulous planning and execution, the devastating power of naval aviation, and the overall strategic context of the island-hopping campaign. While the scale of the destruction at Truk was immense, the operation's impact extended far beyond the immediate
battlefield. By crippling a key Japanese base, disrupting their logistics, and boosting Allied morale, Hailstone marked a crucial turning point, contributing significantly to the eventual Allied victory in the Pacific. The battle's lessons – the importance of
intelligence, coordinated naval operations, and the strategic value of targeting critical logistical hubs – would continue to inform

Allied planning and execution in the months and years that followed. It was not simply a battle won, but a strategic milestone that accelerated the Allies' march towards Japan.

The Turning of the Tide in the Pacific

The destruction wrought upon the Japanese at Truk Lagoon during Operation Hailstone reverberated far beyond the immediate carnage. The sinking of twelve ships, the obliteration of 275 aircraft, and the crippling of the base's infrastructure represented a substantial blow to the Japanese Navy's operational capacity. This was not merely a matter of replacing lost material; the losses inflicted at Truk represented the erosion of a meticulously constructed logistical network that sustained Japanese operations across Micronesia. The loss went beyond mere numbers; it represented a crippling blow to the Japanese ability to wage effective war in the Pacific.

The impact on Japanese logistical capabilities was profound and multifaceted. Truk Lagoon served as a crucial hub for the Japanese supply lines, facilitating the movement of fuel, ammunition, food, and personnel throughout their Pacific holdings. The destruction of fuel and supply depots during Hailstone directly hampered Japanese operations across a wide swath of the Pacific. The Japanese were forced to divert resources to rebuild and resupply Truk, resources that could have been used for offensive operations elsewhere. This diversion of resources inadvertently strengthened Allied positions, allowing them to concentrate their efforts on other strategic objectives.

The loss of experienced aircrews and maintenance personnel further exacerbated the situation. The skilled personnel lost at Truk were not easily replaced, creating a significant shortfall in the Japanese war machine. This shortage extended beyond the immediate losses; the training and experience lost at Truk took years to recover. This depletion of human capital was arguably as damaging as the material losses, undermining the operational effectiveness of the remaining forces. The systematic dismantling of Truk's support infrastructure - workshops, repair facilities, and communication networks - only compounded these challenges, creating a domino effect on Japanese capabilities.

The impact of Operation Hailstone should be considered in the

context of the larger Pacific War. By 1944, the Japanese had suffered a series of significant defeats, including Midway, the Guadalcanal campaign, and the battles in the Solomon Islands. These defeats had already begun to erode Japanese naval power and morale. Hailstone was not a standalone event but rather a critical blow delivered at a moment of already existing Japanese vulnerability. The operation capitalized on their weakened state, exploiting their diminished capacity for resistance and
replenishment. The impact compounded already existing losses, leaving the Japanese Pacific fleet significantly depleted.

The comparatively light resistance encountered by the American forces at Truk during Operation Hailstone was another notable aspect of the battle. This can be attributed to several factors: superior Allied intelligence, the element of surprise, and the
weakened state of Japanese defenses. The Allies' sophisticated intelligence gathering, including code-breaking and reconnaissance efforts, provided them with detailed knowledge of Japanese
deployments, allowing for a precise and devastating attack. The surprise nature of the assault further compounded the Japanese difficulties in mounting an effective defense. The combination of intelligence and surprise caught the Japanese off guard, greatly minimizing their counteroffensive capabilities.

The strategic consequences of Operation Hailstone extended beyond the immediate military gains. The neutralization of Truk as a major Japanese base had a significant psychological impact on the
Japanese military. The swift and decisive nature of the Allied victory served as a powerful demonstration of Allied superiority, further undermining Japanese morale and resolve. The loss of a strategically important base, achieved with relatively low Allied casualties, significantly boosted Allied morale and confidence. This psychological impact, while intangible, was perhaps as crucial as the material losses inflicted on the Japanese. The propaganda value of Hailstone was immense, conveying a clear message of Allied dominance in the Pacific.

The post-Hailstone period saw a dramatic shift in the balance of power in the Pacific theater. The Allies continued their island-hopping campaign, gradually advancing closer to the Japanese home islands. The success at Truk provided invaluable momentum and demonstrated the effectiveness of the strategy. The Allies learned crucial lessons in strategic targeting, naval coordination, and the devastating effect of carrier-based aircraft. The meticulous planning and execution of Hailstone served as a blueprint for future operations, refining Allied strategies and improving coordination between different branches of the military.

Furthermore, the insights gained during Hailstone improved Allied intelligence gathering and analysis. The success of Operation Hailstone further validated and refined the Allied intelligence gathering techniques, providing a roadmap for even more successful operations later in the war. This led to more accurate assessments of Japanese capabilities and better predictions of their reactions, further minimizing Allied losses while maximizing damage to the enemy.

The legacy of Operation Hailstone extends beyond the immediate context of World War II. The lessons learned during the battle, particularly the importance of effective intelligence gathering, precise naval coordination, and strategic targeting of enemy logistical hubs, continue to inform naval doctrine and strategic planning to this day. The battle serves as a case study for the effective use of air power in a combined arms operation and highlights the importance of achieving air superiority as a
prerequisite to successful amphibious landings.

Finally, the underwater graveyard of Truk Lagoon stands as a haunting yet powerful reminder of the brutality of war. The sunken wrecks, visible to divers even today, offer a tangible testament to the devastation of Operation Hailstone and the staggering cost of the Pacific conflict. The silent ships and aircraft on the seabed serve as a stark memorial to the lives lost, both Japanese and American, in the pursuit of victory. This somber legacy serves as a potent reminder of the profound human cost of war and the devastating consequences of military conflict. The transformation of Truk from a powerful Japanese base to a silent underwater graveyard powerfully symbolizes the ultimate Allied triumph in the Pacific. Operation Hailstone, therefore, remains a pivotal event, not only in the military annals of World War II but also as a potent symbol of the Pacific War's destructive power and the Allies' eventual triumph.

The Road to Victory

The strategic ramifications of Operation Hailstone extended far beyond the immediate destruction inflicted upon the Japanese forces at Truk Lagoon. Its impact reverberated across the vast expanse of the Pacific theater, subtly yet significantly altering the trajectory of the war and accelerating the Allied march towards victory. The operation served not merely as a tactical triumph, but as a crucial turning point that reshaped the strategic landscape and profoundly influenced subsequent military decisions.

One of the most immediate consequences of Hailstone was the disruption of Japanese logistical networks in Micronesia. Truk Lagoon, prior to the operation, functioned as a vital hub, supplying Japanese forces throughout the region with essential resources: fuel, ammunition, food, and reinforcements. The destruction of these supply depots, the crippling of repair facilities, and the decimation of airfields effectively severed these crucial supply lines. Japanese forces scattered across the islands found themselves increasingly isolated, starved of vital supplies, and vulnerable to Allied attacks.

This logistical paralysis hindered Japanese offensive capabilities, forcing them into a defensive posture and significantly hindering their ability to mount any meaningful counter-offensive.

The impact on Japanese naval power was equally significant. The loss of twelve ships, including valuable cruisers and destroyers, represented a considerable blow to their already dwindling fleet.

These were not simply ships; they were irreplaceable units with trained crews and accumulated combat experience. Replacing these losses proved extremely difficult for the Japanese, who faced
growing shortages in manpower and material resources. The damage extended beyond the immediate losses; the disruption of shipyards and repair facilities further hampered the Japanese ability to maintain their remaining fleet, effectively slowing down their capacity for repair and replenishment. This operational deficiency further limited the scope and effectiveness of future Japanese naval operations.

The destruction of 275 aircraft, including numerous experienced aircrews, dealt a severe blow to Japanese air power in the Pacific.

The loss of these skilled pilots and ground crews represented an irreplaceable drain on the Japanese military. These were seasoned professionals, often years in training, with experience crucial for successful combat operations. The losses inflicted during Operation Hailstone significantly weakened Japan's ability to defend their remaining bases and significantly undermined their aerial capability throughout the Pacific. The shortage of trained pilots and
maintenance personnel proved a challenge that Japan struggled to overcome, ultimately weakening their offensive and defensive capabilities for the rest of the war.

Operation Hailstone's impact extended beyond the purely military realm. The psychological impact on the Japanese military was substantial. The swift and decisive nature of the Allied victory, achieved with relatively low Allied casualties, served as a stark demonstration of Allied superiority. The loss of Truk, a base
considered impregnable, dealt a severe blow to Japanese morale, already strained by a series of defeats in other sectors of the Pacific. The message was clear: the Allies possessed overwhelming military might and were capable of inflicting devastating blows with
minimal losses. This shattered the image of Japanese invincibility and played a crucial role in undermining Japanese resolve to
continue the war.

The Allied success at Truk had a significant effect on subsequent military operations. The operation served as a successful model for future combined arms operations, showcasing the devastating effectiveness of carrier-based aircraft in neutralizing enemy bases.

This approach would be implemented successfully in other strategically important Pacific islands, contributing significantly to the Allies' island-hopping strategy. Hailstone became a tactical blueprint, meticulously studied and analyzed by Allied planners to refine their future offensive strategies. The operational success at Truk validated the strategic importance of concentrating
overwhelming firepower at strategically vital points, maximizing the damage to the enemy while minimizing Allied losses.

The intelligence gathering and analysis techniques employed during Operation Hailstone proved invaluable in future operations. The precision of the attack, minimizing friendly casualties while maximizing damage to enemy assets, served as testimony to the success of Allied intelligence gathering and code breaking operations. This demonstrated the effectiveness of leveraging high-quality intelligence for precise targeting and surgical strikes, a key factor in the Allies' eventual victory. The lessons learned in the planning and execution of Hailstone further refined Allied intelligence practices and their ability to anticipate enemy movements and responses.

The victory at Truk Lagoon significantly altered the dynamics of the Pacific War. The neutralization of this crucial Japanese stronghold dramatically altered the balance of power, enabling the Allies to advance their island-hopping campaign with greater speed and efficiency. The success of Hailstone provided invaluable momentum to Allied offensives, inspiring increased confidence and bolstering morale among Allied troops. The psychological advantage gained by the operation was arguably as significant as the material losses inflicted on the Japanese.

Beyond its tactical and strategic consequences, Operation Hailstone also held profound symbolic significance. The swift and decisive destruction of the once-formidable Japanese bastion at Truk demonstrated the determination and superior strength of the Allies.

This resonated deeply within both Allied and Axis ranks, shifting the perception of the conflict's trajectory and influencing the overall morale of the warring nations. The narrative of Hailstone, meticulously documented and disseminated, served as a potent symbol of Allied resolve and superiority.

In conclusion, Operation Hailstone's contribution to the Allied path to victory in the Pacific War was multifaceted and far-reaching. The operation not only inflicted significant material damage on the Japanese, crippling their logistical networks and weakening their naval and air power, but it also dealt a substantial blow to Japanese morale and significantly altered the strategic landscape of the Pacific theater. The insights gained during and after the operation—in intelligence gathering, combined arms operations, and the effective use of air power—were invaluable in shaping future Allied strategies, accelerating the path to Japan's eventual surrender. The legacy of Operation Hailstone extends beyond the battlefield, serving as a compelling testament to the power of meticulous planning, superior intelligence, and the unwavering resolve of the Allied forces. It stands as a pivotal event, a chapter in the annals of naval history that significantly contributed to the shaping of the final outcome of World War II in the Pacific. The operation remains a significant case study in modern military strategy, highlighting the crucial interdependencies of intelligence, logistics, and effective execution. Its profound impact on the course of the Pacific War is undeniable, and its lessons continue to resonate in contemporary naval and military doctrine.

Global Implications and Significance

The success of Operation Hailstone resonated far beyond the confines of the Pacific theater, subtly yet profoundly influencing the global dynamics of World War II. Its impact extended to the strategic decisions made by Allied leaders in Europe and the allocation of resources across multiple theaters of conflict. The decisive victory at Truk Lagoon demonstrated the effectiveness of the newly refined strategies employed by the US Navy, particularly the integration of carrier-based air power with other naval assets. This success emboldened Allied commanders and policymakers to adopt similar strategies in other theaters, thus influencing the overall conduct of the war. The lessons learned at Truk – the importance of meticulous planning, superior intelligence, and decisive execution – were quickly disseminated and integrated into the Allied war effort, contributing to victories in other crucial campaigns.

The resources allocated to the Pacific theater, already substantial, increased following Operation Hailstone. The demonstrated effectiveness of the carrier task forces, and the significant weakening of Japanese naval power in the region, freed up resources that could be directed elsewhere. This shift in resource allocation, albeit subtle in some areas, had a measurable impact on the European theater, where the war was still raging. While exact figures on this reallocation are difficult to ascertain definitively from declassified documents, internal memos and official correspondence suggest a subtle but significant reallocation towards the European front. The success in the Pacific, in turn, boosted Allied morale globally, bolstering confidence in the eventual defeat of the Axis powers.

Operation Hailstone had a profound impact on the diplomatic landscape of World War II. The victory at Truk further solidified the United States' position as a leading naval power in the Pacific, strengthening its alliances with Australia and New Zealand. The demonstration of US naval dominance in the Pacific also influenced the strategies of other Allied nations. The British, already involved in a protracted conflict against Nazi Germany, recognized the need to coordinate with the US Navy in the Pacific, facilitating greater sharing of intelligence and military planning. The success of Hailstone provided renewed confidence in the Allied war effort, reinforcing international cooperation against the Axis powers.

The strategic implications of the operation extended beyond immediate military victories. The destruction of Truk Lagoon's infrastructure, including its extensive port facilities and repair yards, significantly hampered Japanese ability to wage war in the Pacific. This disruption, coupled with the substantial loss of naval and air assets, forced Japan into a defensive posture, diverting resources from other critical areas. The loss of manpower, both skilled pilots and experienced naval personnel, represented a burden the Japanese military found increasingly difficult to overcome. These losses, coupled with the psychological impact of the defeat, contributed to Japan's declining military capacity and eventually to their dwindling resources and waning resolve. The operation consequently shortened the war and contributed to the eventual Allied victory.

The technological advancements that underpinned Operation Hailstone's success also had long-term global implications. The successful deployment of new radar technology and improved communication systems showcased the critical role of technological innovation in modern warfare. These advancements weren't just instrumental in the success of the operation itself; they also spurred further research and development, leading to significant
improvements in naval and air warfare capabilities in the years following the war. The lessons learned about the effectiveness of carrier-based aircraft, the integration of air and naval power, and the importance of technological superiority resonated across
international military circles, influencing the development of naval doctrines across the world.

The post-war analysis of Operation Hailstone played a significant role in shaping naval doctrine and military strategy for decades to come. The operation served as a case study, repeatedly examined in military academies and war colleges worldwide. The meticulous planning and execution, the innovative use of carrier-based air power, and the crucial role of intelligence gathering were highlighted as essential components for successful modern naval warfare. The operation's legacy transcends its immediate impact; it continues to inform strategic thinking and military planning to this day, illustrating the enduring power of innovative strategies and advanced technology.

Furthermore, the human cost of Operation Hailstone, though overshadowed by the magnitude of the military victory, warrants careful consideration within the broader context of the war. The loss of Japanese lives, both military personnel and civilians, serves as a sobering reminder of the devastating consequences of war. The operation also underscores the human cost of the Allied victory, as American personnel also suffered casualties. This aspect of the operation highlights the moral complexities of warfare and the need to account for both the immediate and long-term consequences of military actions. The human toll provides context to the broader narrative of the Pacific theater and helps to illustrate the true extent of the conflict's impact on all sides.

The legacy of Operation Hailstone extends beyond military strategy and tactical analysis. The operation's impact on the environment of Truk Lagoon, transforming it into a unique underwater graveyard, underscores the lasting environmental consequences of war. The sunken ships and aircraft now attract divers from all over the world, but they also serve as a somber reminder of the destructive
potential of naval warfare and the enduring impact of human
conflict on the environment. Truk Lagoon's present status, a hauntingly beautiful yet solemn underwater memorial, provides a unique opportunity for reflection on the human and environmental costs of conflict.

In summary, the global implications and significance of Operation Hailstone extend beyond the immediate tactical victory achieved in February 1944. The operation's success influenced strategic
decision-making, resource allocation, diplomatic relations, and technological advancement, and shaped naval doctrine and military strategy for decades to come. Its legacy is embedded within the broader narrative of World War II, illustrating the complex
interplay of military strategy, technological innovation, and human cost that defined the conflict and shaped the post-war world. The

events at Truk Lagoon remain a compelling case study in military history, demonstrating the importance of meticulous planning, effective execution, and the critical role of technological superiority in shaping the course of war and, ultimately, contributing to the Allied victory in the Pacific and the wider global struggle against the Axis powers. Its enduring legacy compels continued analysis and underscores the profound and lasting impact of this pivotal event in naval warfare.

Summary of Key Findings

Operation Hailstone, the devastating American assault on Truk Lagoon in February 1944, stands as a pivotal moment in the Pacific Theater of World War II. This meticulously planned and executed operation crippled Japan's major Pacific base, inflicting significant damage to its naval and air forces, and fundamentally altering the strategic landscape of the war. The book has explored the operation in detail, examining its strategic context, the planning and
execution of the attack, and the lasting consequences of the battle.

The strategic importance of Truk Lagoon cannot be overstated. Serving as a crucial Japanese naval base, it provided a vital hub for resupply, repair, and staging operations across the vast expanse of the Pacific. Its loss dealt a significant blow to the Japanese war effort, disrupting their supply lines, hindering their ability to
project power, and forcing a strategic reassessment of their Pacific campaign. The meticulous intelligence gathering and planning that preceded the operation were instrumental to its success. The Americans accurately assessed the layout of the base, the disposition of Japanese forces, and the vulnerabilities within the seemingly impenetrable defenses. This superior intelligence allowed for a coordinated and devastating attack, maximizing damage while minimizing Allied losses.

The operation itself showcased the power and effectiveness of the newly refined strategies and tactics employed by the U.S. Navy. The integration of carrier-based air power with submarine and surface attacks proved decisive. The waves of aircraft launched from
carriers like the USS Intrepid and Yorktown inflicted catastrophic damage, sinking numerous ships, destroying hundreds of aircraft, and severely crippling the lagoon's infrastructure. This integrated approach highlighted the increasing significance of air power in naval warfare, a trend that would continue to dominate naval strategies throughout the remainder of the war and into the post-war era. The effectiveness of the operation was further amplified by the element of surprise, catching the Japanese largely unprepared and ill-equipped to counter the scale and intensity of the attack. The comparatively light Japanese resistance, a point thoroughly

investigated in the book, resulted from a confluence of factors, including the inadequate early warning systems, underestimation of American capabilities, and the already strained state of the Japanese naval forces in the region.

The repercussions of Operation Hailstone extended far beyond the immediate destruction at Truk Lagoon. The significant loss of Japanese naval vessels, aircraft, and personnel – exceeding twelve ships, 275 aircraft, and an immense number of lives – severely weakened Japan's capacity to wage offensive warfare in the Pacific.

This success bolstered Allied morale globally and reinforced confidence in the eventual Allied victory. The damage inflicted on Truk's infrastructure, including its vital repair yards and port facilities, severely hampered Japan's ability to conduct effective repairs and resupply operations. This disruption further strained their already stretched resources and contributed to their defensive posture for the remainder of the war. The subsequent Allied advances across the Pacific, including the liberation of the Philippines and the subsequent island-hopping campaigns, were significantly aided by the neutralization of Truk Lagoon. The strategic advantage gained at Truk allowed the Allies to concentrate their forces and resources on other critical theaters of operations.

The disruption of Japanese logistics, combined with the psychological blow of the defeat, played a significant role in shifting the momentum of the war decisively in favor of the Allies.

The operation's influence extended to the strategic decisions made by Allied leaders, influencing resource allocation and the overall conduct of the war. The demonstrably successful employment of carrier-based air power prompted Allied powers to further invest in these assets. This reallocation of resources, while not always immediately apparent in official documentation, impacted both the Pacific and European theaters of conflict, contributing to the overall Allied victory.

The technological advancements employed during Operation Hailstone significantly impacted the course of naval warfare. The successful implementation of advanced radar technology, improved communication systems, and more sophisticated navigational tools played a crucial role in the operation's success. The refinement and deployment of these technologies demonstrated their increasing importance in modern naval combat and spurred further research and development, impacting the design and capabilities of naval vessels and aircraft in the years that followed.

The post-war analysis of Operation Hailstone has profoundly influenced naval doctrine and military strategy. The meticulous planning, the innovative use of combined arms, and the crucial role of superior intelligence became central themes in naval warfare training and analysis, shaping the strategic thinking and tactical doctrines of navies worldwide. The operation's success continues to be studied and analyzed in military academies and war colleges, serving as a case study in the importance of planning, execution, and technological superiority in achieving decisive victories. It stands as an enduring testament to the importance of superior intelligence gathering, the careful integration of different military assets, and the power of decisive action in the crucible of modern naval warfare.

The human cost of Operation Hailstone, while often overshadowed by the strategic implications of the victory, remains a crucial aspect of the operation's legacy. The loss of Japanese lives, both military and civilian, serves as a sobering reminder of the devastating consequences of war. The casualty figures, while difficult to obtain with complete accuracy due to incomplete Japanese records, were substantial, representing a tragic loss of human life. The American casualties, though significantly lower due to the effectiveness of the operation's planning, also represent the human cost of war on the Allied side. This aspect of Operation Hailstone, a testament to the human cost of conflict on both sides, underscores the moral complexities of war and the need for ongoing reflection on the consequences of military action.

Beyond the purely military aspects, Operation Hailstone left a lasting environmental impact on Truk Lagoon. The sunken ships and aircraft, now a hauntingly beautiful yet solemn underwater graveyard, serve as a poignant reminder of the destructive power of war. The lagoon's present state, a popular destination for wreck divers, offers a unique opportunity for contemplation on the
devastating environmental costs of conflict. This underwater

memorial serves as a powerful counterpoint to the tactical triumph of the operation, prompting reflection on the long-term consequences of war far beyond its immediate military objectives. The environmental impact of Operation Hailstone, therefore, adds another dimension to the operation's legacy, reminding us that the consequences of conflict extend beyond the battlefield and into the environment.

In conclusion, Operation Hailstone was far more than just a naval battle; it was a turning point in the Pacific War, with significant and lasting global implications. Its success influenced strategic decision-making, resource allocation, diplomatic relations, technological advancements, and the development of naval doctrine for decades to come. The operation's legacy continues to inform military strategy and tactical thinking, demonstrating the power of superior planning, effective execution, and technological innovation in achieving decisive victories in modern warfare. The events at Truk Lagoon remain a compelling case study, highlighting the interplay of military strategy, technological advancement, and human cost that characterized World War II and shaped the post-war world.

The enduring legacy of Operation Hailstone continues to compel further research and analysis, firmly establishing it as one of the most significant naval battles of World War II and a pivotal moment in the Allied path to victory in the Pacific. The haunting beauty of the underwater graveyard at Truk Lagoon serves as both a testament to the destructive power of war and a sobering reminder of the human and environmental cost of conflict.

The Human Cost and Remembrance

The human cost of Operation Hailstone, often overshadowed by the strategic narrative of Allied victory, demands a deeper, more nuanced consideration. While the meticulous planning and decisive execution of the operation represent a triumph of military strategy and technological prowess, the true measure of its impact lies in the irreplaceable loss of human life. The official casualty figures, while offering a glimpse into the scale of the tragedy, inevitably fall short of capturing the full extent of the suffering inflicted upon both the Japanese and American forces. The incompleteness of Japanese records, a consequence of the chaos and destruction of the battle, makes a precise accounting of Japanese losses particularly difficult.

Yet, even incomplete data speaks volumes. The sinking of twelve ships, the destruction of hundreds of aircraft, and the chaotic retreat from the lagoon point to a catastrophic loss of personnel, including countless sailors, airmen, and support personnel. The emotional toll, the separation of families, the grief that haunted survivors and their families for years to come – these are aspects tragically difficult to quantify, yet crucial to understanding the true human cost.

Beyond the immediate loss of life during the battle itself, the consequences extended far beyond the shores of Truk Lagoon. The devastation inflicted upon the Japanese Navy significantly impacted their ability to wage war in the Pacific. The loss of skilled personnel– pilots, navigators, engineers – represented not just immediate casualties but also a critical blow to Japan's long-term war effort. This loss of experienced personnel had a cascading effect, impacting their ability to train and deploy replacement crews effectively, further weakening their capacity for offensive action. The
consequences reached into civilian communities as well. The disruption of supply lines and the general economic collapse following the loss of Truk's infrastructure directly impacted families across the Japanese home islands and its occupied territories, exacerbating the already harsh realities of a nation embroiled in a protracted and increasingly desperate war.

The American casualties, while far less significant in numerical terms due to the success of the surprise attack and the superior intelligence that underpinned Operation Hailstone, nevertheless represent a tangible human cost. American sailors and airmen perished in the operation, their sacrifice a grim reminder that even the most meticulously planned military engagements carry the risk of loss. These men gave their lives in service of their country, contributing to the ultimate Allied victory in the Pacific. Their individual stories, often untold, deserve to be remembered and honored, acknowledging their contributions to the momentous turn of events that unfolded at Truk Lagoon. Analyzing the casualty figures and impact on both sides emphasizes the indiscriminate nature of war and reminds us that victory comes at a heavy human price, regardless of strategic success or technological advancement.

The remembrance of Operation Hailstone must therefore move beyond the purely strategic analysis to embrace a comprehensive understanding of the human experience. The official records, while indispensable for understanding the military context of the operation, often fail to fully convey the human stories of those involved. The personal accounts of survivors, both American and Japanese, if they exist and are accessible, offer invaluable insight into the emotional and psychological impact of the battle. These firsthand narratives illuminate the brutal realities of war – the fear, the uncertainty, the trauma of witnessing death and destruction on a massive scale. Oral histories, letters, diaries, and other personal records, if available, are essential sources that can bring to life the experiences of those who fought and survived at Truk Lagoon.

The lack of easily accessible personal accounts from the Japanese side presents a significant challenge to a comprehensive understanding of the human cost. The sheer scale of the Japanese losses, coupled with the challenges of accessing and translating archival material from that period, presents researchers with difficulties in piecing together a detailed account of their individual stories. This absence of readily available Japanese perspectives highlights the importance of continued research and efforts to uncover and share these untold narratives. The pursuit of these narratives is not only a matter of historical accuracy but also a moral imperative to honor the memory of those lost and to ensure their sacrifices are not forgotten.

Beyond the immediate impact on the combatants, the lingering effects of Operation Hailstone are important to consider. Post-traumatic stress disorder (PTSD), common among veterans of major conflicts, likely affected many survivors, American and Japanese alike. The psychological scars of war can extend for decades,
impacting families and communities long after the guns have fallen silent. This lasting psychological impact underscores the importance of recognizing and addressing the mental health needs of those who participated in, or were affected by, the operation. Understanding and acknowledging this longer-term impact is crucial to a complete understanding of the human cost of Operation Hailstone.

The legacy of Operation Hailstone, therefore, necessitates more than just a military analysis; it calls for a comprehensive
understanding of the human experience of war. The human cost, the individual stories of loss and survival, must be woven into the narrative alongside the strategic significance of the battle. This requires continued archival research, the painstaking collection of personal accounts, and a commitment to presenting a complete and balanced picture of the human dimension of this pivotal battle.

Only through such efforts can we truly understand the enduring legacy of Operation Hailstone and honor the sacrifices made by those who fought and died at Truk Lagoon.

The remembrance of the human cost of Operation Hailstone should not be confined to scholarly analysis or military memorials. It is a matter of shared human experience, transcending national
boundaries and political ideologies. The lessons learned from Truk Lagoon extend beyond the realm of naval strategy. They serve as a powerful reminder of the devastating consequences of war, the importance of diplomacy, and the need for continued efforts to prevent future conflicts. The underwater graveyard at Truk Lagoon, a haunting testament to the destructive power of war, offers a powerful visual representation of the human and environmental costs of conflict. This underwater museum is a testament to the importance of peaceful resolutions to conflict and a constant
reminder of the human price of war. It serves as a site for reflection, a place where visitors can pay respects to the fallen and
contemplate the need for lasting peace.

Remembrance requires active engagement, not just passive observation. It involves the preservation of historical records, the support of research into the human experiences of the conflict, and the education of future generations about the profound human cost of war. The creation of educational programs, museum exhibits, and memorials dedicated to the memory of those lost at Truk Lagoon can ensure that the human cost is not forgotten. These efforts serve not only as tributes to the fallen, but as reminders of the fragility of peace and the critical importance of striving for peaceful resolutions to international conflict. The remembrance of Operation Hailstone, therefore, should not simply be a commemorative act but an
ongoing commitment to learning from the past and striving to build a more peaceful future. The human cost must remain a central element of the story, reminding us of the profound impact war has on individuals, communities, and the world. The continuing legacy of Operation Hailstone is not solely defined by its strategic
implications, but by its lasting human impact, a testament to the need for remembrance and a solemn call for peace.

Truk Lagoon as a War Memorial

The chilling beauty of Truk Lagoon, now a hauntingly serene underwater graveyard, serves as a poignant and enduring war memorial, a silent testament to the ferocity of Operation Hailstone and the human cost of war. The lagoon's transformation from a bustling Japanese naval base to a submerged landscape of wrecked warships and aircraft, encrusted with coral and teeming with marine life, is a stark, yet compelling, reminder of the battle's devastating impact. The sunken vessels, scattered across the lagoon floor, are not merely artifacts of a bygone era; they are the tombs of countless sailors and airmen, their lives extinguished in the maelstrom of conflict. Divers exploring the lagoon's depths encounter a spectral panorama – ghostly silhouettes of warships, once symbols of imperial power, now silent monuments to human fallibility and the destructive capacity of war. The rusted hulks, perforated by bomb blasts and riddled with bullet holes, offer a visceral reminder of the violence unleashed upon this once vibrant hub of Japanese naval power. The stillness of the water, broken only by the occasional movement of marine life, amplifies the somber atmosphere, transforming the lagoon into a place of quiet contemplation and solemn remembrance.

The significance of Truk Lagoon as a war memorial extends beyond its visual impact. It serves as a powerful symbol of the interconnectedness of human experience across national boundaries. The sunken ships, representing the navies of both the United States and Japan, stand as a unified symbol of loss, transcending the historical narratives of victory and defeat. Both sides suffered casualties, leaving behind a legacy of sorrow and shared trauma that continues to resonate through generations. The lack of clear boundaries in this underwater landscape mirrors the blurring of lines that occurs amidst the devastation of war. The underwater world, indifferent to the ideological conflicts of the surface, has embraced the wrecks as part of its intricate ecosystem. This transformation serves as a visual metaphor for the restorative power of nature, even in the face of unprecedented destruction. Yet, the restorative power of nature does not erase the memory of the fallen, instead, it creates a unique environment that allows us to remember the past while acknowledging the enduring power of life itself.

The lagoon's transformation into a popular dive site presents a unique challenge and opportunity. On one hand, the commercialization of the site could be seen as disrespectful, turning a grave into a tourist attraction. However, responsible dive operators and tourism authorities can utilize this opportunity to educate visitors about the historical significance of the site, fostering a deeper understanding of the human cost of war. This approach transforms the lagoon into an educational space where visitors can engage with the past in a meaningful way, honoring the sacrifices made and fostering a greater appreciation for the need for peace. The underwater memorial is not merely a spectacle for recreational pursuits; it is an unparalleled educational resource, offering a powerful and unforgettable learning experience about the complexities and consequences of war.

Beyond the physical reminders of the battle, the oral histories and personal accounts of those who survived Operation Hailstone are crucial to a fuller understanding of the site's significance as a war memorial. These firsthand narratives illuminate the emotional and psychological impact of the battle, providing a human dimension to the otherwise abstract notion of a naval engagement. The stories of survivors, both American and Japanese, offer invaluable insight into the fear, uncertainty, and trauma experienced during and in the aftermath of the battle. These accounts paint a vivid picture of the human experience of war, highlighting not only the physical destruction but also the psychological scars left behind. The fragmented memories, the lingering PTSD, and the enduring grief of survivors are potent reminders of the long-term consequences of war, extending far beyond the immediate battles and skirmishes.

The collection, preservation, and dissemination of these oral histories are essential to ensuring that the human stories associated with Truk Lagoon are not forgotten.

Moreover, Truk Lagoon serves as a memorial beyond the immediate participants in Operation Hailstone. The battle had far-reaching consequences for the entire Pacific theater, shaping the course of the war and influencing the subsequent Allied advances. The

crippling blow dealt to the Japanese fleet at Truk profoundly
impacted the balance of power in the Pacific, paving the way for future
Allied victories. This broader strategic impact renders Truk Lagoon a
symbol of a pivotal turning point in the war, a site where the tide decisively
shifted in favor of the Allied forces. This strategic significance should be
integrated into the interpretation of the site as a memorial, demonstrating its
historical context and its lasting impact on the trajectory of World War II.
Understanding the
strategic context, alongside the human cost, provides a more
holistic and complete understanding of the significance of Truk Lagoon.

The challenge lies in balancing the commemoration of the battle with the
preservation of the environment. The lagoon's delicate ecosystem requires
careful management to ensure its long-term health and sustainability.
Sustainable tourism practices, responsible dive operations, and careful
environmental monitoring are essential to preserving this underwater
memorial for future generations. The goal is not to exploit the site for
profit, but to utilize it as a means of education and remembrance, ensuring
its integrity and
environmental preservation are paramount. This responsible
approach ensures that the lagoon remains a poignant testament to the past,
while also safeguarding its ecological significance for future generations.
The ongoing conversation about responsible tourism and environmental
protection at Truk Lagoon is essential for the site's future as a vital and
lasting war memorial.

In conclusion, Truk Lagoon stands as a powerful and complex war
memorial. It is a place of quiet reflection, where the sunken ships serve as
silent sentinels, bearing witness to the immense human cost of Operation
Hailstone. The lagoon is not just an underwater
graveyard; it is an open-air museum, a classroom, and a poignant reminder
of the futility of war. Its enduring legacy lies not only in its strategic
significance but also in its role as a site of
remembrance, a place where we can confront the human
consequences of conflict and honor the sacrifices made by those who
fought and died at Truk Lagoon. The challenge for future generations is to
ensure that the site is preserved and protected, while also educating visitors
about its profound historical and environmental significance. The
underwater graveyard should be a

powerful stimulus for reflection on the importance of peace and the need to prevent future conflicts, ensuring that the sacrifices made at Truk Lagoon are never forgotten. Only through respectful and responsible management can we ensure that Truk Lagoon continues to serve as a meaningful and lasting war memorial for generations to come. The lagoon, in its poignant stillness, continues to whisper tales of courage, sacrifice, and the enduring human cost of war. It is a testament to the destructive power of conflict, but also to the enduring resilience of the human spirit.

Lessons Learned from the Battle

The Battle of Truk Lagoon, codenamed Operation Hailstone, yielded a wealth of lessons for both the Allied and Axis powers, profoundly shaping naval doctrine and strategic thinking in the latter stages of World War II. For the United States Navy, the operation served as a stark demonstration of the devastating effectiveness of coordinated carrier-based air power. The near-total destruction of the Japanese fleet at Truk, achieved with relatively light losses on the American side, highlighted the vulnerability of surface ships to massed air attacks, even within the supposed safety of a well-defended lagoon. This victory underscored the crucial role of naval aviation in future conflicts, accelerating the shift towards carrier-centric naval strategies and diminishing the relative importance of battleships and cruisers in large-scale engagements. The success of Operation Hailstone solidified the American Navy's understanding of the necessity for overwhelming air superiority as a prerequisite for any successful amphibious assault or major naval operation.

The meticulous planning and execution of Operation Hailstone offered invaluable insights into the complexities of coordinating a large-scale, multi-pronged attack. The seamless integration of carrier aircraft, submarines, and surface vessels exemplified the value of combined arms warfare, a critical lesson learned and subsequently applied in subsequent Pacific campaigns. The pre-battle intelligence gathering, which accurately pinpointed the location and disposition of Japanese assets within Truk Lagoon, proved crucial to the operation's success. This underscored the growing importance of effective reconnaissance and intelligence in modern warfare, paving the way for the development of more sophisticated intelligence-gathering techniques and the emphasis on strategic surprise. The American experience at Truk emphasized that success hinges on accurate and timely intelligence, precise coordination amongst participating forces, and the ability to quickly adapt to unforeseen circumstances.

Analysis of post-battle reports revealed the limitations of relying solely on shore-based anti-aircraft defenses, particularly against the sheer volume and technological sophistication of American carrier aircraft. The Japanese defense of Truk Lagoon, while valiant, ultimately proved insufficient to counter the devastating power of the US Navy's air power. The effectiveness of American dive bombers, torpedo planes, and fighters, coupled with their superior range and payload capacity, exposed the vulnerabilities of Japanese defensive strategies. This lesson significantly influenced subsequent Japanese military planning, prompting a re-evaluation of defensive strategies and an increased emphasis on the development of improved air defense capabilities. The relative lack of effective Japanese radar and communication systems further highlighted the shortcomings of their defensive strategies.

Operation Hailstone also provided crucial insights into the psychological impact of sustained air attacks. The relentless bombing raids inflicted significant damage not only to Japanese ships and infrastructure but also to the morale of the Japanese forces stationed at Truk. The constant barrage of attacks created a climate of fear and uncertainty, undermining the effectiveness of Japanese resistance and accelerating the erosion of their fighting spirit. The psychological impact of this sustained assault served as a valuable lesson for future military strategists, underscoring the importance of not only inflicting material damage but also targeting enemy morale to achieve decisive victory. The near-complete collapse of Japanese air defense and resistance speaks volumes about the efficacy of this psychological warfare aspect.

On the Japanese side, the failure to effectively defend Truk Lagoon against the American air assault highlighted the limitations of their overall Pacific strategy. The concentration of significant naval assets in a single, relatively undefended lagoon, exposed them to devastating attack. This strategic miscalculation underscored the vulnerabilities of concentrating forces in easily targeted locations, a lesson that the Japanese military would struggle to fully internalize throughout the remainder of the war. The inadequacy of Japanese early warning systems and the failure to effectively coordinate defensive efforts, despite intelligence suggesting an impending attack, further exposed systemic weaknesses within the Japanese command structure.

The analysis of Japanese post-battle reports reveals a crucial failing in their assessment of the American capabilities. The Japanese underestimated the range, power, and accuracy of American carrier aircraft, significantly misjudging the extent of the threat posed by Operation Hailstone. This underestimation stemmed from a combination of factors: a lack of up-to-date intelligence on American advancements in naval aviation, an overestimation of their own defensive capabilities, and a cultural predisposition toward optimism and a reluctance to acknowledge potential vulnerabilities. This misjudgment highlights the importance of accurate and realistic intelligence assessments in military planning, highlighting the critical need to avoid wishful thinking and to accurately gauge the capabilities and intentions of the adversary.

Moreover, the Japanese experience at Truk highlighted the limitations of relying on outdated naval doctrine and technology. The age of their aircraft and the lack of sufficient modern fighter aircraft exposed their weakness in aerial combat. The vulnerability of their ships, designed for a different era of naval warfare, underscores the crucial need for continual technological innovation and adaptation to remain competitive in a rapidly evolving military landscape. This need for modernization and adaptability proved crucial, as demonstrated by the subsequent advancements in naval technology and strategy that the Americans capitalized upon during this period and throughout the remainder of the conflict.

Operation Hailstone's impact extended beyond the immediate battlefield. The destruction of the Japanese fleet and the loss of their crucial base at Truk Lagoon irrevocably shifted the balance of power in the Pacific. The operation paved the way for subsequent Allied advances, facilitating the recapture of the Philippines and the eventual island-hopping campaign toward Japan. The lessons learned at Truk, both on the American and Japanese sides, fundamentally altered naval strategy, leading to new approaches in carrier operations, anti-submarine warfare, and the integration of intelligence gathering into overall military planning. The battle served as a pivotal turning point in the Pacific theater, accelerating the Allied advance toward victory and ultimately contributing to Japan's defeat.

The lasting legacy of Operation Hailstone is multifaceted. Beyond the strategic and tactical lessons learned, the battle serves as a stark reminder of the human cost of war. The destruction wrought upon Truk Lagoon resulted in significant loss of life, both amongst the Japanese defenders and the American attackers. The underwater graveyard that Truk Lagoon has become serves as a solemn memorial to those who perished in the battle, a poignant reminder of the devastating impact of conflict and a testament to the human cost of war. The battle's impact extended beyond the immediate loss of life, as surviving participants continue to contend with the psychological scars of warfare, serving as a testament to the deep-seated effects of this intense conflict.

The lessons from Operation Hailstone resonate far beyond World War II. The emphasis on technological superiority, coordinated planning, and the psychological factors of warfare remain crucial considerations in modern military strategy. The battle's enduring legacy underscores the importance of continuous adaptation, effective intelligence gathering, and the integration of multiple arms of service in modern military campaigns. Truk Lagoon remains a stark reminder of the consequences of conflict, a potent symbol that compels ongoing reflection and critical analysis of the factors that lead to war and the importance of pursuing peace. The study of Operation Hailstone offers invaluable insights for military strategists, historians, and anyone seeking to understand the complexities of modern warfare and its enduring implications. The underwater memorial serves as a constant, powerful reminder of the cost of conflict and the importance of peace, urging us to learn from the past and to strive for a better future.

Enduring Legacy and Future Research

The enduring legacy of Operation Hailstone extends far beyond the immediate aftermath of the battle. The strategic and tactical lessons learned during the operation continue to inform naval doctrine and military planning in the 21st century. The overwhelming success of the coordinated carrier air strikes, coupled with the supporting roles of submarines and surface vessels, solidified the importance of combined arms warfare and the decisive advantage of air
superiority in naval engagements. This paradigm shift, directly influenced by Operation Hailstone, fundamentally altered the strategic landscape of naval warfare, diminishing the dominance of battleships and emphasizing the crucial role of aircraft carriers as the primary offensive weapon.

The battle also underscored the critical importance of accurate and timely intelligence. The meticulous pre-battle reconnaissance and intelligence gathering that accurately pinpointed the location and disposition of Japanese assets within Truk Lagoon were crucial factors in the operation's resounding success. This emphasized the need for sophisticated intelligence gathering techniques, advanced surveillance capabilities, and the crucial role of human intelligence in modern warfare. Subsequent conflicts have highlighted the importance of these lessons, underscoring the need for continuous investment in intelligence gathering and analysis to maintain a decisive strategic advantage. The advancements in satellite imagery, signals intelligence, and cyber warfare owe a significant debt to the lessons learned at Truk.

Beyond the tactical and strategic lessons, Operation Hailstone offers profound insights into the psychological dimensions of warfare. The relentless bombing raids inflicted not only material damage but also significantly impacted the morale of the Japanese forces. The psychological impact of sustained air attacks contributed to the breakdown of Japanese resistance, demonstrating the importance of understanding the psychological effect of war on both sides of the conflict. This understanding, fueled by the experiences at Truk Lagoon, has since been integrated into modern military strategies, highlighting the need to consider the psychological impact of warfare on combatants, civilians, and the overall political climate. The study of Operation Hailstone allows for a deeper understanding of the interplay between military strategy and human psychology, vital in today's increasingly complex geopolitical landscape.

Furthermore, the aftermath of Operation Hailstone and its implications for the environment provide an additional dimension to its enduring legacy. The destruction of numerous Japanese vessels in Truk Lagoon created a unique underwater graveyard, a testament to the devastating power of modern warfare. This underwater world, now a popular site for shipwreck divers, serves as a powerful reminder of the human cost of war, a sobering memorial to those who perished in the conflict. The ecological impact of the sunken vessels and their cargo, however, is a topic that requires further investigation. The potential for environmental damage from pollutants and the gradual degradation of the wrecks warrants careful study. This exploration of the environmental impact of Operation Hailstone adds another layer to our understanding of the battle's comprehensive legacy.

The analysis of the Japanese response to Operation Hailstone reveals crucial insights into their military doctrine and strategic decision-making. The concentration of significant naval assets within a single, relatively undefended lagoon demonstrated a strategic vulnerability that was exploited ruthlessly by the Americans. This exposed a critical flaw in Japanese strategic thinking, their underestimation of American capabilities, and their relative lack of adaptability in the face of changing warfare conditions. The Japanese experience at Truk highlights the dangers of complacency and the critical need for continuous adaptation and re-evaluation of military strategies in response to evolving technological advancements and shifting geopolitical realities.

The legacy of Operation Hailstone extends to the realm of naval technology and innovation. The superior technology employed by the U.S. Navy, particularly in naval aviation, played a decisive role in the battle's outcome. This demonstrated the critical importance of technological superiority in modern warfare, spurring significant advancements in aircraft design, radar technology, and anti-submarine warfare capabilities. The post-Truk analysis spurred a

rapid acceleration of technological innovation in these areas, transforming naval warfare in the years that followed. The
technological dominance exhibited by the Americans underscored the necessity for continuous research and development to maintain a competitive edge in the global military landscape.

Despite the wealth of information available, significant avenues for further research and study remain open. The detailed examination of individual pilot accounts, and naval records would offer new insights into the lived experience of those who participated in the battle, adding crucial details to the human narrative of the conflict.

A more thorough investigation into the Japanese perspective, particularly incorporating less accessible Japanese wartime accounts and documents, would provide a more complete understanding of their strategic decision-making and their responses to the unfolding battle. Further research should also delve into the long-term environmental impact of the sunken ships, examining the potential consequences of pollution and the ecological changes occurring within the lagoon's ecosystem. A comparative analysis of Operation Hailstone with other major naval battles of World War II, such as the Battle of Midway or the Battle of Leyte Gulf, would yield valuable insights into the unique aspects of this pivotal
engagement. This comparative approach would illuminate the evolution of naval warfare strategies and highlight the distinctive factors that contributed to the success or failure of various military operations.

Operation Hailstone's legacy continues to shape our understanding of naval warfare. The technological advancements, strategic
decisions, and human experience of this pivotal battle provide invaluable lessons for military strategists and historians alike. The battle's lasting significance compels continued research and study, ensuring that the lessons learned at Truk Lagoon remain relevant in the context of modern military conflicts and geopolitical realities. The investigation into the battle's impact should not be confined to its immediate military consequences but should also include
explorations of its long-term social, economic, and environmental impacts. The detailed study of Operation Hailstone provides a fertile ground for interdisciplinary research, bridging the gaps between military history, environmental science, and social studies

to create a comprehensive understanding of this pivotal moment in World War II history. The battle itself, and its consequences, offer valuable insights into a range of topics, from intelligence gathering and the evolving role of naval aviation to the psychological impact of war and its long-term effects on the environment and the individuals involved. The continued investigation of this complex event is essential to a comprehensive understanding of the complexities of modern warfare and its lasting implications. The study of Operation Hailstone is therefore not just a historical exercise but a valuable contribution to the ongoing dialogue concerning the prevention of future conflicts and the responsible conduct of warfare. Truk Lagoon, a silent testament to the horrors and consequences of war, serves as a constant reminder of the importance of peaceful conflict resolution and the preservation of global peace.

Glossary

Aircraft Carrier: A warship designed to deploy and recover aircraft.

Battleship: A large, heavily armored warship armed with large-caliber guns.

Combined Arms Warfare: The coordinated use of different military branches (army, navy, air force) in a single operation.

Cruiser: A medium-sized warship typically armed with a mix of guns and anti-aircraft weaponry.

Destroyer: A smaller warship designed primarily for anti-submarine and anti-aircraft defense.

Kamikaze: Japanese suicide attacks using aircraft loaded with explosives.

Submarine: A warship designed to operate underwater.

Truk Lagoon: A large, sheltered lagoon in the Caroline Islands, used as a major Japanese naval base during World War II.

Made in the USA
Columbia, SC
27 March 2025